PROJECT MANHATTAN- THE UNTOLD STORY OF THE MANHATTAN PROJECT

ADEEB JAMAL

This book, Project Manhattan: The Untold Story of the Manhattan Project, is dedicated to the countless individuals who shaped one of the most transformative and complex chapters in human history.

To the brilliant scientists, engineers, and thinkers who pushed the boundaries of knowledge, venturing into uncharted territory to unlock the secrets of the atom. Your relentless pursuit of discovery, even in the face of moral and ethical dilemmas, changed the course of history forever.

To the thousands of workers, soldiers, and administrators who labored in secrecy, often unaware of the monumental impact of their contributions. Your sacrifices, perseverance, and commitment laid the foundation for achievements that have been both celebrated and questioned.

To the people of Hiroshima and Nagasaki, whose lives were forever altered by the devastating consequences of this project. Your suffering stands as a stark reminder of the immense responsibility that accompanies scientific progress and the profound need for compassion and reflection in the application of power.

To the families of those involved, who endured separation, uncertainty, and the weight of secrets. Your strength and support enabled this unprecedented undertaking, even as you bore its burdens in silence.

To the generations that followed, who live in a world shaped by the legacy of the Manhattan Project. This book is for you—to help understand the lessons of the past and to inspire thoughtful consideration of the choices that shape our future.

Finally, to those who dare to dream of a world where science and humanity coexist harmoniously, where innovation serves not to destroy but to build a better tomorrow. Let this book serve as a testament to the complexities of progress and the unyielding need for ethical responsibility in all our endeavors.

This dedication is a reflection of the past, a tribute to the present, and a call for wisdom, empathy, and accountability as we continue to shape the world of tomorrow. - Adeeb Jamal (Author)

Contents

Foreword

It is with great pride and admiration that I write this foreword for Project Manhattan: The Untold Story of the Manhattan Project, a remarkable work by my student and mentee, Adeeb Jamal. Adeeb's relentless curiosity and dedication to uncovering the intricacies of one of history's most significant scientific endeavors are evident on every page of this book.

The Manhattan Project was not just a monumental achievement in science and engineering; it was a turning point in human history. To understand its complexities, both technical and ethical, requires not only knowledge but also a profound sense of responsibility to interpret its legacy with nuance and care. Adeeb has achieved this balance, weaving together the historical, scientific, and human elements of the project with exceptional skill.

Having mentored Adeeb during his formative years, I have witnessed his intellectual growth and unyielding passion for exploration. Whether it is his deep dives into quantum computing, his insightful research papers, or his practical applications of cybersecurity principles, Adeeb's work is always characterized by thorough research, critical thinking, and an unrelenting pursuit of excellence. This book is no exception.

Through this work, Adeeb has not only told the story of the Manhattan Project but has also raised important questions about the nature of progress, the responsibility of scientists, and the dual-edged power of innovation. His ability to blend meticulous research with thoughtful analysis makes this book a valuable contribution to our understanding of the past and a guide for navigating the challenges of the future.

As a mentor, it is immensely fulfilling to see Adeeb channel his talents and energy into such meaningful endeavors. His journey from a curious student to a published author and researcher is a testament to his resilience, ambition, and hard work. I am confident that his contributions will continue to inspire others to think deeply

about the role of science and technology in shaping our world.

I invite you, the reader, to explore this compelling narrative and to engage with the questions it poses. The story of the Manhattan Project is one of triumph and tragedy, of genius and uncertainty, and of progress and its consequences. Adeeb's thoughtful examination of these themes will leave you not only informed but also profoundly moved.

Congratulations, Adeeb, on this outstanding achievement. I am honored to have been a part of your journey, and I look forward to seeing the remarkable contributions you will undoubtedly make in the years to come.

— Anadi Kirti Pratap
(Mentor and Teacher of Adeeb Jamal)

Preface

T*he Manhattan Project was a defining chapter in human history—a fusion of scientific ingenuity, political strategy, and moral complexity that forever changed the world. This book, Project Manhattan: The Untold Story of the Manhattan Project, is my attempt to unravel the layers of this extraordinary endeavor, exploring its triumphs, tragedies, and lasting impact on society.*

My fascination with the Manhattan Project began as a spark of curiosity. How did an idea born in the minds of brilliant scientists evolve into one of the most ambitious and consequential undertakings of the 20th century? How did the efforts of thousands—many working in secrecy—converge to unlock the atom's energy, a force capable of both unprecedented progress and unimaginable destruction?

Writing this book has been a journey through history, science, and humanity. It has taken me deep into archives, letters, and firsthand accounts of those who lived and breathed this project. While many accounts focus on the monumental achievement of creating the world's first nuclear weapons, my goal has been to tell the whole story—one that includes the human element, the ethical dilemmas, and the untold contributions of countless individuals.

In these pages, you will find more than just the well-documented milestones of the Manhattan Project. You will meet the visionaries who brought it to life, the unsung heroes who toiled in the shadows, and the people whose lives were irrevocably changed by its consequences. You will also confront the broader implications of this project, from the dawn of the nuclear age to the enduring questions it poses about the balance between progress and responsibility.

This book is not an attempt to glorify or vilify the Manhattan Project. Instead, it is a thoughtful exploration of its complexities, offering readers a chance to form their own understanding of its legacy. It is a story of science and ambition, but also of sacrifice and introspection—a story that reminds us of the dual-edged nature of human innovation.

As I wrote, I often reflected on the lessons the Manhattan Project holds for us today. We live in an age of rapid technological advancements, where the power of discovery is matched by the necessity for ethical foresight. This book is both a tribute to those who shaped history and a call to future generations to wield knowledge with wisdom and care.

I am deeply grateful to the many individuals who supported this work—my mentors, teachers, and readers whose insights and encouragement made this book possible. Their contributions have helped shape this narrative into what I hope will be a compelling and thought-provoking account of the Manhattan Project.

I invite you to join me on this journey into the untold story of the Manhattan Project. Together, let us uncover the lessons of the past and reflect on their significance for the present and the future.

— Adeeb Jamal (Author)

(Author of Titans of Trade and Power and Project Manhattan, Researcher and writer of 4 research papers and Certified Professional in Cybersecurity Analytics and Project Management from Microsoft and Google.)

Acknowledgements

Writing Project Manhattan: The Untold Story of the Manhattan Project has been a deeply enriching and transformative journey, one that would not have been possible without the support, guidance, and inspiration of many individuals and organizations.

First and foremost, I am profoundly grateful to my mentor and teacher, Anadi Kirti Pratap, whose unwavering encouragement, intellectual guidance, and belief in my potential have been instrumental in shaping this work. Your mentorship has been the cornerstone of my academic and personal growth, and for that, I will always be indebted.

To my parents, my mother, Asma Jamal, and my father, Ateeque Jamal, your unconditional love, sacrifices, and unwavering belief in me have been my greatest sources of strength. You have instilled in me the values of perseverance, curiosity, and integrity, all of which have guided me throughout this journey. This book is as much a tribute to your support as it is a culmination of my efforts.

I extend my heartfelt gratitude to the historians, scientists, and archivists whose meticulous documentation of the Manhattan Project served as the backbone of this book. Your dedication to preserving history has enabled countless individuals, including myself, to explore and understand this pivotal chapter in human history.

A special acknowledgment goes to the editorial team and reviewers who offered their invaluable feedback and insights, refining this work into what it is today. Your expertise and patience were essential in bringing this project to fruition.

To my friends and colleagues, thank you for your support, thoughtful discussions, and understanding during the countless hours I dedicated to this book. Your camaraderie has been a source of energy and inspiration.

Lastly, to the readers of this book—you are the reason this story is told. Thank you for taking the time to engage with this narrative and for seeking to understand the profound complexities of the Manhattan Project. It is my hope that this book inspires reflection, dialogue, and a deeper appreciation for the intertwined paths of science, history, and humanity.

This work is a culmination of shared efforts, encouragement, and inspiration from many individuals. To each of you, whether mentioned here or in spirit, I owe my deepest gratitude.

— Adeeb Jamal

(Author of Titans of Trade and Power and Project Manhattan, Researcher and writer of 4 research papers and Certified Professional in Cybersecurity Analytics and Project Management from Microsoft and Google.)

Prologue

In the quiet of an unassuming office in 1939, a letter was drafted—its words a delicate thread weaving together science and urgency. Addressed to President Franklin D. Roosevelt, it bore the weight of a monumental revelation: the discovery of nuclear fission and its potential to unleash a power unlike any the world had ever seen. That letter, signed by physicist Albert Einstein and his colleague Leó Szilárd, would become the spark that ignited one of the most ambitious, secretive, and transformative endeavors in human history—the Manhattan Project.

The story of the Manhattan Project is not simply the tale of a technological achievement; it is a window into the soul of humanity. It is a story of collaboration and division, of intellect and intuition, of ambition and doubt. It is the story of individuals—scientists, engineers, soldiers, and laborers—whose efforts, whether motivated by duty, fear, or curiosity, culminated in the creation of the first atomic bombs.

This journey begins in an era of global instability, where the dark shadow of war loomed over nations. The fear of Nazi Germany achieving nuclear capability drove the United States to mobilize its greatest minds, resources, and ingenuity. In secluded laboratories and makeshift towns, the seeds of scientific discovery were cultivated with unprecedented urgency.

But the Manhattan Project was more than a scientific experiment—it was a human endeavor. For every calculation scribbled on a blackboard, there was a moment of doubt. For every breakthrough, there was a question of morality. What began as a race for survival transformed into a reckoning with the profound consequences of wielding such destructive power.

This book is an invitation to step into that world. Through these pages, you will journey into the laboratories at Los Alamos, the bustling industrial complex at Oak Ridge, and the barren testing grounds of the Nevada desert. You will witness the collaboration of minds like Robert Oppenheimer, Enrico Fermi, and Niels Bohr, whose genius shaped the project's direction, and the untold stories of countless individuals whose contributions were equally vital yet often overlooked.

More than a historical account, this book aims to uncover the untold story—the emotional weight, ethical dilemmas, and enduring legacy of the Manhattan Project. Its impact echoes through time, not only in the shadow of Hiroshima and Nagasaki but also in the policies, fears, and hopes that define the modern era.

As you embark on this journey, consider not just the achievements but the questions they leave behind: How should humanity wield the knowledge it possesses? What price are we willing to pay for security and progress? And what lessons can we draw from the choices made during one of the most pivotal moments in history?

The Manhattan Project was a fusion of brilliance and burden, a testament to both the heights of human ingenuity and the depths of our ethical quandaries. This is its story—untold, unraveled, and unflinchingly human.

CHAPTER ONE

THE WORLD BEFORE THE ATOM

The state of science before the Manhattan Project-

The state of science before the Manhattan Project was shaped by a mixture of rapidly advancing theoretical knowledge, experimental breakthroughs, and the ongoing tensions of a world on the brink of war. The period leading up to the Manhattan Project, roughly from the late 19th century to the early 1940s, witnessed a massive evolution in scientific understanding, particularly in the fields of nuclear physics, chemistry, and engineering. These advancements would lay the groundwork for the development of nuclear weapons during World War II.

1. The Rise of Modern Physics-

Before the Manhattan Project, science had already undergone a significant transformation, particularly in the field of physics. The turn of the 20th century saw the dismantling of classical Newtonian mechanics, with Albert Einstein's theory of relativity, Max Planck's work on quantum theory, and Niels Bohr's contributions to atomic structure radically altering our understanding of the universe.

The Theory of Relativity-

Einstein's special theory of relativity (1905) and general theory of relativity (1915) were pivotal in the development of modern physics. The former introduced the groundbreaking idea that time and space are not fixed entities but are relative to the observer. This theory revolutionized our understanding of the universe, especially in the realms of high velocities and gravitational forces. In the latter, Einstein's general theory of relativity expanded upon the concept of gravitation, describing gravity not as a force but as a curvature of spacetime caused by massive objects.

While relativity would later prove fundamental to understanding atomic physics, it was Einstein's work on mass-energy equivalence—famously expressed in the equation $E=mc2E = mc^2E=mc2$—that directly contributed to the birth of the atomic age. This equation implied that mass and energy were interchangeable and that small amounts of mass could be converted into vast amounts of energy, which would become crucial for the development of nuclear power and weapons.

Quantum Mechanics-

At the same time, quantum mechanics was emerging as another paradigm-shifting theory. In 1900, Max Planck proposed that energy is emitted in discrete quantities, or "quanta," marking the birth of quantum theory. This idea was expanded by Einstein in 1905, who demonstrated the photoelectric effect, which showed that light could be understood as both a wave and a particle, laying the foundation for quantum mechanics.

In the years following, physicists such as Niels Bohr, Werner Heisenberg, and Erwin Schrödinger would further develop quantum mechanics, leading to a deeper understanding of atomic and subatomic particles. Heisenberg's uncertainty principle (1927), which postulated that one could not simultaneously know both the position and momentum of a particle with absolute precision, and Schrödinger's wave equation (1926), which described the behavior of quantum particles, were groundbreaking developments. These ideas played a direct role in the later discovery of nuclear fission.

The Discovery of the Neutron and the Atomic Nucleus-

In the 1920s, physicists were beginning to understand the structure of the atom. In 1911, Ernest Rutherford's famous gold foil experiment revealed the existence of a dense atomic nucleus, challenging the prevailing plum pudding model. By the 1930s, scientists had determined that the atom was made up of a nucleus, composed of protons and neutrons, surrounded by electrons.

The discovery of the neutron by James Chadwick in 1932 was crucial. Neutrons were electrically neutral particles that could penetrate atomic nuclei, facilitating the process of nuclear fission. This discovery, combined with the growing knowledge of atomic structure, created the conditions for a new era in atomic research.

2. The Emergence of Nuclear Fission-

The most significant scientific discovery in the lead-up to the Manhattan Project was the discovery of nuclear fission in 1938. The story of this discovery begins with the work of Lise Meitner and Otto Hahn, who were conducting experiments with uranium. Hahn and Fritz Strassmann had observed that bombarding uranium with neutrons resulted in the splitting of uranium atoms, releasing a tremendous amount of energy. Lise Meitner, who had been forced to flee Nazi Germany due to her Jewish heritage, and her nephew Otto Frisch provided the theoretical explanation for this process, showing that it was indeed a fission reaction, where the nucleus of an atom splits into smaller fragments, releasing large amounts of energy.

This discovery raised the possibility that nuclear reactions could be controlled and harnessed for both energy production and, more ominously, the creation of powerful weapons. The potential for a self-sustaining nuclear chain reaction, where the products of one fission event would trigger further fission events, became clear. The implications were enormous: if controlled, this process could provide a nearly limitless source of energy; if unleashed, it could lead to the creation of a devastating weapon.

The concept of nuclear fission was quickly recognized as a breakthrough, but it was not yet clear how to harness the energy released in a controlled manner. Researchers around the world began to explore how to trigger and sustain a chain reaction, but the technology was still in its infancy.

3. The Role of Scientists and Governments-

While the theoretical groundwork for nuclear physics was being laid, it was the political and military tensions of the 1930s and 1940s that would bring science and technology to bear on the development of nuclear weapons. The rise of Nazi Germany, under the leadership of Adolf Hitler, prompted a series of events that would directly lead to the establishment of the Manhattan Project.

The German Threat-

In the 1930s, German physicists such as Werner Heisenberg, Otto Hahn, and others were making significant progress in understanding nuclear fission. However, the rise of the Nazi regime raised concerns that Germany might be the first nation to develop a nuclear weapon. In 1938, when the discovery of nuclear fission was made, the possibility of harnessing this process for destructive purposes was clear, and many physicists feared that the Germans would be able to create an atomic bomb.

In 1939, a letter written by Albert Einstein and physicist Leo Szilard to U.S. President Franklin D. Roosevelt warned of the potential for Nazi Germany to develop nuclear weapons. The letter, which was signed by Einstein but primarily drafted by Szilard, described the potential for an atomic bomb and urged the U.S. to begin similar research efforts. This letter was instrumental in pushing the U.S. government to take the threat seriously and eventually led to the establishment of the Manhattan Project.

The Establishment of the Manhattan Project-

In response to growing fears about German progress, the U.S. government established the Manhattan Project in 1942, a secret research and development effort aimed at building an atomic bomb before Nazi Germany could do so. The project brought together the brightest minds in physics, engineering, and chemistry from across the United States, Europe, and even Japan. The goal was clear: develop the atomic bomb before it could be used against the Allies.

J. Robert Oppenheimer was appointed as the scientific director of the Manhattan Project, and the team of researchers included renowned physicists such as Enrico Fermi, Leo Szilard, and Niels Bohr. The project would be carried out at multiple sites across the U.S., including the Los Alamos Laboratory in New Mexico, where the actual development of the bomb would take place.

4. The Precursor Discoveries: From U235 to the First Chain Reaction-

The road to the atomic bomb involved a series of discoveries and technological innovations. One of the critical discoveries was the identification of uranium-235 (U-235), an isotope of uranium that could sustain a nuclear chain reaction. Natural uranium contains only about 0.7% U-235, with the rest being uranium-238, which is not suitable for sustaining a chain reaction. Researchers would need to develop methods to enrich uranium to increase the concentration of U-235.

Meanwhile, experiments with nuclear reactors began to show that a controlled chain reaction was possible. In 1942, Enrico Fermi and his team at the University of Chicago successfully built the first self-sustaining nuclear chain reaction in a reactor called Chicago Pile-1. This breakthrough demonstrated that it was possible to produce a controlled release of nuclear energy, providing the scientific foundation for the development of nuclear reactors and, ultimately, nuclear weapons.

5. The State of Science and Technology on the Eve of the Manhattan Project-

By the time the Manhattan Project officially began in 1942, science was already at the cusp of an atomic revolution. The groundbreaking discoveries in quantum mechanics, nuclear physics, and chemistry had provided the knowledge necessary to build the atomic bomb. However, there were still immense technical and practical challenges to overcome. Scientists were faced with the need to enrich uranium, build large-scale reactors, and develop methods for constructing a bomb that could unleash the power of the atom.

The world had entered an age where the potential for mass destruction through scientific knowledge was more apparent than ever before. The state of science before the Manhattan Project was one of anticipation and uncertainty, with the looming threat of war pushing the urgency of scientific innovation. The knowledge and discoveries made in the years preceding the project would change the world forever, opening the door to both the peaceful use of nuclear energy and the devastating power of atomic weapons.

In the final analysis, the state of science before the Manhattan Project was one of unprecedented progress. The 1930s and 1940s saw the convergence of brilliant minds, cutting-edge discoveries, and intense political pressures that would result in one of the most important and controversial scientific projects in history. As the atomic age dawned, the role of science in shaping the future of humanity would never be the same.

Early discoveries in nuclear physics-

Early Discoveries in Nuclear Physics-
The development of nuclear physics was one of the most profound and transformative intellectual achievements of the 20th century. The early discoveries in this field, including Einstein's famous equation, Rutherford's pioneering findings on atomic structure, and other key contributions, laid the foundation for the eventual development of nuclear technology, including both nuclear energy and weapons. These discoveries were not isolated but part of a series of interrelated scientific

breakthroughs, spanning over several decades, that challenged and ultimately overturned previous understandings of the atom, the forces of nature, and the very fabric of the universe.

1. The Early Concept of the Atom-

Before the advent of nuclear physics, the concept of the atom had already undergone significant development. In ancient Greece, philosophers like Democritus postulated that matter was composed of indivisible particles called "atomos," though these ideas were largely philosophical rather than scientific. It was not until the early 19th century that scientific thinking about the atom began to gain traction, especially through the work of John Dalton, who developed the atomic theory. Dalton's model, published in 1808, proposed that each element consisted of atoms of a single, unique type and that chemical reactions were essentially the rearranging of these atoms.

By the late 19th century, scientists had begun to develop more precise models of atomic structure. Experiments with electricity and magnetism led to the discovery of the electron by J.J. Thomson in 1897. Thomson's "plum pudding" model of the atom suggested that electrons were embedded in a positively charged "soup" within an atom, a model that was soon to be disproven.

2. The Discovery of the Nucleus-

One of the most important milestones in the development of nuclear physics was Ernest Rutherford's discovery of the atomic nucleus. In 1909, Rutherford and his colleagues, Hans Geiger and Ernest Marsden, conducted the famous gold foil experiment, in which they fired alpha particles (helium nuclei) at a thin sheet of gold. Most of the alpha particles passed through the gold foil without any deflection, which was consistent with the prevailing model of the atom at the time. However, a small number of particles were deflected at large angles, and some even bounced back toward the source.

Rutherford's interpretation of these results was revolutionary. He concluded that the atom was mostly empty space, with a tiny, dense, positively charged nucleus at its center, which repelled the positively charged alpha particles. This was in stark contrast to Thomson's "plum pudding" model, where the positive charge was assumed to be spread out over the entire atom. Rutherford's nuclear model of the atom, proposed in 1911, demonstrated that the atom was not indivisible, as once thought, but contained a central core, or nucleus, around which the much lighter electrons orbited.

This discovery was foundational in the development of nuclear physics, as it introduced the concept of a nucleus and suggested that much of the atom's mass and its positive charge were concentrated in this small, dense core. Rutherford's work on the nucleus would lay the groundwork for further discoveries in atomic structure and later advances in nuclear reactions.

The Discovery of the Proton-

Following Rutherford's discovery of the nucleus, the next major step was the identification of the proton. In 1917, Rutherford conducted experiments in which he bombarded nitrogen gas with alpha particles and observed the emission of hydrogen nuclei. This led him to propose the existence of a new particle, which he called the proton. Unlike electrons, which were much lighter, protons were positively charged and much heavier. This discovery confirmed the nucleus as not only the center of positive charge but also as the repository of much of the atom's mass.

The identification of the proton, combined with Rutherford's earlier work on the nucleus, provided the first accurate picture of the atom's internal structure, revealing a dense, positively charged core surrounded by electrons in orbit.

3. The Neutron and the Foundation of Nuclear Physics-

While the discovery of the proton was crucial in advancing atomic theory, the next great breakthrough came in 1932, with the discovery of the neutron by James Chadwick. Chadwick's work filled in an important gap in Rutherford's model: while the proton accounted for the positive charge in the nucleus, the nucleus still had to account for the rest of the atom's mass. The discovery of the neutron, a particle with approximately the same mass as the proton but with no electric charge, completed the picture of the atomic nucleus as being made up of protons and neutrons.

The neutron's lack of electric charge made it particularly important in nuclear reactions. Unlike protons, neutrons could penetrate atomic nuclei without being repelled by the electric charge, making them ideal for triggering nuclear fission reactions. This discovery by Chadwick opened the door to further investigations into nuclear reactions and played a central role in the later development of nuclear energy and weapons.

4. The Birth of Quantum Theory-

While Rutherford and others were making groundbreaking discoveries in nuclear physics, developments in quantum mechanics were also reshaping the understanding of atomic and subatomic particles. At the turn of the 20th century, classical physics, based on Newtonian mechanics and electromagnetism, was no longer sufficient to explain the behavior of matter at the atomic scale. This led to the development of quantum mechanics, which would play a central role in the future of nuclear physics.

In 1900, Max Planck introduced the concept of quantized energy, which proposed that energy could only be emitted or absorbed in discrete amounts, or "quanta." This radical idea was initially developed to explain black-body radiation but would later become the foundation of quantum mechanics. Albert Einstein expanded on Planck's work in 1905 with his theory of the photoelectric effect, which showed that light could behave as both a wave and a particle, a concept that would later become central to quantum theory.

The development of quantum mechanics was further advanced by physicists such as Niels Bohr, Werner Heisenberg, and Erwin Schrödinger. In 1913, Bohr proposed his model of the atom, in which electrons occupied fixed orbits around the nucleus, with the energy of each orbit being quantized. This model explained the spectral lines observed in hydrogen and was a key step in the development of quantum theory.

Heisenberg's uncertainty principle (1927) and Schrödinger's wave equation (1926) were further breakthroughs in understanding atomic behavior. Heisenberg's uncertainty principle stated that one could not simultaneously know both the position and momentum of a particle with absolute precision, while Schrödinger's wave equation provided a mathematical framework for describing the behavior of quantum particles as waves. These developments would be crucial for understanding the behavior of subatomic particles like electrons, protons, and neutrons.

5. Einstein's Equation and the Concept of Mass-Energy Equivalence-

One of the most important contributions to nuclear physics came from Albert Einstein's theory of special relativity, particularly his famous equation E=mc2, published in 1905. This equation showed that mass and energy are interchangeable; that is, mass can be converted into energy and vice versa. The equation, E=mc2, tells us that the energy (E) of an object is equal to its mass (m) times the square of the speed of light (c2).

Einstein's equation was groundbreaking because it showed that a small amount of mass could be converted into a tremendous amount of energy. This idea became a key part of nuclear physics. In nuclear fission and fusion reactions, small amounts of mass are indeed converted into large amounts of energy, as seen in the functioning of the atomic bomb and nuclear reactors. Though Einstein himself did not work on the development of nuclear weapons, his equation provided the theoretical foundation for understanding how nuclear reactions could unleash such enormous amounts of energy.

6. Nuclear Fission: The Discovery That Changed the World-

In 1938, the discovery of nuclear fission by Otto Hahn and Fritz Strassmann was a pivotal moment in nuclear physics. Hahn and Strassmann were experimenting with uranium and bombarding it with neutrons when they observed that the uranium nucleus split into two smaller nuclei, releasing energy. The discovery was groundbreaking because it demonstrated that the nucleus could be divided into smaller parts, releasing a massive amount of energy in the process.

Lise Meitner, who had collaborated with Hahn and Strassmann, and her nephew Otto Frisch were the first to understand the significance of the discovery, proposing that the fission of uranium was due to the splitting of the nucleus into smaller fragments. This discovery marked the beginning of a new era in nuclear physics. It was quickly realized that a chain reaction, where the products of one fission reaction could cause further fission reactions, could be achieved. This knowledge would later prove to be central to the development of nuclear weapons.

7. The Development of Nuclear Technology-

The discovery of nuclear fission opened the door to the development of nuclear energy and weapons. Scientists quickly recognized that the energy released during fission could be harnessed for both peaceful and destructive purposes. The concept of a chain reaction led to the idea of a nuclear bomb, a weapon capable of producing an explosion of unprecedented power.

In the years following the discovery of fission, scientists around the world, including those involved in the Manhattan Project, worked tirelessly to understand and control nuclear reactions. The development of nuclear reactors, including the first successful chain reaction initiated by Enrico Fermi and his team in 1942, was a direct result of these early discoveries.

The early discoveries in nuclear physics, from Rutherford's identification of the nucleus to Einstein's mass-energy equivalence and the discovery of nuclear fission, provided the intellectual foundation for the atomic age. These breakthroughs not only transformed the scientific understanding of matter and energy but also changed the course of history, leading to the development of nuclear energy and weapons. The legacy of these discoveries continues to shape the modern world, with both beneficial and harmful consequences, as nuclear technology plays a central role in energy production, medicine, and geopolitics.

The geopolitical climate leading to World War II-

The Geopolitical Climate Leading to World War II-

The outbreak of World War II in 1939 was the culmination of a long series of events and tensions that developed over several decades. The geopolitical climate in the interwar years was marked by a combination of unresolved issues from the First World War, the global economic depression of the 1930s, the failure of international diplomacy, and the rise of totalitarian regimes bent on territorial expansion. World War II was not merely the product of a single event but the result of a confluence of multiple factors, many of which had been brewing for decades. The war was not a sudden eruption but the consequence of a failure to address rising tensions and an inability to resolve geopolitical disputes effectively.

In order to understand how the world descended into a global conflict in 1939, it is crucial to examine the key events and issues that contributed to the political instability and rising militarism of the 1930s. This involves an exploration of the aftermath of World War I, the interwar years of economic crises and political turbulence, the rise of aggressive nationalist and fascist movements, and the inability of the international community to maintain peace.

1. The Legacy of World War I and the Treaty of Versailles-

World War I (1914-1918) fundamentally reshaped the political and territorial structure of Europe. The war caused immense destruction, with millions of soldiers and civilians killed, and vast portions of Europe's landscape decimated. The Treaty of Versailles, which officially ended the war in 1919, aimed to ensure a lasting peace and prevent future conflicts by imposing harsh penalties on Germany, the primary instigator of the war. However, the treaty's terms sowed the seeds of resentment and dissatisfaction, setting the stage for future conflict.

The Treaty of Versailles held Germany solely responsible for the war and demanded significant territorial and economic reparations. It imposed severe military restrictions on the German army, forbidding conscription and limiting the number of troops. It also demilitarized the Rhineland, forbade Germany from uniting with Austria (Anschluss), and forced the country to surrender its overseas colonies. The reparations that Germany was required to pay were enormous, and the economic burden created immense hardship for the German population. These conditions were seen as humiliating and unjust by many Germans, including Adolf Hitler, who would later use the Treaty of Versailles as a rallying cry for his rise to power.

The collapse of several empires, including the Austro-Hungarian Empire, the Ottoman Empire, and Tsarist Russia, further contributed to the instability in Europe. The Treaty of Versailles and its associated peace treaties created new states, such as Czechoslovakia, Poland, and Yugoslavia, but these new countries were often ethnically diverse and plagued by internal tensions. This created a powder keg of potential conflicts, with many national groups seeking to either assert their independence or rejoin their ethnic kin in neighboring states. This was especially the case in regions like Central and Eastern Europe, where the new borders created by the Treaty of Versailles left many ethnic minorities dissatisfied with their political status.

The League of Nations was created in the aftermath of the war as an international body to promote peace and cooperation among nations. However, its effectiveness was severely hampered by the absence of the United States and the inability of the League to take decisive action in response to acts of aggression by the rising totalitarian states. The U.S. Senate rejected membership in the League, believing that isolationism was the best course for America. This absence of American influence allowed aggressive nations such as Germany, Italy, and Japan to expand their territories with minimal international opposition.

2. Economic and Political Instability in the 1920s and 1930s-

The years following World War I were marked by political instability and economic hardship in many countries, especially in Europe. The global economy struggled to recover from the effects of the war, and the early 1920s were characterized by inflation, high unemployment, and widespread poverty. The Great Depression of the 1930s, which began with the U.S. stock market crash in 1929, had a devastating global impact. It exacerbated existing economic problems and contributed to the rise of extremist political movements in many countries.

In Germany, the economic situation was particularly dire. Hyperinflation in 1923 wiped out the savings of the middle class, and the country's economy remained fragile throughout the 1920s. The Great Depression hit Germany hard, with unemployment soaring to over 30%. The inability of the Weimar Republic to effectively address these economic challenges created widespread disillusionment with the democratic government. This discontent allowed Adolf Hitler and the Nazi Party to rise to prominence, as they promised to restore national pride and prosperity through radical nationalist and militarist policies.

In Italy, the situation was similarly unstable. Mussolini's Fascist regime came to power in 1922, capitalizing on the economic difficulties and the political chaos that followed World War I. Mussolini promised to restore Italy's former glory through authoritarian rule, territorial expansion, and military strength. He was able to consolidate power and suppress political opposition, using propaganda and violent tactics to maintain control.

In Japan, the economic difficulties of the 1920s and 1930s helped fuel the rise of militarist factions within the government. The Japanese military had a significant influence on the government, and it increasingly advocated for territorial expansion as a solution to Japan's economic woes. This expansionist policy led Japan to invade Manchuria in 1931 and eventually to launch a full-scale invasion of China in 1937.

3. The Rise of Totalitarian Regimes-

The interwar period saw the rise of several totalitarian regimes that sought to challenge the existing international order. The most notable of these were the Nazi regime in Germany, Fascist Italy, and militarist Japan. These regimes were united by their commitment to expansionism, authoritarian rule, and the rejection of democratic norms.

Nazi Germany and the Rise of Adolf Hitler-

Adolf Hitler and the Nazi Party came to power in Germany in 1933. Hitler's ideology, known as Nazism, was based on extreme nationalism, anti-Semitism, and the desire to expand Germany's territory. He rejected the principles of the Treaty of Versailles and sought to overturn its provisions, particularly the restrictions on Germany's military. Hitler's ultimate goal was to establish a Greater Germany, which would include the territories of Austria, Czechoslovakia, and large parts of Eastern Europe. He believed that the German people needed more living space (Lebensraum), which could only be achieved through military conquest.

Hitler's rise was facilitated by the economic turmoil of the Great Depression and the weakness of the Weimar Republic. He used his oratory skills to rally the German people, promising to restore national pride and rebuild the economy. Once in power, Hitler moved quickly to consolidate his control over the government, eliminating political opposition and establishing a totalitarian state. The Nazi regime pursued a policy of aggressive expansionism, reoccupying the Rhineland in 1936, annexing Austria in 1938, and demanding the Sudetenland from

Czechoslovakia. These actions were met with little resistance from Britain and France, who followed a policy of appeasement in an attempt to avoid another war.

Fascist Italy and Benito Mussolini-

Benito Mussolini, who came to power in Italy in 1922, established the first fascist regime in Europe. Mussolini's regime was characterized by extreme nationalism, militarism, and authoritarian rule. Like Hitler, Mussolini sought to restore national pride and establish a new Roman Empire. He pursued aggressive territorial expansion, beginning with the invasion of Ethiopia in 1935. Mussolini also sought to strengthen Italy's position in the Mediterranean by forming alliances with Germany and Japan.

Mussolini's fascism was based on the idea that the state should have total control over all aspects of society, including the economy, culture, and political life. Mussolini used propaganda, violence, and repression to maintain control, suppressing political opposition and dismantling democratic institutions.

Militarist Japan and Expansionism in Asia-

In Japan, the rise of militarism in the 1930s was closely tied to the country's desire for territorial expansion. Japan had experienced significant economic challenges during the 1920s, and the Great Depression exacerbated the country's problems. The Japanese military, which had long been a powerful force in the government, increasingly advocated for expansion in Asia as a means of securing resources and establishing Japan as a dominant power in the region.

Japan's first major act of aggression came in 1931, when it invaded Manchuria, a resource-rich region in northeastern China. The international community condemned the invasion, but the League of Nations was unable to take any meaningful action. Japan's actions were part of a broader plan to establish a Greater East Asia Co-Prosperity Sphere, a bloc of nations under Japanese control that would be free from Western influence. This expansionist policy eventually led to Japan's invasion of China in

1937 and its eventual entry into World War II.

4. The Failure of the League of Nations and Appeasement-

The League of Nations, established after World War I as an international body aimed at preventing future conflicts, was largely ineffective in the interwar period. The absence of the United States and the League's inability to take decisive action in the face of aggression by the Axis powers weakened its credibility and authority. The League failed to prevent the rise of fascism in Europe and Asia and was unable to halt the territorial expansion of Germany, Italy, and Japan.

The policy of appeasement, particularly adopted by Britain and France, also played a significant role in enabling the Axis powers to grow stronger. In the 1930s, as Hitler began his territorial expansion, Britain and France hoped to avoid another war by making concessions to Germany. The most notable example of this policy was the Munich Agreement of 1938, in which Britain and France allowed Hitler to annex the Sudetenland in exchange for a promise of no further territorial expansion. This appeasement ultimately failed, as Hitler continued his aggressive actions, culminating in the invasion of Poland in 1939.

5. The Molotov-Ribbentrop Pact and the Outbreak of War-

The final catalyst for World War II was the signing of the Molotov-Ribbentrop Pact between Nazi Germany and the Soviet Union in August 1939. This non-aggression pact shocked the world, as the two countries had been ideological enemies. The pact included a secret protocol that divided Eastern Europe into spheres of influence, enabling Hitler to invade Poland without fear of Soviet intervention. The invasion of Poland on September 1, 1939, marked the official beginning of World War II, as Britain and France declared war on Germany in response.

The geopolitical climate leading to World War II was the result of a complex set of factors, including the unresolved consequences of World War I, economic instability, the rise of totalitarian regimes, and the failure of diplomacy. The aftermath of World War I created a fragile and unstable peace, and the harsh conditions of the Treaty of Versailles sowed the seeds of resentment, particularly in Germany. The rise of aggressive nationalist movements in Germany, Italy, and Japan, coupled with the inability of the international community to prevent further aggression, ultimately led to the outbreak of the most destructive conflict in human history. The failure of the League of Nations, the policy of appeasement, and the Molotov-Ribbentrop Pact all contributed to the conditions that made war inevitable. The world would never be the same again after 1939, as the conflict that followed reshaped global politics, economics, and society.

Theoretical breakthroughs by scientists like Leo Szilard and Enrico Fermi-

The development of nuclear technology and the subsequent creation of the atomic bomb during World War II were not the result of a singular discovery, but rather a series of interconnected theoretical breakthroughs by visionary scientists. Among these were Leo Szilard and Enrico Fermi, whose pioneering work laid the foundation for the atomic age. Their contributions, coupled with the efforts of other physicists and chemists, ultimately led to the realization of the nuclear chain reaction and the advent of the Manhattan Project, which would change the course of history.

1. The Rise of Nuclear Physics and the Birth of Modern Atomic Theory-

At the dawn of the 20th century, the world of atomic science was rapidly transforming. The early atomic model, which had remained largely unchanged since the time of Dalton and Democritus, was on the verge of a radical change. In the years following the discovery of X-rays by Wilhelm Roentgen in 1895, and radioactivity by Henri Becquerel in 1896, scientists began to realize that the atom, long considered indivisible, was far more complex than previously thought.

The work of J.J. Thomson, who discovered the electron in 1897, shifted scientific thinking away from the idea of indivisible atoms and toward a more complex understanding of atomic structure. However, it was Ernest Rutherford's groundbreaking experiments in the early 1900s that truly shattered the old paradigm. In 1911, Rutherford conducted his famous gold foil experiment, which led to the discovery of the atomic nucleus. This was a pivotal moment in the development of nuclear physics. Rutherford showed that the atom consisted of a tiny, dense, positively charged nucleus at its center, surrounded by a cloud of electrons. This revelation would pave the way for further exploration into the nature of atomic nuclei and their interactions.

The next major breakthrough came with the discovery of the neutron by James Chadwick in 1932. Until that point, the nucleus was thought to be made up only of protons, the positively charged particles discovered by Rutherford. Chadwick's discovery of the neutron, a particle with no electric charge but with roughly the same mass as the proton, added another layer of complexity to the atom. The neutron played a crucial role in the development of nuclear physics, as it could interact with the nucleus without being repelled by the positive charge of the protons. This made neutrons the ideal candidates for initiating nuclear reactions, a discovery that would prove essential for the development of nuclear energy and weapons.

With the discovery of the neutron, the stage was set for the development of nuclear theory, and scientists were soon able to explore the possibility of harnessing the immense energy locked within the atom.

2. Leo Szilard and the Concept of the Nuclear Chain Reaction-

One of the most crucial theoretical breakthroughs came from Leo Szilard, a Hungarian-born physicist who became one of the key figures in the development of nuclear energy and weapons. Szilard's work in the 1930s centered around the idea of the nuclear chain reaction, a process in which nuclear fission could be triggered in a controlled manner, sustaining a reaction that would release an immense amount of energy.

In 1933, Szilard realized that neutrons could cause uranium atoms to split, releasing more neutrons in the process. This observation was a crucial step in the understanding of how a nuclear chain reaction could be initiated. If enough uranium atoms were present, the released neutrons could induce fission in other uranium atoms, creating a self-sustaining reaction. Szilard's insight was groundbreaking because it provided the theoretical foundation for the development of both nuclear reactors and atomic bombs.

Szilard was quick to recognize the potential military applications of his discovery. He understood that a sustained chain reaction could release enormous amounts of energy, which could be harnessed for destructive purposes. In 1934, Szilard patented the concept of a nuclear reactor, but his initial work focused on the development of a nuclear-powered submarine, rather than weapons. He envisioned a peaceful application of nuclear energy, but his ideas were soon to be redirected toward the urgent problem of nuclear weapons development in the face of rising tensions in Europe.

Szilard's role in the development of the atomic bomb was also crucial. In 1938, German scientists Otto Hahn and Fritz Strassmann discovered nuclear fission in uranium, showing that when uranium nuclei were bombarded with neutrons, they split into smaller nuclei and released a large amount of energy. This discovery confirmed Szilard's earlier theories and opened up new possibilities for nuclear energy. Fearing that Nazi Germany might use this knowledge to build an atomic bomb, Szilard approached Albert Einstein in 1939 with a warning. In a letter drafted by Szilard and signed by Einstein, they urged U.S. President Franklin D. Roosevelt to fund research into the development of nuclear weapons before the Nazis could develop one. This letter was instrumental in galvanizing U.S. efforts toward the eventual creation of the Manhattan Project.

Szilard's intellectual contributions to nuclear physics were immense. His theoretical understanding of the chain reaction and his ability to see the potential for both peaceful and military applications of nuclear energy would shape the course of history. His foresight and actions helped to set the stage for the development of the atomic bomb, and his legacy remains a central part of the story of the Manhattan Project.

3. Enrico Fermi and the Discovery of Neutron-Induced Fission-

While Leo Szilard was laying the groundwork for the nuclear chain reaction, Italian physicist Enrico Fermi was making his own major contributions to nuclear theory. Fermi's experiments with neutrons in the 1930s led to a number of important discoveries, including the realization that uranium could undergo fission when bombarded with neutrons.

Fermi's work was instrumental in understanding how neutrons could induce fission in uranium and other elements. In 1934, Fermi and his colleagues began bombarding elements with neutrons, and their work led to the discovery that some elements, such as uranium, could absorb neutrons and then undergo fission, splitting into smaller nuclei. Fermi's experiments demonstrated the potential of neutron-induced fission, which was critical for the development of nuclear reactors and, eventually, the atomic bomb.

In 1938, Otto Hahn and Fritz Strassmann in Germany made the breakthrough discovery that uranium could be split into two smaller nuclei upon neutron bombardment, releasing a large amount of energy. This discovery was pivotal because it showed that nuclear fission could be controlled and harnessed. Fermi's work, which had already shown the role of neutrons in inducing fission, now helped to explain the mechanics of the process in greater detail.

Fermi's work also demonstrated the importance of using slow neutrons, rather than fast neutrons, to initiate fission. He discovered that slowing down neutrons using a material like paraffin wax made them more effective in inducing fission. This insight was crucial for the development of the first nuclear reactors, as it showed that neutrons could be moderated, or slowed down, to create a sustained chain reaction. Fermi's work laid the foundation for the construction of the first nuclear reactor, the Chicago Pile-1, which was built as part of the Manhattan Project.

Fermi's experiments also led to the realization that uranium-235, a specific isotope of uranium, was particularly susceptible to fission. This was an important discovery because uranium-235 was the material that would be used in the construction of the atomic bomb. Fermi's work with uranium-235 and other isotopes helped to refine the understanding of nuclear reactions, and his contributions were essential to the development of the atomic bomb.

4. The Manhattan Project and the Birth of the Atomic Bomb-

The theoretical breakthroughs made by Leo Szilard, Enrico Fermi, and other physicists were critical in laying the groundwork for the creation of the atomic bomb. By the early 1940s, it was clear that nuclear fission could release immense amounts of energy, and scientists understood that the key to harnessing that energy lay in controlling the nuclear chain reaction.

In response to the growing fear that Nazi Germany was developing its own atomic bomb, the U.S. government initiated the Manhattan Project in 1942. Led by General Leslie Groves and scientific director J. Robert Oppenheimer, the project brought together some of the most brilliant minds in physics, chemistry, and engineering to solve the technical challenges of building a nuclear bomb.

The Manhattan Project aimed to produce two types of atomic bombs: one using uranium-235 and the other using plutonium-239. The project's scientists were tasked with designing a bomb that would release an enormous amount of energy in a single, catastrophic explosion. To achieve this, they needed to create a critical mass of fissile material—enough uranium-235 or plutonium-239 to sustain a chain reaction.

The first major hurdle was producing sufficient quantities of uranium-235 and plutonium-239. Uranium-235 is naturally rare, making up only about 0.7% of natural uranium. The rest is made up of uranium-238, which is not suitable for fission. The project's scientists had to develop a method for enriching uranium-235, which was accomplished using a variety of techniques, including gaseous diffusion and electromagnetic separation. Meanwhile, plutonium-239 was produced in a nuclear reactor, specifically designed for this purpose.

One of the most critical achievements of the Manhattan Project was the construction of the first nuclear reactor, Chicago Pile-1, which became the site of the first controlled nuclear chain reaction. On December 2, 1942, Fermi and his team achieved a self-sustaining reaction, confirming that it was possible to release nuclear energy in a controlled manner. This was a key step toward developing both nuclear energy and the atomic bomb.

After several years of research and development, the Manhattan Project scientists successfully built and tested the world's first atomic bomb. On July 16, 1945, the Trinity test took place in the New Mexico desert. The explosion, caused by the detonation of a plutonium bomb, was the first demonstration of nuclear power on such a massive scale. The success of the Trinity test paved the way for the use of atomic bombs on Japan, marking the end of World War II.

5. The End of One Era and the Beginning of Another-

The theoretical breakthroughs made by scientists like Leo Szilard and Enrico Fermi were essential in shaping the course of history. Szilard's conception of the nuclear chain reaction and Fermi's work on neutron-induced fission laid the intellectual groundwork for the development of nuclear energy and weapons. Their insights, along with the contributions of many other scientists, enabled the United States to create the atomic bomb, which altered the nature of warfare and international relations.

The Manhattan Project was not just a scientific achievement; it was a momentous event that forever changed the world. The successful development of the atomic bomb brought an end to World War II but also ushered in the nuclear age, a period of intense scientific, political, and ethical challenges. The discoveries made by Szilard, Fermi, and their colleagues remain central to modern physics and continue to shape the way we think about the atom, energy, and the future of warfare. The legacy of their work serves as a reminder of the immense power that scientific discoveries hold, for both good and ill.

The initial recognition of nuclear energy's potential for warfare-

The Initial Recognition of Nuclear Energy's Potential for Warfare-

The recognition of nuclear energy's potential for warfare represents one of the most significant moments in human history, with repercussions that continue to shape global politics, ethics, and security to this day. What began as a scientific breakthrough with the potential to provide new forms of energy and revolutionize the world, quickly evolved into a force of immense destructive power. Nuclear energy's path from a fascinating scientific discovery to a weapon of mass destruction was marked by a combination of intellectual breakthroughs, political developments, and historical events, each of which contributed to the growing recognition of nuclear energy's potential for warfare.

1. The Rise of Nuclear Science and Early Discoveries-

The story of nuclear energy's potential for warfare begins with the discovery of radioactivity in the late 19th century. In 1896, the French scientist Henri Becquerel discovered that uranium emitted radiation without any external energy source, an observation that sparked a wave of scientific interest in the mysterious properties of atomic substances. This discovery was quickly followed by the pioneering work of Marie and Pierre Curie, who identified and isolated radium and polonium, two highly radioactive elements. Their discoveries laid the foundation for further research into the atom's internal structure, revealing that atoms were not indivisible as once believed, but consisted of smaller, more powerful particles.

By the early 20th century, scientists had begun to explore the structure of the atom in greater detail. The most crucial breakthrough came in 1911 when Ernest Rutherford, a New Zealand-born physicist, discovered the nucleus at the center of the atom. This revelation fundamentally changed the understanding of atomic science, showing that the atom contained vast amounts of energy concentrated in its nucleus. Rutherford's findings opened the door to new possibilities in both peaceful applications, like energy generation, and potentially destructive uses, such as nuclear weapons.

In the following years, the concept of the atom and its components—the electron, proton, and neutron—became more refined. In 1932, James Chadwick discovered the neutron, which would prove to be essential in later developments related to nuclear energy and weapons. Scientists began to realize that if the nucleus of certain atoms could be split, it would release enormous amounts of energy. The idea that this energy could be harnessed for practical purposes began to take shape, but at this stage, the idea of weaponizing nuclear energy was far from being realized.

2. The Discovery of Nuclear Fission and Its Weaponized Potential-

The pivotal moment in the journey toward recognizing the potential of nuclear energy for warfare came in 1938 when German scientists Otto Hahn and Fritz Strassmann discovered nuclear fission. They found that when uranium atoms were bombarded with neutrons, they split into smaller nuclei, releasing a tremendous amount of energy. This discovery, combined with the theoretical framework developed by Lise Meitner and Otto Frisch, who explained the process and its potential for a chain reaction, opened up the possibility that this nuclear process could be controlled and harnessed.

Initially, this discovery was seen primarily in terms of its potential for energy generation. The idea of controlled nuclear fission reactions capable of producing large amounts of energy was a highly attractive concept. However, for a small group of scientists, the destructive possibilities of nuclear fission became increasingly evident. As early as 1939, physicists such as Leo Szilard recognized the immense power that could be released through uncontrolled fission reactions. The implications of this discovery for warfare became clear as they imagined the potential for creating a bomb with the explosive power to obliterate entire cities.

Leo Szilard, who had worked extensively on the problem of nuclear chain reactions, quickly realized that fission could be harnessed to create a weapon of unprecedented destructive power. Szilard, an immigrant physicist from Hungary, was acutely aware of the global political climate. By the late 1930s, Adolf Hitler's regime in Nazi Germany had shown increasing interest in scientific advancements, including the military applications of atomic energy. Szilard feared that Germany might be able to develop an atomic bomb, and his concerns were compounded by reports from other European scientists about the progress of nuclear research in Germany.

3. The Einstein-Szilard Letter: A Turning Point-

In 1939, Szilard sought the help of one of the most famous figures in the scientific community: Albert Einstein. Together, they wrote a letter to U.S. President Franklin D. Roosevelt, urging him to take immediate action to support nuclear research in the United States. The letter warned that nuclear fission could be used to create a powerful new weapon and that it was essential for the U.S. to invest in atomic research to stay ahead of Nazi

Germany, which might already be pursuing such a weapon. The Einstein-Szilard letter, signed by Einstein, who was widely admired for his work in theoretical physics, was sent to Roosevelt in October 1939, shortly after the outbreak of World War II.

The letter had a profound effect on the U.S. government. It convinced Roosevelt to establish the Advisory Committee on Uranium, a group tasked with investigating the potential applications of nuclear energy. The letter also sparked a broader conversation within the U.S. government and the scientific community about the need to explore the military potential of atomic energy. While many scientists were initially more focused on peaceful applications, the threat posed by Nazi Germany made it clear that nuclear energy had the potential to reshape the balance of global power.

This was the first significant formal recognition at the highest levels of government that nuclear energy could be weaponized. In 1941, the U.S. and the United Kingdom began sharing information on nuclear research, setting the stage for closer collaboration. Scientists from both countries, including Niels Bohr, who had fled Nazi-occupied Denmark, became central figures in the growing effort to understand and harness the power of nuclear fission.

4. The Manhattan Project: The Development of the Atomic Bomb-

As the war in Europe escalated, the United States accelerated its efforts to build an atomic bomb, leading to the creation of the Manhattan Project in 1942. The Manhattan Project was a massive, top-secret research and development program aimed at developing nuclear weapons before Germany could create them. The project brought together some of the brightest minds in the world, including scientists such as J. Robert Oppenheimer, Enrico Fermi, and Niels Bohr.

By 1942, under the direction of General Leslie Groves, the Manhattan Project focused on several critical areas: enriching uranium, building the reactors necessary to sustain nuclear chain reactions, and designing the bombs themselves. Scientists realized that the key to creating a viable atomic bomb was to obtain a sufficient amount of fissile material, specifically uranium-235 or plutonium-239. In 1942, the team successfully achieved the first self-sustaining nuclear chain reaction in the world at the University of Chicago. This moment, known as the Chicago Pile-1 experiment, confirmed that nuclear reactions could be controlled and used to produce energy. Soon after, the project focused on turning this new knowledge into a weapon.

The development of the atomic bomb was a race against time. With the United States' entry into the war following the attack on Pearl Harbor in December 1941, the threat of Nazi Germany achieving nuclear weapon capability was a looming concern. However, by 1944, it became clear that the Germans had fallen behind in their nuclear program due to a lack of resources, infighting among scientists, and strategic missteps. Despite this, the U.S. continued to push forward, determined to build the bomb before Japan could potentially access the technology.

5. The Trinity Test and the First Use of Nuclear Weapons-

In July 1945, the first successful test of an atomic bomb, codenamed "Trinity," took place in the New Mexico desert. The explosion released a massive amount of energy, equivalent to 20 kilotons of TNT, and marked the birth of the nuclear age. The Trinity test was a defining moment in the history of warfare, as it demonstrated that nuclear energy, once a concept of theoretical physics, had now become a weapon capable of annihilating entire cities.

The success of the Trinity test was followed by the decision to use atomic bombs on Japan. Despite Germany's surrender in May 1945, Japan had not yet given up, and the war in the Pacific was far from over. The U.S. believed that the use of nuclear weapons could bring about a quick end to the war, saving millions of lives that would have been lost in a prolonged invasion of Japan.

On August 6, 1945, the first atomic bomb, "Little Boy," was dropped on Hiroshima. The bomb, a uranium-based device, detonated with devastating force, killing an estimated 140,000 people by the end of the year. Three days later, a second bomb, "Fat Man," was dropped on Nagasaki. The bomb, made from plutonium, caused immediate destruction and killed an estimated 70,000 people.

The use of atomic bombs on Hiroshima and Nagasaki forced Japan to surrender, bringing an end to World War II. However, it also signaled the dawn of a new and terrifying era in warfare. The recognition of nuclear energy's potential for warfare had been fully realized, and the consequences of this realization would be felt for generations.

6. The Dual Nature of Nuclear Energy-

The recognition of nuclear energy's potential for warfare had profound implications for global security, ethics, and international relations. The atomic bomb was not just a military weapon; it was a symbol of the new world order, where the power to destroy entire cities and alter the course of human history rested in the hands of a few nations. The atomic bomb introduced a new form of warfare, one in which deterrence and the threat of annihilation became central to global politics.

While the atomic bomb was developed as a weapon of war, its potential for peaceful applications—such as nuclear energy for power generation—remained a key aspect of its legacy. In the years following World War II, nuclear energy became a symbol of both progress and fear. It represented the possibility of limitless energy, but also the risk of catastrophic destruction.

In the Cold War that followed, the nuclear arms race between the United States and the Soviet Union led to the creation of even more powerful nuclear weapons, including the hydrogen bomb. The recognition of nuclear energy's potential for warfare shaped not only the geopolitics of the 20th century but also the ethical debates surrounding the use of atomic weapons. As nations around the world sought to control the spread of nuclear technology, the dual nature of nuclear energy—its ability to power cities and destroy civilizations—remained a central concern.

The Legacy of Nuclear Energy's Weaponization-

The initial recognition of nuclear energy's potential for warfare marked a profound shift in human history. What began as a series of scientific discoveries in the early 20th century led to the development of one of the most powerful and destructive forces ever harnessed by humanity. The journey from nuclear discovery to weaponization was driven by a combination of scientific breakthroughs, political fears, and the recognition of nuclear energy's power.

Today, the legacy of nuclear energy's weaponization continues to shape international relations, military strategy, and the ethical questions surrounding the use of nuclear technology. The atomic bomb changed the nature of warfare forever and introduced the world to the terrifying possibility of global annihilation. At the same time, nuclear energy remains a powerful tool that, if used responsibly, has the potential to provide clean energy to a growing world. The recognition of nuclear energy's dual potential—as both a source of immense power and as a weapon of mass destruction—remains one of the defining challenges of the modern era.

CHAPTER TWO

THE SPARK – FROM THEORY TO ACTION

Einstein-Szilard letter to President Roosevelt-

The Einstein-Szilard letter to President Franklin D. Roosevelt, written on August 2, 1939, is one of the most crucial documents in the history of the atomic bomb and the development of nuclear weapons. It set in motion a series of events that would ultimately lead to the establishment of the Manhattan Project and the development of nuclear weapons by the United States during World War II. The letter was written by Leo Szilard, a Hungarian-born physicist, with the signature of Albert Einstein, one of the most renowned scientists of the 20th century.

Background to the Letter-

The early discoveries in nuclear physics and the increasing understanding of nuclear fission had raised the possibility of harnessing atomic energy in ways that could be used for both peaceful and military purposes. By the late 1930s, physicists had already begun to recognize the destructive potential of nuclear fission, which could be triggered by bombarding uranium atoms with neutrons. In 1938, German scientists Otto Hahn and Fritz Strassmann discovered the process of nuclear fission, and the subsequent theoretical work by Lise Meitner and Otto Frisch showed that the fission of uranium could produce a chain reaction, releasing enormous amounts of energy.

Physicists, especially those who had fled Nazi Germany, were acutely aware of the potential for this scientific breakthrough to be turned into a weapon. As tensions in Europe escalated, many of them feared that Nazi Germany, under the leadership of Adolf Hitler, could be the first to develop a nuclear bomb, which would grant them an overwhelming military advantage.

One of the most vocal scientists concerned with this issue was Leo Szilard, who had been working on theories related to nuclear chain reactions. He was deeply worried about the possibility of Nazi Germany making significant advances in nuclear weaponry. Having fled Germany himself, Szilard feared the consequences of a nuclear-armed Nazi regime. Recognizing the urgency of the situation, Szilard decided to take action by reaching out to the U.S. government. He believed that the United States, with its scientific and industrial capabilities, was the only nation that could develop atomic weapons in response to the Nazi threat.

Szilard's concerns were not just based on theoretical knowledge. By the time he wrote the letter to Roosevelt, Nazi Germany had begun to advance in the field of nuclear research, and there were reports that German scientists had already initiated studies on uranium and its potential military applications. If Germany succeeded in harnessing atomic energy, the consequences for the balance of power in Europe and the world would be catastrophic. This understanding led Szilard to conclude that the U.S. had to act immediately to prevent the Nazis from obtaining such a devastating weapon.

Szilard's Concerns and Einstein's Role-

Szilard had already made efforts to warn key American scientific figures, but he recognized that only a letter signed by Albert Einstein, the most famous scientist in the world, would get the attention of President Roosevelt and other high-ranking officials in the U.S. government. Einstein, despite his relatively limited direct involvement in atomic physics, had a deep understanding of the significance of the scientific discoveries and the geopolitical stakes at play.

Szilard approached Einstein with his concerns, and Einstein, after careful consideration, agreed to lend his name to the cause. Einstein's fame would ensure that the letter would not be dismissed, and his support would give the issue the weight it needed to be taken seriously by the U.S. government. In the early months of 1939, Szilard and Einstein discussed the potential dangers of nuclear fission being used to create a weapon, and Einstein, though he had a moral opposition to war, agreed that the threat from Nazi Germany required immediate action.

The decision to sign the letter was not an easy one for Einstein. Though a pacifist at heart, Einstein recognized that the stakes were too high to ignore the possibility of nuclear weapons falling into the hands of a totalitarian regime. Both men understood the devastating potential of nuclear energy, but they also saw the need for the U.S. to act quickly, as they feared that the Nazis were already making strides toward a bomb of their own.

Einstein and Szilard had also discussed the potential ethical consequences of creating such a weapon. While they both hoped the atomic bomb would never be used in combat, they knew that the threat of its use might be enough to deter hostile powers. Their motivations were complex, encompassing both a fear of Nazi Germany's scientific advancements and an understanding of the power that nuclear energy represented. Though Einstein would later express regret over his involvement in the bomb's development, at the time, he saw the need to act.

The Content of the Letter-

The Einstein-Szilard letter was drafted by Szilard, with Einstein's endorsement, and sent to President Roosevelt on August 2, 1939. The letter was short but powerful, warning the president of the dangers posed by the discovery of nuclear fission and urging immediate action to begin research into atomic energy for military purposes. The key points in the letter were:

Discovery of Nuclear Fission and Its Potential: The letter explained the recent discovery of nuclear fission by German scientists and highlighted that the process of splitting uranium atoms released enormous amounts of energy. The letter further explained that this discovery could lead to the creation of a new type of weapon, much more powerful than any that had been seen before. The authors emphasized that the energy released by a chain reaction in uranium could be harnessed for destructive purposes, creating a bomb of unprecedented power.

The Nazi Threat: Szilard and Einstein expressed their growing concern that Nazi Germany could already be working on developing an atomic bomb. The letter noted that, since Germany had been conducting research into uranium and had a strong scientific community, it was possible that the Nazis might already be making significant progress in their attempts to harness nuclear energy for military purposes. The letter warned that Germany's scientific community might be ahead of the United States in this regard, which would give them a decisive advantage in the war.

Urgency for Action: The letter stressed the urgency of the situation, urging President Roosevelt to take immediate action to ensure that the United States would not fall behind in the race to develop nuclear weapons. Szilard and Einstein recommended that the U.S. government fund research into nuclear fission and begin large-scale efforts to explore the creation of atomic bombs. They also suggested that the U.S. needed to establish a committee to study the possibilities of nuclear fission, with a focus on developing a nuclear weapon.

Call for Collaboration and Investment: In addition to urging the U.S. government to fund research, the letter also called for collaboration between American and European scientists who were already conducting nuclear research. Szilard and Einstein believed that bringing together the brightest minds in nuclear physics would be crucial for the successful development of an atomic bomb. They also noted that the U.S. government should invest in facilities and resources that would enable the rapid progress of research.

The letter's tone was urgent but measured, emphasizing the need for immediate action without resorting to hyperbole or alarmism. Szilard and Einstein both recognized the potential for scientific progress but also understood the devastating consequences if nuclear fission were used as a weapon. They called on President Roosevelt to take leadership on this issue and ensure that the United States was not left behind in the global race to harness atomic energy.

The Einstein-Szilard letter was a carefully worded document that balanced scientific warning with strategic foresight. Szilard's experience as a physicist and his understanding of the political climate of the time played a crucial role in the letter's design. It conveyed the need for urgent action but avoided creating a panic. Instead, it focused on the necessity of preparedness and foresight in the face of an emerging global threat.

The Immediate Response to the Letter-

Upon receiving the letter, President Roosevelt took the matter seriously. While Roosevelt had already been briefed on the possibilities of nuclear fission by his advisors, the Einstein-Szilard letter was the catalyst that prompted the U.S. government to take the next steps. Roosevelt, recognizing the importance of the situation, responded quickly. In October 1939, he authorized the creation of the Advisory Committee on Uranium, which was tasked with investigating the scientific and military implications of nuclear fission.

The committee's early efforts focused on understanding the practicalities of nuclear fission and its potential military applications. Although the committee was initially small and had limited resources, it quickly became clear that more significant efforts were required to explore the possibility of an atomic bomb. By 1940, discussions with Britain and Canada had begun, and the groundwork for a large-scale collaborative effort was laid.

The Manhattan Project, the top-secret program to develop an atomic bomb, was officially launched in 1942. It brought together the brightest minds in physics, chemistry, and engineering, including many scientists who had fled Nazi Europe. The project's goal was clear: to develop a nuclear weapon before the Axis powers could achieve the same. The program was carried out under tight security and ultimately led to the successful testing of the first atomic bomb in July 1945 at the Trinity Test in New Mexico.

The response to the letter highlighted the recognition of the letter's foresight and urgency. Roosevelt's decision to act upon the letter's recommendations was pivotal, as it enabled the United States to engage in a race against Nazi Germany and the Axis powers to develop atomic weapons. The letter's advocacy for scientific collaboration across borders also helped foster the international cooperation that would later define the Manhattan Project and its transatlantic partnerships.

The Long-Term Impact of the Einstein-Szilard Letter-

The Einstein-Szilard letter had far-reaching consequences beyond the immediate development of the atomic bomb. It marked the beginning of the U.S. government's active involvement in nuclear research and set the stage for the Cold War-era arms race between the United States and the Soviet Union. The use of nuclear weapons in World War II, particularly the bombing of Hiroshima and Nagasaki, raised ethical questions that continue to be debated to this day.

The letter also highlighted the complex relationship between science and politics, particularly in times of war. It demonstrated how scientific discoveries, when combined with political urgency, can lead to rapid technological advancements with profound implications for both national security and global peace. The legacy of the Einstein-Szilard letter continues to resonate in discussions about nuclear nonproliferation, the ethics of scientific research, and the responsible use of technology.

, the Einstein-Szilard letter remains one of the most significant documents in the history of science and warfare. It not only alerted the United States government to the dangers of nuclear weapons but also helped to catalyze the creation of the atomic bomb. The letter underscores the potential of science to shape the course of history and the responsibility of scientists to consider the ethical implications of their work. The events set in motion by this letter ultimately led to the development of nuclear weapons and the creation of the Manhattan Project, which would forever alter the landscape of global warfare.

Formation of the Advisory Committee on Uranium-

Formation of the Advisory Committee on Uranium: Paving the Way for the Manhattan Project

The formation of the Advisory Committee on Uranium in 1939 marked one of the critical moments in the early stages of the development of nuclear energy for military purposes, leading to the eventual creation of the Manhattan Project. The committee was not a singular, isolated effort, but rather a response to the growing realization that the power of nuclear fission could have significant military implications, particularly in the context of the geopolitical landscape of World War II. The committee's formation was largely influenced by the correspondence between Leo Szilard and Albert Einstein, as well as the broader scientific community's growing awareness of the potential destructive power inherent in the discovery of uranium fission.

The groundwork for the Advisory Committee was laid in response to increasing concerns among the scientific community regarding the potential military applications of nuclear energy, and especially the possibility that Nazi Germany, under the leadership of Adolf Hitler, might pursue the development of nuclear weapons. In this climate, the United States government realized the necessity of investigating nuclear fission with urgency and establishing a scientific effort to explore the technology's military potential. The Advisory Committee on Uranium would ultimately serve as a central organizing body to assess the feasibility of a uranium-based weapon, offer recommendations for scientific direction, and push for the resources needed to make such a weapon a reality.

The Early Role of the Committee and Its Key Scientists-

Initially, the committee's mandate was to evaluate the possibility of uranium fission and whether it could be harnessed for a practical military application. The committee was formed by the National Academy of Sciences under the direction of Harold Urey, a physicist and chemist who had contributed significantly to the field of nuclear physics. Urey's involvement helped provide the early direction for uranium research, as he was well-versed in the chemistry of uranium and had a deep understanding of the challenges involved in isolating and enriching uranium. He was also an advocate for ensuring that the U.S. government invested adequately in this emerging field of research.

A key aspect of the committee's role was to bring together prominent scientists who would eventually play central roles in the Manhattan Project. This group of individuals included physicists such as Enrico Fermi, Leo Szilard, J. Robert Oppenheimer, and Arthur Compton, all of whom would go on to make significant contributions to nuclear research during the war. The collaborative nature of the committee brought together some of the best minds in physics and chemistry, though their backgrounds varied greatly. Some, like Szilard, had been exiled from Europe due to the rise of Nazi fascism, while others, like Urey and Oppenheimer, were American-born scientists deeply entrenched in the academic landscape.

Szilard, a Hungarian-born physicist, was instrumental in emphasizing the military potential of uranium fission. His experiences in Europe, where he had witnessed the rise of fascism and the persecution of scientists under the Nazi regime, made him especially attuned to the urgency of preventing nuclear weapons from falling into the wrong hands. He believed that the United States had a moral obligation to pursue nuclear research before Nazi Germany could develop such weapons. Szilard's ability to combine his deep scientific knowledge with a keen geopolitical awareness made him a driving force within the committee, and his work would later lead to the creation of the letter to President Franklin D. Roosevelt, urging the U.S. to initiate a large-scale research effort into nuclear weapons development.

One of the key accomplishments of the Advisory Committee on Uranium was its early recognition of the potential applications of uranium fission for military purposes. While much of the committee's work was speculative and theoretical, its conclusions led to the early mobilization of resources for further research into uranium enrichment and the development of a nuclear reactor capable of sustaining a chain reaction. The committee's report confirmed that uranium could indeed undergo fission, releasing a vast amount of energy in the process, and recommended that the U.S. government fund research into harnessing this energy for military purposes.

Challenges in Early Nuclear Research-

Despite the enthusiasm surrounding the potential of uranium fission, the committee and the broader scientific community faced significant scientific and technical challenges in the early stages of nuclear research. The concept of uranium fission was still relatively new, and many of the fundamental principles surrounding it were not fully understood. For instance, while the theoretical basis for nuclear fission was relatively well established by 1939, the process of isolating the necessary isotopes for fission, particularly Uranium-235, presented a huge obstacle.

Uranium in its natural state is predominantly Uranium-238, which is far less likely to undergo fission when struck by neutrons. In contrast, Uranium-235 is the isotope that can be most easily induced to undergo fission, releasing a tremendous amount of energy. However, the two isotopes are chemically identical, making it extremely difficult to separate them using traditional methods of chemistry. Researchers would need to develop innovative technologies to separate these isotopes in sufficient quantities for use in a nuclear reaction. This would eventually require the development of advanced processes like gaseous diffusion and electromagnetic isotope separation, which would be central to the success of the Manhattan Project.

In addition to these technical hurdles, the sheer scale of the resources required to develop a nuclear weapon posed a challenge. The committee's recommendations indicated that the effort would require extensive government funding and a concerted coordination of efforts between academic institutions, private industry, and the U.S. military. Recognizing the need for an organized and centralized approach to nuclear research, the U.S. government began to take action, ultimately leading to the establishment of the Manhattan Project.

The Advisory Committee's Impact on Policy and Further Research-

While the Advisory Committee on Uranium itself did not directly conduct experiments or develop technologies, its influence on U.S. policy and its role in guiding the direction of research were pivotal. The committee's conclusions led to a significant shift in the way the U.S. government viewed nuclear research. Prior to the formation of the committee, nuclear physics had been a largely academic pursuit, with little involvement from the U.S. government or military. The formation of the committee and its subsequent findings, however, made it clear that the development of nuclear weapons was not only feasible but necessary to ensure national security in the face of a potential nuclear arms race with Nazi Germany.

The committee's work led directly to the National Defense Research Committee (NDRC), which was tasked with organizing the nation's research efforts and overseeing the development of technologies for the military. Under the NDRC, research into uranium enrichment, reactor design, and weapon development began in earnest. Key figures in the Manhattan Project, such as J. Robert Oppenheimer, were brought on board to lead the scientific efforts, and the project quickly expanded as new research facilities were built at locations like Los Alamos in New Mexico and Oak Ridge in Tennessee. These facilities would become the heart of the Manhattan Project, where some of the brightest minds in science and engineering worked to create a working nuclear weapon.

The Long Road to the Manhattan Project-

The formation of the Advisory Committee on Uranium was just the beginning of the journey that would lead to the development of the atomic bomb. The committee helped to catalyze a rapid and unprecedented expansion of research into nuclear physics, which, in turn, led to the establishment of the Manhattan Project. While the project's ultimate success would not come until the early 1940s, the committee's efforts laid the groundwork for the groundbreaking scientific achievements that followed. The creation of the committee also reflected the growing sense of urgency among scientists and policymakers, as they recognized the magnitude of the threat posed by nuclear weapons and the need for immediate action.

, the Advisory Committee on Uranium played a pivotal role in the early stages of nuclear weapons development. By bringing together top scientific minds, mobilizing government resources, and highlighting the importance of uranium research, the committee set the stage for the creation of the Manhattan Project and the eventual development of the atomic bomb. Its legacy remains a testament to the power of collaboration and the far-reaching impact of scientific inquiry in times of global conflict.

Initial funding and establishment of the Uranium Committe-

Initial Funding and Establishment of the Uranium Committee: A Pivotal Moment in Nuclear Research-

The establishment of the Uranium Committee (later known as the Advisory Committee on Uranium) in 1939 was a watershed moment in the development of nuclear research in the United States. It marked the beginning of a concentrated effort by the U.S. government to explore the possibilities of nuclear energy and, more critically, nuclear weapons. The story of the Uranium Committee's formation is a complex tale, one that involves the convergence of scientific discovery, geopolitical tensions, and a shift in American military policy. It was the outcome of several critical factors, including growing concerns about the potential applications of atomic energy, the early recognition of nuclear fission's military value, and the drive to prevent Nazi Germany from gaining access to this dangerous new technology.

While the scientific groundwork for the study of atomic energy had been laid in Europe and the United States during the early 20th century, it wasn't until the late 1930s that the scientific community began to appreciate the full implications of uranium fission for both energy and weapon development. The year 1938 saw the discovery of uranium fission by German scientists Otto Hahn and Fritz Strassmann, a breakthrough that was quickly followed by theoretical explanations from Lise Meitner and Otto Frisch. This discovery hinted at the possibility of releasing vast amounts of energy from the nucleus of the uranium atom. With the rise of Adolf Hitler and the growing militarization of Nazi Germany, the potential of harnessing this energy for weapons became an immediate concern for scientists around the world. The specter of a Nazi atomic bomb, which could have devastating consequences, drove a sense of urgency in the scientific community.

The formation of the Uranium Committee was directly influenced by a series of key events and individuals who helped catalyze the early U.S. response to the discovery of uranium fission. Central to this story was the Einstein-Szilard letter to

President Franklin D. Roosevelt, which warned of the potential for nuclear weapons development by Nazi Germany and urged the U.S. government to initiate its own research into atomic energy. This letter, sent in 1939, served as a catalyst for U.S. involvement in nuclear research and played a significant role in the establishment of the Uranium Committee.

The Political and Scientific Context: A World on the Brink of War-

In the years leading up to the formation of the Uranium Committee, the world was already on the brink of global conflict. World War II was looming large, and tensions were rising between major powers, particularly in Europe. The Nazi regime was aggressively expanding its reach, and its technological advancements were seen as a potential threat to democratic nations. Meanwhile, the discovery of nuclear fission was still in its infancy, and its military applications were not yet fully understood, but the implications were becoming increasingly clear. The fact that nuclear fission could release such an enormous amount of energy, coupled with the realization that it could be used to create weapons of mass destruction, led many to fear that the development of atomic weapons could alter the course of the war.

The United States, despite its initial reluctance to engage in the European conflict, was becoming more aware of the growing threat posed by Nazi Germany's military ambitions. The rise of fascism and the rapid militarization of Germany under Hitler prompted several prominent scientists, including Albert Einstein and Leo Szilard, to take action. Both scientists were deeply concerned about the potential for nuclear weapons in the hands of Nazi Germany. Szilard, in particular, had already begun to understand the practical applications of nuclear fission and the risks associated with it. He realized that nuclear weapons could potentially give the Nazi regime a tremendous advantage in the war.

In late 1938, Szilard wrote a letter to Albert Einstein, urging him to sign a petition addressed to President Roosevelt, warning him about the possibility of Nazi Germany developing nuclear weapons. Einstein, who was one of the most well-known and respected scientists in the world at the time, added his signature to the letter, which was then sent to Roosevelt in October 1939. The letter, which was titled "The Letter to the President," outlined the potential for the development of atomic weapons and recommended that the United States take immediate steps to begin research into the possibilities of uranium fission and its military applications.

Einstein and Szilard's letter had a profound impact on the U.S. government's response to the emerging threat posed by nuclear weapons. It was widely regarded as the catalyst that sparked the U.S. government's interest in nuclear research, leading to the formation of the Uranium Committee. The letter's influence was immediate, as President Roosevelt was deeply concerned by the potential for Nazi Germany to develop nuclear weapons. The letter prompted Roosevelt to take action, and soon after, the Advisory Committee on Uranium was formed.

The Role of the Advisory Committee on Uranium-

The Uranium Committee was formed in response to the pressing need for scientific research into the military applications of nuclear fission. Its primary goal was to evaluate the potential for using uranium as a source of energy for weapons. The committee was tasked with investigating the feasibility of producing an atomic bomb, and its formation marked the beginning of a concerted effort by the U.S. government to explore nuclear technology. The committee was not a scientific body in itself but rather an advisory group that brought together prominent physicists, chemists, and engineers who could advise the government on the next steps in nuclear research.

The committee's formation was largely driven by the growing concerns among U.S. policymakers about the military implications of nuclear fission. In 1939, as tensions between the United States and Germany continued to escalate, there was a sense of urgency surrounding the need to prevent Nazi Germany from gaining an atomic weapon. At the time, the United States was still grappling with the implications of uranium fission and had not yet established a comprehensive program to investigate its military potential. The formation of the Uranium Committee represented a direct response to this gap in the U.S. government's understanding of the potential of nuclear weapons.

The committee's first major task was to explore the scientific basis for nuclear fission and assess the feasibility of developing an atomic bomb. This process began with basic research into the properties of uranium and its ability to sustain a chain reaction. Early on, it became clear that the most significant technical challenge would be isolating and concentrating the isotope Uranium-235, which was the key to achieving a sustained nuclear reaction. The committee's early work focused on understanding the behavior of uranium atoms and investigating the practical challenges associated with enriching uranium.

One of the first steps in this process was identifying the key scientific figures who would guide the U.S. government's nuclear research efforts. Among the most important of these was Harold Urey, a prominent chemist who had already won the Nobel Prize in Chemistry in 1934 for his work on isotopes. Urey was tasked with organizing the early research efforts into uranium enrichment and the feasibility of nuclear weapons. Alongside Urey, several other physicists and chemists contributed to the early stages of the Uranium Committee's work. Enrico Fermi, an Italian physicist who had already made significant contributions to nuclear theory, was also brought into the fold. His expertise in nuclear reactions and his experience with working with neutrons made him a valuable addition to the group.

In addition to Fermi and Urey, a number of other physicists, including J. Robert Oppenheimer and Leo Szilard, became involved in the project. These scientists would play critical roles in the later stages of nuclear research, including the construction of the first nuclear reactors and the eventual development of the atomic bomb. The Uranium Committee's work paved the way for the creation of the Manhattan Project, which would later become the formal, large-scale U.S. effort to develop atomic weapons.

Initial Funding and Its Challenges-

One of the early challenges faced by the Uranium Committee was securing funding for its work. Despite the growing concerns about nuclear weapons and the potential for an atomic bomb, the U.S. government was initially hesitant to allocate significant funds to such an uncertain and untested field of research. However, the Einstein-Szilard letter had already sparked Roosevelt's interest in the subject, and as a result, the president authorized a modest initial appropriation for the committee's work.

In the early stages, funding for nuclear research came from a combination of government sources and private institutions. The National Academy of Sciences and other research institutions provided a portion of the necessary funds, but it was clear that larger, more sustained financial support would be needed to carry out the ambitious research agenda set forth by the Uranium Committee. Eventually, the government recognized that a significant investment would be required to fully explore the potential of nuclear energy, both for power generation and for weapons. This recognition of the need for greater financial commitment eventually led to the creation of the Manhattan Engineering District (also known as the Manhattan Project), which would be funded at an unprecedented level and would become the centerpiece of the U.S. effort to develop nuclear weapons.

The establishment of the Uranium Committee and the allocation of funding for nuclear research marked the beginning of a long and intense period of scientific investigation and technological development that would ultimately result in the creation of the atomic bomb. However, the funding and support for this research would continue to evolve as the scale of the project expanded. What began as a modest and tentative effort, with limited financial resources, would quickly grow into one of the largest and most secretive scientific endeavors in history, one that would change the course of the Second World War and the future of global geopolitics.

The Birth of Nuclear Weapons Development-

The creation of the Uranium Committee and the initial funding for its research were the first steps in what would become the U.S. effort to develop atomic weapons. The urgency of the situation, coupled with the scientific and geopolitical context of the late 1930s, pushed the U.S. government to take swift action to explore the military potential of nuclear fission. The committee's work, which was grounded in the scientific expertise of leading physicists and chemists, laid the groundwork for the larger and more organized Manhattan Project, which would ultimately lead to the successful creation of the atomic bomb.

In the years that followed, the United States would channel immense resources into nuclear research, culminating in the successful detonation of the first atomic bomb in 1945. The initial efforts of the Uranium Committee, combined with the scientific acumen and ingenuity of researchers like Oppenheimer, Fermi, and Szilard, would change the world forever, ushering in the age of nuclear weapons and fundamentally altering the trajectory of world history.

The role of Vannevar Bush and the National Defense Research Committee (NDRC)-

Introduction to Vannevar Bush's Role and the Formation of the NDRC-

The United States, in the period leading up to World War II, faced a rapidly changing technological landscape, and this change was especially evident in the realm of physics. In the years leading up to the war, significant breakthroughs in nuclear physics, such as the discovery of nuclear fission in 1938, laid the foundation for what would eventually become the atomic bomb. While the threat of war loomed, the realization that nuclear energy could be harnessed for destructive purposes was still in its infancy.

Vannevar Bush, a prominent engineer and inventor, emerged as a central figure in the effort to transition theoretical nuclear research into practical wartime technology. Bush, who was appointed in 1940 as the head of the Office of Scientific Research and Development (OSRD) by President Franklin D. Roosevelt, brought a fresh vision of how the United States should mobilize its scientific resources. Prior to this role, Bush had already gained considerable acclaim for his contributions to the field of electrical engineering and for his leadership of the Massachusetts Institute of Technology (MIT)'s engineering programs. However, it was his organizational skills and ability to coordinate efforts on a national scale that would make him a central figure in U.S. wartime science.

The formation of the National Defense Research Committee (NDRC) under Bush's direction was the direct response to the increasing need for scientific coordination and innovation to support the U.S. military effort. The NDRC was tasked with overseeing all scientific efforts related to national defense, focusing on advanced technologies like radar, jet propulsion, and atomic energy. The committee would play a crucial role in managing scientific research and steering it toward military applications during World War II.

Bush's Vision: Organizing U.S. Scientific Effort in Wartime-

Vannevar Bush understood that the rapid pace of technological advancements required a centralized effort to harness the talents of the nation's scientists, engineers, and academic institutions. Before the creation of the OSRD, the U.S. had not yet developed the infrastructure necessary to rapidly apply scientific research to military needs. The National Defense Research Committee was formed in June 1940 to begin organizing such a framework. Initially, it focused on a broad range of technologies, from the development of chemical weapons to advancements in radar. However, as the possibility of nuclear weapons grew more pressing, the NDRC would eventually find itself playing a critical role in the coordination of nuclear weapons research.

One of the fundamental aspects of Bush's leadership was his ability to recognize the need for collaboration across multiple disciplines. While the idea of a "Manhattan Project" would not come to fruition until later, Bush had already laid the groundwork for cross-disciplinary scientific cooperation through his work with the NDRC. The scientific community at the time was a patchwork of institutions, many of which were not in close communication with one another. As a result, scientific discoveries were often made in isolation, with little effort toward practical application.

To address this, Bush's leadership in organizing the NDRC was key in bringing together top scientists from different fields, including physics, chemistry, and engineering. For instance, Niels Bohr, Leo Szilard, and Enrico Fermi—scientists whose research in nuclear physics would be integral to the development of atomic energy—were brought into the fold, despite being separated by vast geographical distances. Similarly, the U.S. military was heavily involved in the NDRC's work, ensuring that the research being conducted had immediate military implications. This hybrid model of civilian-led, government-supported research became the hallmark of the U.S. approach to wartime scientific efforts.

Moreover, Bush's insistence on the importance of applied science—science that had practical value—was crucial in ensuring that wartime scientific efforts were focused on producing immediate results. This framework of focusing on practical, usable technology enabled the NDRC to prioritize research on nuclear energy and weapons, a field that was still in its infancy.

The Advisory Committee on Uranium and the Early Stages of the Atomic Bomb-

The scientific community's awareness of the military potential of nuclear fission began to crystallize during the late 1930s and early 1940s. A series of key discoveries, such as the identification of uranium fission and the theoretical understanding of how it could be used to generate an explosive chain reaction, captured the attention of leading physicists. In 1939, scientists like Leo Szilard and Albert Einstein sent an urgent letter to President Franklin D. Roosevelt, warning that Nazi Germany might be on the verge of developing an atomic bomb.

In response to this growing concern, Roosevelt established the Advisory Committee on Uranium under the NDRC in 1940. The committee was tasked with investigating the potential of uranium as a source of energy and weapons. The advisory committee, which included figures such as Lyman J. Briggs and Ernest O. Lawrence, quickly realized that atomic energy could be harnessed for military applications. This marked the beginning of what would eventually become the Manhattan Project.

In the early stages, the committee faced substantial uncertainty. While the theoretical principles of nuclear fission were well understood, the practical aspects—such as how to sustain a chain reaction, how to enrich uranium, and how to safely harness the energy—were still far from clear. Moreover, the committee had to contend with the reality that the resources required for large-scale nuclear research were immense. Uranium was scarce, and it was not immediately clear whether the necessary technology to isolate and enrich Uranium-235 existed.

At the time, the most advanced laboratory work on uranium enrichment and fission was occurring in Europe, particularly in Germany. The NDRC's focus, therefore, became both a matter of advancing scientific understanding and of ensuring that the United States would remain ahead of Nazi Germany in the race to develop nuclear weapons.

The committee's work eventually laid the foundation for the creation of the Manhattan Project—a highly secretive and intense scientific effort that would bring together the world's leading physicists, engineers, and military personnel to work toward the development of the atomic bomb.

Vannevar Bush's Leadership and the Expansion of the U.S. Nuclear Program-

Bush's role as the director of OSRD proved instrumental in ensuring that nuclear research was given priority. Under his leadership, the U.S. government made substantial investments in the infrastructure and scientific resources necessary to support large-scale nuclear research. Bush understood that the Manhattan Project—which would officially begin in 1942 under the guidance of General Leslie Groves—needed not only brilliant minds but also the resources to build the massive facilities required for uranium enrichment and plutonium production.

To this end, Bush helped secure funding for the construction of the Los Alamos Laboratory, led by J. Robert Oppenheimer, and the Oak Ridge National Laboratory, which would focus on uranium isotope separation. He also played a pivotal role in the establishment of the Hanford Site, where plutonium production would take place. The sheer scale of these operations would have been impossible without Bush's coordination and leadership, as well as his ability to navigate the complex relationship between civilian scientists, the military, and industry.

Bush's personal influence went beyond organizational matters. His ability to identify and assemble key players was key in the formation of the Manhattan Project. The selection of Oppenheimer as the head of Los Alamos, for example, was a decision that would define the direction of the project. Oppenheimer's leadership and scientific vision would shape the design and construction of the first atomic bombs. Similarly, Bush recognized the importance of scientists like Fermi, Szilard, and Niels Bohr, whose early contributions were crucial to the theoretical underpinnings of nuclear fission.

The Post-War Legacy: Vannevar Bush's Vision for Science in America-

While Bush's contributions during the war were monumental, his influence did not end with the defeat of the Axis powers. Bush's vision for the role of science in post-war America would shape U.S. science policy for decades. His 1945 report, "Science: The Endless Frontier," laid the intellectual foundation for the creation of the National Science Foundation (NSF), an institution dedicated to funding scientific research and supporting innovation.

In this report, Bush argued that science should be a central part of U.S. policy, not only for its military applications but also for its potential to address national challenges in fields ranging from public health to economics. The creation of the NSF and Bush's emphasis on government investment in scientific research would have lasting effects, particularly during the Cold War era when technological competition with the Soviet Union would drive the need for continuous innovation in science and defense technologies.

Moreover, Bush's advocacy for the responsible use of scientific discoveries in the service of humanity was one of his most important post-war contributions. His recognition of the power of nuclear weapons—both for peace and for destruction—would inform future international efforts toward nuclear regulation and arms control.

The Enduring Impact of Vannevar Bush and the NDRC-

Vannevar Bush's leadership during World War II and his role in overseeing the formation of the National Defense Research Committee were fundamental to the development of nuclear weapons and the broader efforts to harness science for military purposes. His work ensured that the United States was at the forefront of the race to develop the atomic bomb and provided the organizational structure necessary for effective wartime science.

Bush's organizational brilliance, combined with his ability to unite diverse scientific disciplines and coordinate efforts between the military and civilian sectors, made the atomic bomb a reality. His post-war contributions, particularly his vision for the future of U.S. science and technology, helped lay the foundation for America's continued leadership in science and innovation in the 20th century.

Today, the legacy of Bush's leadership is still felt in the ways that science and technology continue to intersect with military and civilian spheres. The NDRC, under Bush's guidance, helped pave the way for the modern era of scientific collaboration and innovation, leaving a profound and lasting mark on history.

Early experiments on uranium and plutonium fission-

Early Experiments on Uranium and Plutonium Fission-

The discovery of nuclear fission in the late 1930s was one of the most significant events in modern science. It altered the trajectory of physics and chemistry and had profound implications for global geopolitics and the course of history. The early experiments on uranium and plutonium fission not only revealed the fundamental mechanisms of atomic structure but also set in motion the development of nuclear energy and weapons, which became central to the outcome of World War II and shaped the future of international relations and military power. To truly appreciate the impact of these experiments, it is crucial to trace the steps leading up to and following the discovery of nuclear fission, from the initial observations to the large-scale developments that would eventually produce the atomic bomb.

The Discovery of Nuclear Fission (1938)-

The foundations of nuclear fission began with a series of key discoveries, culminating in 1938 with the groundbreaking work of German chemists Otto Hahn and Fritz Strassmann. Their experiment, though accidental, opened a new chapter in the study of nuclear reactions. While conducting an experiment that involved bombarding uranium with neutrons, Hahn and Strassmann found that the uranium nucleus split, resulting in the formation of smaller atoms—specifically barium. This unexpected result puzzled the scientists, as they had not anticipated such a reaction in uranium, an element known for its heavy nucleus.

The discovery caught the attention of Austrian-Swedish physicist Lise Meitner, who had worked with Hahn earlier but had fled Germany due to the rise of the Nazi regime. In January 1939, Meitner, along with her nephew Otto Frisch, provided a theoretical explanation for Hahn and Strassmann's results. Meitner and Frisch realized that the uranium nucleus had been split into two smaller nuclei, a process now understood as nuclear fission. They proposed that when a uranium atom absorbed a neutron, it became unstable and split, releasing a large amount of energy. This discovery revolutionized the understanding of atomic structure and had profound implications for both science and technology. The energy released in nuclear fission was found to be far greater than the energy produced by chemical reactions, and this realization raised questions about how to harness fission for power generation—or potentially, weaponization.

The significance of this discovery was not lost on the scientific community. Within a year of Meitner and Frisch's theoretical explanation, researchers had confirmed that fission could be initiated and controlled. What followed was a series of experiments designed to understand the nature of the process, identify other materials that could undergo fission, and ultimately explore how this newfound energy could be used.

The Fissionability of Uranium-

Uranium, a heavy metal, had long been studied for its potential uses, but its nuclear properties had not been fully understood. Researchers quickly realized that the isotope Uranium-235 (U-235) was the key to the fission process. While naturally occurring uranium is a mixture of isotopes, with Uranium-238 (U-238) being the dominant isotope (accounting for over 99% of natural uranium), only U-235 was capable of undergoing fission with relative ease. U-235 was the isotope that released energy when it absorbed a neutron, making it a potential source of enormous energy. However, the small percentage of U-235 in natural uranium posed a major challenge for the large-scale production of fissionable material.

The low natural abundance of U-235 meant that methods for uranium enrichment would be necessary to produce enough U-235 to sustain a chain reaction, a process known as critical mass. Researchers soon began investigating methods for isolating and concentrating U-235, including the use of gaseous diffusion, electromagnetic separation, and liquid thermal diffusion. Each of these methods had its challenges, but their development was crucial for the Manhattan Project—the U.S. government's top-secret initiative to develop an atomic bomb during World War II.

The realization that U-235 could be used for nuclear fission opened new scientific questions about how to control and utilize this energy. The discovery of uranium's fission properties was foundational, but it was also clear that further experiments and technological innovations would be needed to unlock its full potential.

Plutonium: The Emergence of a New Fissile Material-

While uranium's potential for fission was well-established, it was soon realized that another material—plutonium—could also be used to sustain a nuclear chain reaction. In 1940, Glenn T. Seaborg and his colleagues at the University of California, Berkeley, discovered Plutonium-239 (Pu-239), a fissile isotope produced by bombarding uranium-238 (U-238) with neutrons. This discovery proved to be pivotal, as plutonium-239 not only had a higher probability of undergoing fission than U-235, but it could also be produced in nuclear reactors through the irradiation of U-238, making it a practical material for nuclear weapons.

The ability to produce plutonium in large quantities offered a new avenue for the development of atomic bombs. Unlike U-235, which required extensive enrichment processes, plutonium could be bred in reactors, making it a potentially more feasible material for bomb production. The discovery of plutonium thus introduced new challenges and questions about its use and handling, as plutonium is highly radioactive and requires specialized procedures for extraction and purification.

Early Nuclear Experiments: The Role of Neutrons and Chain Reactions-

One of the most significant challenges in understanding nuclear fission was the investigation of how neutrons interacted with atomic nuclei to induce fission. Neutrons, which are electrically neutral particles, were capable of penetrating atomic nuclei and causing them to split. The phenomenon of neutron-induced fission formed the basis for the concept of a chain reaction, where each fission event could produce additional neutrons, which in turn could cause further fission events. The key to harnessing fission for energy or weapons purposes lay in understanding how to control this chain reaction.

The concept of a self-sustaining chain reaction became central to nuclear experimentation, particularly in the quest to build a nuclear reactor that could produce more energy than it consumed. This was the aim of Enrico Fermi and his colleagues, who worked on building the first experimental nuclear reactors. Fermi, an Italian physicist who had emigrated to the U.S., played a pivotal role in the early stages of nuclear experimentation. He and his team were the first to build a nuclear reactor that achieved a self-sustaining chain reaction. The Chicago Pile-1

(CP-1) reactor, constructed under the bleachers of the University of Chicago's football stadium in 1942, was the world's first nuclear reactor to produce energy from a controlled chain reaction.

Fermi's experiments demonstrated that the chain reaction could be controlled by manipulating the materials around the reactor, such as graphite (which slowed down neutrons) and uranium (which absorbed them). This principle of moderating and controlling the speed of neutrons was crucial for the future development of nuclear reactors, both for civilian energy purposes and for the production of weapons-grade material.

The Path to the Manhattan Project-

The success of Fermi's experiments led directly to the formation of the Manhattan Project in 1942. The project was launched as a response to the growing concern that Nazi Germany might be the first to develop a nuclear weapon. Scientists from a wide range of disciplines were brought together to work on the development of the atomic bomb. Among the many problems they faced were how to scale up the production of uranium-235 and plutonium-239 to the necessary quantities for a weapon, how to design a reactor capable of producing these materials in large quantities, and how to develop methods of enriching uranium.

In addition to uranium and plutonium, the development of nuclear weapons also required the production of heavy water (a form of water with a higher concentration of deuterium, or hydrogen-2, used as a neutron moderator in reactors), the construction of massive reactors, and the development of methods for separating isotopes. The Manhattan Project's success would not have been possible without the contributions of leading physicists such as Robert Oppenheimer, Niels Bohr, Leo Szilard, and Hans Bethe, who worked together to solve the numerous scientific and technical challenges posed by the development of nuclear weapons.

The Role of Early Nuclear Reactors in Weapons Production-

The construction of reactors capable of producing plutonium became a central goal of the Manhattan Project. The Hanford Site in Washington State was selected for the large-scale production of plutonium. Here, a series of reactors were built to irradiate uranium-238, converting it into plutonium-239. The reactors used a design similar to that of Fermi's Chicago Pile-1, but on a much larger scale. These reactors produced plutonium at a rate that made it feasible to produce the material needed for the development of atomic bombs.

At the same time, Oak Ridge National Laboratory in Tennessee was tasked with the production of enriched uranium-235. The site employed a range of enrichment methods, including gaseous diffusion, electromagnetic separation, and liquid thermal diffusion, to separate uranium-235 from uranium-238.

These reactors and enrichment facilities, operating under the tightest security, were critical to the success of the Manhattan Project. They enabled the large-scale production of fissile materials—uranium-235 and plutonium-239—which were used in the bombs dropped on Hiroshima and Nagasaki in 1945.

The Development of Nuclear Weapons and the Trinity Test-

By the mid-1940s, scientists at the Manhattan Project had succeeded in building both uranium and plutonium-based bombs. In July 1945, the first successful test of a nuclear bomb was conducted in the deserts of New Mexico, known as the Trinity Test. This explosion was a direct result of the experiments on uranium and plutonium fission, as it was the product of a plutonium-based nuclear bomb. The success of the test marked the culmination of years of experimentation, research, and development.

The Trinity Test not only proved that nuclear fission could be harnessed for weapons production but also signaled the beginning of a new era in warfare. The destructive power of nuclear weapons would change the geopolitical landscape and lead to the Cold War and the subsequent development of nuclear arsenals by both the United States and the Soviet Union.

The early experiments on uranium and plutonium fission were fundamental to the development of nuclear energy and weapons. From the discovery of fission by Hahn and Strassmann in 1938 to the synthesis of plutonium by Seaborg and his team, these experiments laid the groundwork for one of the most transformative scientific and technological revolutions of the 20th century. The development of nuclear reactors and the production of enriched uranium and plutonium made possible the creation of atomic bombs, which played a decisive role in the outcome of World War II. The legacy of these early experiments continues to shape the world today, both in terms of energy production and the ongoing concerns about the proliferation of nuclear weapons and their ethical implications.

CHAPTER THREE

BUILDING THE FRAMEWORK – ORGANIZATION AND LEADERSHIP

Creation of the Manhattan Engineer District (MED)-

The Creation of the Manhattan Engineer District (MED)-

The Manhattan Engineer District (MED), later popularly known as the Manhattan Project, was a pivotal turning point in both military history and the trajectory of global science and technology. It was an unprecedented effort that brought together the brightest scientific minds, vast industrial resources, and immense political will to develop the world's first nuclear weapons during World War II. The creation of the MED was not merely a bureaucratic or military action; it was a monumental endeavor that would forever alter the global balance of power, influence ethical debates, and redefine the role of science in warfare.

This expanded account delves into the intricate details surrounding the formation of the MED, exploring its historical context, organizational structure, challenges, contributions of key figures, and the far-reaching consequences of its creation. Through this lens, we uncover the depth and complexity of one of the most transformative projects in human history.

Historical Context and Early Developments-

The roots of the Manhattan Engineer District lie in the groundbreaking discoveries of nuclear physics in the early 20th century. The identification of nuclear fission by German scientists Otto Hahn and Fritz Strassmann in 1938, and its theoretical explanation by Lise Meitner and Otto Frisch, revealed the immense energy potential locked within the nucleus of the atom. By splitting heavy elements such as uranium, scientists could release energy on a scale far greater than that of conventional explosives.

This discovery soon became a matter of grave concern to physicists worldwide. The rise of Nazi Germany and its aggressive expansionism under Adolf Hitler posed an existential threat to global stability. Many physicists, particularly those who had fled Europe due to persecution, were alarmed by the possibility that Germany might exploit nuclear fission to develop a superweapon. Among these physicists, Hungarian-born Leo Szilard emerged as a leading voice, recognizing both the destructive potential of nuclear energy and the urgency of preempting German advancements.

In 1939, Szilard, along with his colleague Eugene Wigner, persuaded Albert Einstein to co-sign a letter addressed to U.S. President Franklin D. Roosevelt. This now-famous Einstein-Szilard letter highlighted the strategic importance of uranium and the possibility of a nuclear bomb. The letter catalyzed the U.S. government's initial interest in nuclear research, leading to the establishment of the Advisory Committee on Uranium. However, early efforts were scattered and underfunded, reflecting a lack of understanding of the technical challenges and the urgency of the task.

The Path to Centralized Leadership-

As World War II intensified, the need for a coordinated approach to nuclear research became evident. Reports from the British MAUD Committee, which concluded that an atomic bomb was feasible and could potentially be developed within a few years, provided additional impetus. In response, the U.S. established the Office of Scientific Research and Development (OSRD) in 1941, with Vannevar Bush at its helm. Bush, a visionary leader and advocate for scientific mobilization, played a pivotal role in convincing Roosevelt of the necessity of a large-scale, government-funded nuclear weapons program.

By 1942, the Army Corps of Engineers was tasked with overseeing the construction and industrial aspects of the project. To formalize these efforts, the Manhattan Engineer District was established in August 1942. Its headquarters were initially located in New York City, reflecting the Corps' administrative divisions, but the project's scope quickly expanded far beyond Manhattan.

Organizational Structure of the MED-

The Manhattan Engineer District was designed to integrate scientific research, industrial production, and military oversight into a unified effort. Its structure was as follows:

1. Leadership-

The MED was initially under the command of Colonel James C. Marshall, who began organizing the logistical and administrative groundwork. However, recognizing the need for more dynamic leadership, the project was soon placed under Brigadier General Leslie R. Groves. Groves, an experienced military engineer known for his work on large-scale construction projects like the Pentagon, brought unparalleled organizational skills, decisiveness, and authority to the MED. His leadership was instrumental in turning the project into a disciplined and efficient operation.

2. Scientific Oversight-

The scientific aspect of the project was spearheaded by leading physicists, most notably J. Robert Oppenheimer, who was appointed director of the Los Alamos Laboratory. Los Alamos became the intellectual and experimental hub where theoretical concepts were translated into practical designs for atomic weapons. Other key figures included Enrico Fermi, who oversaw the creation of the first self-sustaining nuclear chain reaction at the University of Chicago, and Ernest Lawrence, whose work on electromagnetic separation methods was critical for uranium enrichment.

3. Industrial Production-

The MED's industrial efforts were unparalleled in scale and complexity. To produce the fissile materials necessary for nuclear weapons, the project established massive facilities at multiple sites:

Oak Ridge, Tennessee: Focused on uranium enrichment through gaseous diffusion, electromagnetic separation, and thermal diffusion.

Hanford, Washington: Dedicated to the production of plutonium using nuclear reactors.

Los Alamos, New Mexico: Responsible for assembling and testing the bomb designs.

4. Security and Secrecy-

Secrecy was paramount to the MED's success. The project's leaders implemented strict compartmentalization, ensuring that most workers only knew about their specific tasks without understanding the broader objective. Measures included extensive background checks, code names for facilities, and military policing of the sites.

Key Contributions and Early Progress-

The MED's formation marked the beginning of a new phase of intense research and development. Among its early accomplishments were:

The Chicago Pile-1 Experiment: On December 2, 1942, a team led by Enrico Fermi achieved the first controlled nuclear chain reaction. This milestone demonstrated the feasibility of harnessing nuclear energy and provided critical data for reactor design.

Uranium Enrichment: The MED oversaw the development of multiple methods for enriching uranium-235, a fissile isotope that constitutes only 0.7% of natural uranium. The electromagnetic separation method, developed by Ernest Lawrence, and gaseous diffusion techniques proved essential for producing weapons-grade uranium.

Plutonium Production: At the Hanford site, the construction of large-scale nuclear reactors enabled the production of plutonium-239, an alternative fissile material. This work was critical for the design of the second bomb, "Fat Man."

Challenges and Overcoming Obstacles-

The MED faced numerous challenges, many of which were unprecedented in scale and complexity:

1. Scientific and Technical Uncertainty-

At the outset, many aspects of nuclear physics and engineering were poorly understood. Scientists had to address fundamental questions about critical mass, chain reactions, and bomb design, often through trial and error.

2. Logistical Demands-

The project required vast quantities of raw materials, specialized equipment, and skilled labor. Procuring and transporting these resources during wartime posed significant logistical hurdles.

3. Maintaining Secrecy-

The scope of the project made it difficult to keep operations concealed. Despite rigorous security measures, Soviet espionage infiltrated the project, as later revealed by the activities of spies like Klaus Fuchs and the Rosenbergs.

4. Ethical and Political Tensions-

Some scientists, including Szilard and Bohr, expressed reservations about the moral implications of nuclear weapons. These concerns occasionally created tensions within the project's leadership.

Significance and Legacy-

The creation of the Manhattan Engineer District was a watershed moment in the history of science, technology, and warfare. By the time the atomic bombs were dropped on Hiroshima and Nagasaki in August 1945, the MED had achieved its objective, bringing an end to World War II. However, its success came at a profound cost, including massive loss of life, environmental devastation, and the ushering in of the nuclear age.

The MED's legacy is multifaceted, encompassing:-

Scientific Advancements: The project accelerated advancements in nuclear physics, materials science, and engineering, laying the groundwork for future innovations in energy and medicine.

Geopolitical Impact: The advent of nuclear weapons reshaped international relations, leading to the Cold War and the establishment of nuclear deterrence as a cornerstone of global security.

Ethical Debates: The use of atomic bombs continues to provoke debate about the morality of nuclear warfare and the responsibilities of scientists and governments.

In hindsight, the Manhattan Engineer District represents both the pinnacle of human ingenuity and the profound challenges of wielding such power responsibly. Its creation was a testament to what can be achieved through coordinated effort, but it also serves as a cautionary tale about the consequences of technological progress in the absence of ethical foresight.

General Leslie Groves' appointment and leadership style-

General Leslie Groves' Appointment and Leadership Style-

The appointment of General Leslie Groves to oversee the Manhattan Project marked a transformative moment in the history of science and military strategy. Groves, a seasoned officer in the U.S. Army Corps of Engineers, was uniquely suited to lead this massive and unprecedented undertaking. His combination of bureaucratic expertise, engineering acumen, and a strict, results-oriented leadership style proved indispensable in steering the Manhattan Project to its ultimate success.

Early Career and Preparation for Leadership-

Leslie Richard Groves was born in Albany, New York, in 1896, and his upbringing in a disciplined military household shaped his character. After attending the U.S. Military Academy at West Point, Groves embarked on a career in the Army Corps of Engineers. He quickly earned a reputation as a capable and efficient officer, known for his ability to tackle large, complex projects.

One of Groves' most notable pre-Manhattan achievements was his role in overseeing the construction of the Pentagon, a massive and ambitious project that served as the headquarters for the Department of Defense. Completed in record time, the Pentagon showcased Groves' talent for managing extensive resources, coordinating teams, and navigating bureaucratic challenges. This accomplishment demonstrated his capacity to lead high-stakes initiatives and contributed to his selection for the Manhattan Project.

Appointment to the Manhattan Project-

In September 1942, Groves was appointed to lead the Manhattan Engineer District (MED), the military organization responsible for developing the atomic bomb. His initial reaction to the assignment was one of reluctance, as he viewed the project as a detour from the more traditional wartime engineering duties he preferred. However, upon recognizing the strategic importance of the endeavor, Groves embraced his role with characteristic determination.

Groves was promoted to Brigadier General shortly after his appointment, underscoring the significance of his new responsibilities. His military background, engineering expertise, and unyielding work ethic made him the ideal candidate to oversee a project of such magnitude and complexity.

Leadership Style: Authoritarian and Results-Oriented

Groves' leadership style was marked by an authoritarian approach that demanded precision, efficiency, and unwavering commitment from his subordinates. He maintained strict control over all aspects of the Manhattan Project, from scientific research to construction and security. Groves was known for his decisiveness and his ability to cut through bureaucratic red tape, often taking direct action to ensure progress.

A critical element of Groves' leadership was his insistence on excellence. He held his team to the highest standards and was unafraid to make difficult decisions, even if they proved unpopular. His demanding nature earned him the respect of some and the ire of others, but his effectiveness was undeniable.

Talent Recruitment and Collaboration

One of Groves' most significant contributions was his ability to identify and recruit top talent. He recognized that the success of the Manhattan Project depended on assembling a team of the brightest minds in science, engineering, and industry. Among his most notable recruits was J. Robert Oppenheimer, who served as the scientific director of the Los Alamos Laboratory.

Despite initial reservations about Oppenheimer's political affiliations and lack of administrative experience, Groves saw in him a rare combination of intellectual brilliance and the ability to inspire and coordinate diverse scientific teams. This decision proved pivotal, as Oppenheimer's leadership at Los Alamos was instrumental in the project's success.

Groves also fostered collaboration between the military, academia, and industry. He understood the value of integrating expertise from different fields and worked to create an environment where scientists and engineers could focus on their work without undue interference. This delicate balance of control and delegation was a hallmark of his leadership style.

Organizational and Logistical Mastery-

Under Groves' direction, the Manhattan Project evolved into a sprawling operation that involved multiple research and production sites across the United States. Each site had a specific purpose, and Groves ensured that they worked in concert to achieve the project's overarching goals.

Key facilities included:-

Los Alamos Laboratory (New Mexico): Focused on weapon design and theoretical physics.

Oak Ridge (Tennessee): Specialized in uranium enrichment through gaseous diffusion and electromagnetic separation.

Hanford Site (Washington): Produced plutonium using nuclear reactors.-

Groves' engineering background was invaluable in addressing the technical challenges associated with these facilities. For example, the construction of the K-25 gaseous diffusion plant at Oak Ridge was a monumental task that required innovative solutions to unprecedented problems. Groves' ability to mobilize resources, coordinate teams, and maintain focus ensured that these facilities were completed on time and within the necessary specifications.

Emphasis on Security and Secrecy-

The Manhattan Project's success depended on its ability to remain hidden from public view and potential adversaries. Groves implemented rigorous security measures to protect against espionage and information leaks. Personnel operated on a strictly need-to-know basis, and comprehensive background checks were conducted to ensure loyalty.

Groves also worked closely with counterintelligence agencies to identify and mitigate potential threats. These efforts extended to monitoring the activities of foreign scientists and diplomats who might pose a risk. While these measures created an atmosphere of intense secrecy, they were essential to safeguarding the project's objectives.

Challenges and Problem-Solving-

The Manhattan Project faced numerous challenges, including technical setbacks, resource constraints, and the need to maintain morale among a diverse and highly skilled workforce.

Groves' ability to address these issues was critical to the project's success.

For example, the production of enriched uranium and plutonium required innovative approaches and substantial trial-and-error experimentation. Groves worked closely with scientific and industrial teams to overcome these obstacles, often pushing for solutions that seemed impossible at the time. His relentless drive and refusal to accept failure inspired his team to achieve breakthroughs that ultimately made the atomic bomb a reality.

Key Achievements and Legacy

Under Groves' leadership, the Manhattan Project achieved its ambitious goal of developing the world's first atomic bombs. The successful detonation of the Trinity device in July 1945 demonstrated the project's feasibility, and the subsequent bombings of Hiroshima and Nagasaki in August 1945 brought World War II to a dramatic conclusion.

Groves' legacy is a complex one. While his authoritarian leadership style drew criticism, his ability to manage a project of unparalleled scope and significance is widely recognized. The Manhattan Project set a precedent for large-scale, multidisciplinary scientific and military collaborations, and Groves' role in its success remains a testament to his vision and determination.

General Leslie Groves' appointment to the Manhattan Project marked a turning point in the development of nuclear weapons. His leadership style, characterized by decisiveness, meticulous oversight, and a relentless focus on results, was instrumental in transforming the project from a theoretical endeavor into a tangible reality. Groves' contributions to the Manhattan Project not only shaped the outcome of World War II but also left an enduring impact on the fields of science, engineering, and military strategy.

Selection of J. Robert Oppenheimer as the scientific director-

The selection of J. Robert Oppenheimer as the scientific director of the Los Alamos Laboratory, the core research and design facility of the Manhattan Project, was one of the most critical decisions in the development of the atomic bomb. This choice was not only a turning point in the history of the Manhattan Project but also a defining moment in the history of science and warfare. The decision to appoint Oppenheimer reflected a blend of pragmatic considerations, personal connections, and an appreciation for his unique abilities to navigate the challenges of a groundbreaking and highly secretive scientific endeavor. This chapter delves deeply into the circumstances, deliberations, and implications surrounding Oppenheimer's selection and his transformative impact on the project.

The Context of the Manhattan Project and Early Challenges-

In the early stages of the Manhattan Project, the U.S. government and military leaders recognized that the success of the atomic bomb program depended on assembling an extraordinary team of scientists. These individuals would need to possess not only exceptional expertise in physics, chemistry, and engineering but also the ability to work collaboratively under extreme pressure and secrecy.

By 1942, the project had grown from a theoretical exploration of nuclear fission into a full-scale effort to build a functioning atomic weapon. The establishment of the Manhattan Engineer District (MED) under General Leslie Groves signaled the transition to a more organized and goal-oriented approach. However, the project still faced numerous challenges, including logistical coordination, resource allocation, and the integration of diverse scientific disciplines. It became evident that the scientific efforts needed a central figure to unify the researchers and provide clear leadership.

J. Robert Oppenheimer: A Rising Star in Theoretical Physics-

J. Robert Oppenheimer, born in 1904 in New York City, was a theoretical physicist of exceptional intellect and charisma. Educated at prestigious institutions such as Harvard University, the University of Cambridge, and the University of Göttingen, Oppenheimer had established himself as a leading figure in the emerging field of quantum mechanics by the 1930s. His contributions to theoretical physics, particularly in areas such as quantum field theory and cosmic ray research, earned him widespread respect within the scientific community.

Despite his brilliance, Oppenheimer was an unconventional choice for a leadership position in a project of this magnitude. Unlike many of his peers, he lacked extensive administrative experience and had not previously managed large-scale research efforts. Moreover, his reputation as an intellectual maverick and his association with leftist political causes raised concerns among some government officials and military leaders.

The Deliberation Process-

The decision to appoint a scientific director for the Los Alamos Laboratory involved careful consideration and input from key figures in the Manhattan Project. General Leslie Groves, who had been appointed to oversee the entire project, played a central role in evaluating potential candidates. Groves understood that the scientific director needed to be someone who could inspire and manage a diverse team of researchers while maintaining the rigorous pace required to meet wartime deadlines.

Several prominent scientists were considered for the role, including Ernest Lawrence, the inventor of the cyclotron, and Arthur Compton, a Nobel laureate in physics. While both men had impressive credentials and leadership experience, they were ultimately deemed more valuable in their existing roles within the project's decentralized structure. Lawrence, for example, was deeply involved in uranium enrichment research at the Radiation Laboratory in Berkeley, while Compton was overseeing work on plutonium production at the Metallurgical Laboratory in

Chicago.

Oppenheimer emerged as a leading candidate due to a combination of factors:-

Interdisciplinary Expertise: Oppenheimer's broad knowledge of physics allowed him to bridge gaps between theoretical and experimental researchers. His ability to engage with complex problems across multiple disciplines was a key asset for a project that required seamless integration of diverse scientific efforts.

Personal Relationships: Oppenheimer's connections with other prominent physicists, many of whom were already involved in the Manhattan Project, bolstered his candidacy. Figures like Hans Bethe, Edward Teller, and Enrico Fermi respected Oppenheimer's intellect and believed he could unite the scientific team.

Vision and Communication Skills: Oppenheimer possessed a rare combination of intellectual depth and eloquence. He had a knack for articulating complex ideas clearly and compellingly, which was crucial for rallying support and maintaining focus among the researchers.

Groves' Intuition: General Groves, despite initial reservations about Oppenheimer's lack of administrative experience, was impressed by his sharp mind and persuasive demeanor. Groves also recognized that Oppenheimer's understanding of the scientific challenges aligned well with the project's objectives.

Addressing Security Concerns-

One of the most contentious aspects of Oppenheimer's appointment was his political background. During the 1930s, he had been associated with various leftist causes and had connections to individuals affiliated with the Communist Party. These associations raised red flags for military officials and government agencies tasked with ensuring the project's security.

To address these concerns, Groves ordered a thorough investigation into Oppenheimer's background. Despite uncovering evidence of past political affiliations, Groves decided to proceed with the appointment. He believed that

Oppenheimer's value to the project outweighed the potential risks and took personal responsibility for the decision. This move demonstrated Groves' pragmatic approach to leadership and his willingness to take calculated risks to achieve the project's goals.

Establishing Los Alamos Laboratory-

Once appointed as scientific director, Oppenheimer faced the daunting task of building the Los Alamos Laboratory from the ground up. Located in a remote area of New Mexico, the site was chosen for its isolation, which provided both security and the space needed for large-scale experiments.

Oppenheimer's leadership was instrumental in shaping the laboratory's structure and culture. He worked tirelessly to recruit top scientists from around the world, leveraging his personal connections and reputation to assemble a team of unparalleled talent. Notable recruits included Hans Bethe, who became the head of the Theoretical Division, and Richard Feynman, a brilliant young physicist who brought innovative approaches to problem-solving.

The laboratory was organized into divisions focusing on specific aspects of bomb design and production, such as theoretical physics, explosives, and instrumentation. Oppenheimer fostered a collaborative environment that encouraged open communication and cross-disciplinary cooperation. Despite the intense pressure and secrecy surrounding the project, he managed to create a sense of shared purpose among the scientists.

Leadership Style and Challenges-

Oppenheimer's leadership style was characterized by a combination of intellectual engagement, personal charm, and a deep commitment to the project's success. He was known for his ability to inspire confidence and motivate his team, often leading by example and immersing himself in the scientific work.

However, his tenure as scientific director was not without challenges. The intense demands of the project took a toll on his health, and he often worked long hours with little rest. He also faced tensions within the scientific community, particularly with Edward Teller, who advocated for the development of a hydrogen bomb rather than focusing solely on the fission bomb.

The Legacy of Oppenheimer's Appointment-

The decision to appoint J. Robert Oppenheimer as scientific director proved to be a pivotal moment in the Manhattan Project's history. Under his leadership, the Los Alamos Laboratory achieved groundbreaking scientific and engineering milestones, culminating in the successful detonation of the first atomic bomb at the Trinity test site in July 1945.

Oppenheimer's role in the Manhattan Project cemented his place in history as one of the most influential figures in modern science. His ability to navigate the complexities of the project, both scientific and organizational, demonstrated the importance of visionary leadership in achieving ambitious goals. However, his legacy remains complex, as the ethical implications of the atomic bomb continue to be debated.

,The selection of J. Robert Oppenheimer as the scientific director of the Los Alamos Laboratory was a decision that profoundly shaped the course of the Manhattan Project and the development of nuclear weapons. His unique combination of intellectual brilliance, leadership qualities, and the ability to inspire collaboration made him an indispensable figure in one of history's most significant scientific endeavors. Oppenheimer's appointment serves as a testament to the power of individual leadership in overcoming extraordinary challenges and achieving unprecedented breakthroughs.

Key figures: Edward Teller, Hans Bethe, Ernest Lawrence, and others-

The Manhattan Project was not just a monumental scientific and engineering achievement; it was also a convergence of some of the brightest minds in physics, chemistry, and engineering from around the world. Key figures such as Edward Teller, Hans Bethe,

Ernest Lawrence, and others played crucial roles in advancing the theoretical and practical work that led to the development of the atomic bomb. Each of these individuals brought unique expertise, perspectives, and contributions to the project, helping to overcome the numerous scientific and logistical challenges that arose.

Edward Teller: The Father of the Hydrogen Bomb-

Edward Teller, a Hungarian-American physicist, is often remembered for his advocacy of the hydrogen bomb, a vision that extended beyond the immediate goals of the Manhattan Project. Born in 1908 in Budapest, Teller displayed a prodigious talent for mathematics and physics from a young age. After completing his education in Europe, including a Ph.D. under Werner Heisenberg, Teller immigrated to the United States in the 1930s due to the rise of Nazism.

Teller's involvement in the Manhattan Project began when he was recruited to Los Alamos. Initially, he contributed to theoretical work on nuclear fission and the design of fission bombs. However, Teller soon became preoccupied with the concept of a thermonuclear weapon—a hydrogen bomb that would use nuclear fusion rather than fission as its primary mechanism. This focus created tension within the Los Alamos team, as most scientists, including J. Robert Oppenheimer, believed that the immediate priority should be the development of a workable fission bomb.

Despite these conflicts, Teller's contributions were significant. He worked on equations related to bomb efficiency and explosive yields and engaged in high-level discussions on theoretical physics. Teller's insistence on exploring thermonuclear reactions laid the groundwork for post-war advancements in hydrogen bomb technology. His controversial legacy reflects his complex personality—a blend of brilliance, determination, and a willingness to challenge consensus.

Hans Bethe: Mastermind of Theoretical Physics-

Hans Bethe, a German-American physicist, was one of the most respected scientists of his era and a key figure in the Manhattan Project. Born in 1906 in Strasbourg, then part of Germany, Bethe earned his doctorate in theoretical physics at the University of Munich under Arnold Sommerfeld. His early work on quantum mechanics, nuclear reactions, and astrophysics established him as a leading figure in his field.

At Los Alamos, Bethe was appointed head of the Theoretical Division, a role that placed him at the center of the project's scientific efforts. His division was responsible for the mathematical and theoretical calculations required to design and optimize the atomic bomb. Bethe's leadership was marked by his ability to synthesize complex ideas, mentor younger scientists, and maintain a collaborative atmosphere under immense pressure.

Bethe's contributions included critical work on implosion dynamics, neutron transport, and the efficiency of nuclear chain reactions. His calculations ensured that the bomb designs were not only theoretically sound but also practical for large-scale production. Bethe's meticulous approach and intellectual rigor earned him the admiration of his peers, and he remained a central figure in nuclear science long after the Manhattan Project ended.

Ernest Lawrence: Pioneer of Big Science-
Ernest O. Lawrence, an American physicist, revolutionized experimental physics through his invention of the cyclotron, a device that accelerated particles to high energies for nuclear reactions. Born in 1901 in South Dakota, Lawrence's groundbreaking work at the University of California, Berkeley, earned him the Nobel Prize in Physics in 1939.

Lawrence's role in the Manhattan Project was multifaceted. He directed the Radiation Laboratory at Berkeley, where he oversaw research on uranium enrichment and isotope separation—critical components for producing fissile material. Lawrence's laboratory became a hub for innovation, as his team developed electromagnetic separation techniques using devices like the calutron, an adaptation of the cyclotron.

Beyond his technical contributions, Lawrence was a tireless advocate for the project, leveraging his connections with government and industry to secure resources and funding. His ability to bridge the gap between academia and the military-industrial complex was instrumental in the project's success. Lawrence's efforts exemplified the emergence of "big science," where large-scale, interdisciplinary collaborations became the norm.

Other Key Figures-

While Teller, Bethe, and Lawrence were among the most prominent figures, the Manhattan Project benefited from the contributions of many other brilliant minds:

Enrico Fermi: Known as the "architect of the nuclear age," Fermi's work on neutron moderation and chain reactions was foundational. He led the team that achieved the first self-sustaining nuclear chain reaction at the University of Chicago's Metallurgical Laboratory.

Leo Szilard: A visionary physicist and one of the earliest advocates for nuclear research, Szilard co-authored the Einstein-Szilard letter, which urged President Roosevelt to pursue atomic research. His work on reactor design and plutonium production was pivotal.

Richard Feynman: A young and dynamic physicist, Feynman contributed to theoretical calculations and bomb design at Los Alamos. His innovative problem-solving approach and enthusiasm inspired many of his colleagues.

Niels Bohr: A Danish physicist and Nobel laureate, Bohr provided critical insights into nuclear fission and the structure of the atom. His discussions with Oppenheimer and others helped refine the theoretical underpinnings of the project.

John von Neumann: A mathematical genius, von Neumann applied his expertise in fluid dynamics and shock wave theory to the implosion design of the plutonium bomb. His contributions were essential to the success of the "Fat Man" device.

Leslie Groves: Although not a scientist, General Groves' leadership and organizational skills were crucial. He provided the administrative and logistical framework that allowed the scientific team to focus on their work.

Klaus Fuchs: A German-born physicist who worked at Los Alamos, Fuchs made significant contributions to bomb design. However, his legacy is overshadowed by his role as a Soviet spy, which had profound implications for post-war geopolitics.

George Kistiakowsky: A chemist and explosives expert, Kistiakowsky led the effort to develop the explosive lenses required for the implosion method. His work ensured the precise detonation of the plutonium bomb.

Robert Serber: A close collaborator of Oppenheimer, Serber was responsible for translating complex theories into practical designs. He authored the "Los Alamos Primer," a series of lectures that introduced new recruits to the principles of atomic bomb design.

Collaborative Dynamics and Challenges-

The diverse backgrounds and personalities of these key figures created both opportunities and challenges. The collaborative environment at Los Alamos fostered innovation, as scientists shared ideas and built upon each other's work. However, the intense pressure to deliver results, coupled with the secrecy of the project, sometimes led to conflicts and misunderstandings.

Oppenheimer's leadership played a crucial role in managing these dynamics. His ability to mediate disputes, delegate responsibilities, and inspire his team ensured that the project remained focused on its goals. The collective efforts of these individuals and their teams ultimately culminated in the successful development and deployment of atomic weapons, reshaping the course of history.

Legacy-

The contributions of Edward Teller, Hans Bethe, Ernest Lawrence, and their colleagues extended far beyond the Manhattan Project. Their work laid the foundation for the fields of nuclear physics, quantum mechanics, and big science. However, the ethical implications of their achievements continue to spark debate, highlighting the complex relationship between scientific progress and societal impact.

The Manhattan Project serves as a testament to the power of collaboration and the enduring influence of visionary scientists. The legacy of these key figures reminds us of the profound responsibilities that come with scientific discovery and the need to balance innovation with ethical considerations.

Coordination between government, military, and scientific institutions-

The Manhattan Project was a groundbreaking initiative that required unprecedented collaboration between government agencies, military leadership, and the scientific community. The seamless integration of these entities was essential to overcoming the immense scientific, engineering, and logistical challenges of developing nuclear weapons during World War II. The success of this endeavor not only demonstrated the potential of interdisciplinary cooperation but also set the stage for future large-scale scientific and technological projects.

Government Leadership and Oversight-

The United States government's involvement in the Manhattan Project began with the recognition of the potential threat posed by Nazi Germany's nuclear ambitions. The Einstein-Szilard letter, delivered to President Franklin D. Roosevelt in 1939, was a key catalyst. This letter, written by physicist Leó Szilárd and signed by Albert Einstein, warned of the possibility of Germany developing an atomic bomb and urged the United States to accelerate its own research efforts.

In response, Roosevelt established the Advisory Committee on Uranium, later evolving into the Office of Scientific Research and Development (OSRD) under the leadership of Vannevar Bush. The OSRD was instrumental in bridging the gap between civilian scientific research and military needs. Bush's ability to navigate political and bureaucratic challenges ensured that the project received the necessary funding and support.

The OSRD's creation of the National Defense Research Committee (NDRC) further streamlined efforts by centralizing oversight of scientific and technological research relevant to national defense. The NDRC worked closely with the War Department and other governmental bodies to align priorities and coordinate resources. This collaboration was critical in addressing the multifaceted demands of the Manhattan Project, from uranium enrichment to the construction of specialized facilities.

Military Oversight and Organization-

The military's role in the Manhattan Project was managed by the U.S. Army Corps of Engineers, which established the Manhattan Engineer District (MED) to oversee the project's logistical and operational aspects. General Leslie Groves, appointed to lead the MED, was a driving force behind the project's success. Groves's leadership style, characterized by decisiveness and a relentless focus on results, proved essential in coordinating the diverse elements of the project.

Groves's responsibilities included site selection, procurement of materials, and security. He oversaw the rapid construction of facilities such as Los Alamos in New Mexico, Oak Ridge in Tennessee, and Hanford in Washington. These sites were strategically chosen for their geographic isolation, access to resources, and logistical feasibility. The construction of these facilities was a monumental task, requiring the mobilization of thousands of workers and overcoming significant engineering challenges.

The military's emphasis on security was another critical aspect of the project. The highly classified nature of the Manhattan Project necessitated strict protocols to prevent leaks and espionage. Groves implemented measures such as compartmentalization of information and rigorous background checks to ensure that sensitive details remained secure. Despite these efforts, the project was not immune to breaches, as evidenced by the activities of Soviet spies such as Klaus Fuchs.

Scientific Institutions and Leadership-

The scientific community was the intellectual backbone of the Manhattan Project, providing the expertise and innovation needed to achieve its ambitious goals. Leading universities and research laboratories across the United States became hubs of activity, contributing to various aspects of nuclear research and development.

At the heart of the project was the Los Alamos National Laboratory, established in 1943 under the leadership of physicist J. Robert Oppenheimer. Los Alamos served as the primary site for the design and assembly of nuclear weapons. Oppenheimer's ability to attract and coordinate a team of world-class scientists was critical to the project's success. His leadership fostered a culture of collaboration and innovation, enabling researchers to tackle complex challenges such as neutron transport, critical mass calculations, and bomb design.

Other institutions also played significant roles. The University of California, Berkeley, was a key center for research on uranium enrichment, spearheaded by physicist Ernest Lawrence and his Radiation Laboratory. Lawrence's development of the cyclotron and electromagnetic separation techniques were pivotal in producing enriched uranium for the bomb.

Similarly, the University of Chicago's Metallurgical Laboratory, led by Arthur Compton, conducted groundbreaking work on nuclear reactors and plutonium production. The first controlled nuclear chain reaction, achieved under the leadership of Enrico Fermi at the university's Stagg Field in 1942, was a landmark achievement that demonstrated the feasibility of nuclear energy.

International contributions also played a crucial role in the project. Many of the scientists involved, including Edward Teller, Hans Bethe, and Niels Bohr, were immigrants who brought expertise from European research traditions. Their diverse perspectives enriched the project and underscored the global nature of scientific progress.

Integration and Collaboration-

Coordinating the efforts of government, military, and scientific institutions required robust communication and management strategies. Regular meetings, progress reports, and cross-disciplinary teams helped ensure alignment of objectives and facilitated problem-solving. The Scientific Panel, composed of leading researchers such as Oppenheimer, Fermi, and Compton, served as an advisory body to General Groves, providing critical insights into technical challenges and project timelines.

The project's classified nature added a layer of complexity to coordination. Strict security protocols limited information sharing, creating challenges for collaboration. However, these measures were deemed necessary to protect against espionage and ensure the project's success. The balance between maintaining secrecy and fostering collaboration was a delicate one, requiring careful management.

Challenges and Tensions-

Despite its successes, the Manhattan Project faced numerous challenges in coordinating its diverse components. Differences in priorities and working styles often led to tensions between scientists and military personnel. While scientists valued intellectual freedom and open exchange of ideas, the military's hierarchical structure and emphasis on secrecy sometimes created friction.

Resource allocation was another significant challenge. The project demanded immense quantities of manpower, materials, and funding, all of which were in high demand due to the ongoing war effort. Balancing these competing demands required careful planning and prioritization.

The urgency of the project's timeline also placed immense pressure on all involved. Deadlines were often aggressive, necessitating long hours and rapid problem-solving. This high-pressure environment, while driving innovation, also led to stress and occasional conflicts among team members.

Legacy of Coordination-

The Manhattan Project's success demonstrated the potential of coordinated efforts between government, military, and scientific institutions. It established a model for future large-scale endeavors, such as the Apollo program and the Human Genome Project. The project also highlighted the importance of interdisciplinary collaboration in addressing complex challenges.

Moreover, the Manhattan Project reshaped the relationship between science and national policy. It underscored the value of investing in scientific research and integrating it into strategic decision-making. The project's legacy continues to influence contemporary discussions on the role of science and technology in addressing global challenges, from climate change to public health.

, the coordination between government, military, and scientific institutions was a cornerstone of the Manhattan Project's success. By aligning their efforts and leveraging their unique strengths, these entities achieved a remarkable feat of innovation and collaboration. The lessons learned from this experience continue to resonate, offering insights into the power and potential of interdisciplinary cooperation.

CHAPTER FOUR

THE SECRET CITIES – FACILITIES AND OPERATIONS

Los Alamos Laboratory: Research hub for bomb design-

The Los Alamos Laboratory, also known as Project Y, was established in 1943 as the primary research hub for the design and development of nuclear weapons under the Manhattan Project. Located in the remote highlands of New Mexico, the laboratory became a focal point for some of the most brilliant scientific minds of the 20th century. Its creation marked a pivotal step in the journey toward harnessing nuclear energy for warfare, and its success was the result of exceptional scientific collaboration, innovation, and coordination.

Origins and Site Selection-

The decision to establish a central laboratory for bomb design was driven by the need to consolidate research efforts and enhance coordination. Prior to the establishment of Los Alamos, work on nuclear weapons was dispersed across various institutions, leading to inefficiencies and challenges in communication. General Leslie Groves, the military leader of the Manhattan Project, and J. Robert Oppenheimer, the project's scientific director, identified the need for a single, secure site where scientists could work collaboratively.

Oppenheimer's familiarity with the region played a key role in the selection of Los Alamos. He had spent time in New Mexico and appreciated its isolation, which provided both security and a conducive environment for intense scientific work. The site's remoteness also minimized the risk to civilian populations in the event of an accident.

The selection process involved extensive evaluations of potential sites. Factors such as accessibility, climate, and the availability of water and other resources were carefully considered. Los Alamos, previously the location of a boys' school, met these criteria and was deemed ideal for the project's needs. The site's prior use as an educational institution also meant that some basic infrastructure was already in place, which facilitated its rapid transformation into a scientific hub.

Construction and Infrastructure-

The development of the Los Alamos site was a massive logistical undertaking. Within months, a sprawling facility was built, complete with laboratories, workshops, residential housing, and recreational amenities to support the scientists and their families. The laboratory's design emphasized functionality and security, with restricted access and strict protocols to maintain secrecy.

Despite its rapid construction, the site faced challenges such as harsh weather conditions, limited resources, and the need to accommodate a growing workforce. Housing was often cramped, and the remote location made it difficult to obtain supplies. Nevertheless, these hurdles were overcome through meticulous planning and the dedication of those involved in the project.

The laboratory's infrastructure was designed to support a wide range of scientific activities. State-of-the-art equipment was installed to facilitate research in physics, chemistry, metallurgy, and engineering. Specialized facilities, such as high-explosives testing sites and radiochemistry laboratories, were built to address the unique challenges of bomb design. The site also included administrative offices, a library, and spaces for social and recreational activities, which helped foster a sense of community among the residents.

Leadership and Organization-

J. Robert Oppenheimer's leadership was instrumental in shaping the culture and success of Los Alamos. Known for his intellectual brilliance and ability to inspire others, Oppenheimer created an environment that encouraged collaboration and innovation. He fostered open communication among scientists while maintaining the discipline required to meet tight deadlines.

The laboratory's organizational structure was designed to facilitate interdisciplinary collaboration. Scientists from diverse fields, including physics, chemistry, engineering, and metallurgy, worked in close proximity, enabling the exchange of ideas and rapid problem-solving. Teams were formed to address specific challenges, such as neutron transport, implosion dynamics, and materials testing. These teams operated under the guidance of senior scientists, who provided oversight and ensured that efforts were aligned with the project's objectives.

In addition to Oppenheimer, other key leaders at Los Alamos played crucial roles in its success. General Leslie Groves provided the military oversight and logistical support necessary to maintain the project's momentum. His ability to navigate bureaucratic challenges and secure resources ensured that the laboratory had the tools and materials it needed to succeed. Scientists such as Hans Bethe, Edward Teller, and Richard Feynman brought their expertise and creativity to the project, contributing to its groundbreaking achievements.

Scientific Achievements-

The research conducted at Los Alamos led to significant breakthroughs in nuclear physics and weapon design. Among the key achievements were:

Theoretical Modeling: Scientists developed advanced mathematical models to understand the behavior of nuclear reactions, critical mass requirements, and energy release mechanisms. These models provided the foundation for the design of both uranium- and plutonium-based bombs.

Implosion Method: The implosion method, used in the design of the plutonium bomb (Fat Man), was a major focus at Los Alamos. This approach required precise calculations and innovative engineering to achieve symmetrical compression of the plutonium core. The development of explosive lenses, which directed shock waves inward, was a critical aspect of this work.

Materials Science: Researchers investigated the properties of fissile materials, such as uranium-235 and plutonium-239, and developed methods for their purification and handling. The laboratory also explored the use of high explosives and other materials to optimize bomb design and performance.

Testing and Validation: Extensive testing was conducted to validate theoretical models and refine bomb designs. The Trinity test, conducted in July 1945 in the New Mexico desert, marked the culmination of these efforts and demonstrated the success of the implosion method. This test provided critical data on the bomb's explosive yield, radiation effects, and overall performance.

Innovation in Engineering: Engineers at Los Alamos developed specialized tools and techniques to address the unique challenges of bomb assembly and delivery. This included the design of bomb casings, detonation systems, and mechanisms for initiating nuclear reactions.

Challenges and Tensions-

The intense pace of work at Los Alamos created a high-pressure environment that often led to tensions among scientists and between the scientific and military leadership. Differences in priorities and working styles sometimes caused friction. For example, scientists' desire for thorough research and experimentation occasionally clashed with the military's urgency to produce a functional weapon.

Additionally, the classified nature of the project imposed restrictions on communication, both within the laboratory and with the outside world. Scientists were often isolated from their families and had limited access to information unrelated to their specific tasks. These conditions, while necessary for security, added to the personal and professional challenges faced by the workforce.

Despite these challenges, the collaborative spirit at Los Alamos ultimately prevailed. The laboratory's culture of innovation and problem-solving enabled it to overcome obstacles and achieve its objectives. The dedication and resilience of the scientists, engineers, and support staff were instrumental in the project's success.

Legacy and Impact-

The work conducted at Los Alamos during the Manhattan Project not only led to the development of the first nuclear weapons but also laid the foundation for post-war advancements in nuclear science and technology. The laboratory became a symbol of scientific achievement and a testament to the power of collaboration.

The success of Los Alamos also raised ethical questions about the use of nuclear weapons and the responsibilities of scientists in military research. These debates continue to influence discussions on the role of science in society and the balance between innovation and ethical considerations.

In the decades following the Manhattan Project, Los Alamos National Laboratory evolved into a premier research institution, contributing to a wide range of scientific fields, from energy research to national security. Its legacy serves as a reminder of the profound impact of interdisciplinary collaboration and the enduring importance of addressing the societal implications of scientific advancements.

The lessons learned at Los Alamos continue to resonate in the scientific community. The laboratory's success demonstrated the potential of large-scale, mission-oriented research efforts to achieve transformative results. It also highlighted the importance of balancing technical excellence with ethical considerations, a challenge that remains relevant in the modern era.

In summary, the Los Alamos Laboratory was the epicenter of innovation and collaboration during the Manhattan Project. Its establishment and success exemplified the power of collective effort in achieving monumental scientific and technological breakthroughs. The laboratory's contributions not only shaped the outcome of World War II but also left an indelible mark on the trajectory of modern science and global geopolitics. The story of Los Alamos serves as a testament to the remarkable achievements that can be realized when vision, leadership, and teamwork converge in the pursuit of a common goal.

Oak Ridge: Uranium enrichment using gaseous diffusion and electromagnetic separation-

1. Introduction: The Need for Uranium Enrichment in the Manhattan Project-

The Oak Ridge National Laboratory (ORNL), located in Oak Ridge, Tennessee, was one of the most significant sites in the development of the atomic bomb during the Manhattan Project. The United States' effort to build an atomic bomb was sparked by concerns that Nazi Germany could be the first to harness the destructive potential of atomic energy. The Nazis' early work on nuclear fission and chain reactions, including the discovery of uranium fission by Otto Hahn and Fritz Strassmann, led to fears of a nuclear arms race. In 1939, physicist Leó Szilárd, together with Albert Einstein, urged the United States government to pursue atomic research in response to these growing concerns, culminating in the creation of the Manhattan Project.

The success of the atomic bomb, however, relied on overcoming a critical obstacle: uranium enrichment. Natural uranium contains only about 0.7% uranium-235 (U-235), the fissile isotope necessary for sustaining a nuclear chain reaction, with the remaining 99.3% composed of uranium-238 (U-238), which does not readily undergo fission. This low concentration of U-235 meant that innovative techniques were required to isolate and concentrate it into sufficient quantities. The development of these techniques would form the crux of the uranium enrichment efforts at Oak Ridge.

Among the most prominent methods of uranium enrichment employed were gaseous diffusion and electromagnetic separation. Both techniques made use of the slight mass difference between U-235 and U-238 to separate the two isotopes, but each method had its own challenges, innovations, and significance in the broader effort of the Manhattan Project. This section delves into these two methods, their technical underpinnings, the challenges faced in their implementation, and the legacy they left in the fields of nuclear science and technology.

2. The K-25 Plant and Gaseous Diffusion: The Largest Enrichment Facility of Its Time-

Gaseous diffusion, a method based on the diffusion of uranium hexafluoride (UF6) gas through porous barriers, was one of the first and most prominent approaches for uranium enrichment at Oak Ridge. The underlying principle behind gaseous diffusion was relatively simple: lighter gas molecules, such as U-235, move faster than heavier molecules, such as U-238, due to their lower mass. As UF6 gas was passed through porous barriers, U-235 molecules would diffuse through the barriers slightly faster than U-238 molecules, thereby concentrating U-235 on the other side of the barrier.

This principle was first suggested by chemists Harold Urey and Gilbert N. Lewis, who recognized that uranium could be chemically separated in its gaseous form. Despite the seeming simplicity of this idea, the gaseous diffusion process posed significant engineering challenges due to the need for high-efficiency barriers and the large volumes of gas that needed to be processed.

The K-25 Plant:-

The K-25 Plant, located in Oak Ridge, was the largest gaseous diffusion plant of its time. Construction of K-25 began in 1943 and was completed in 1944. The plant would go on to play a central role in providing the enriched uranium required for the Manhattan Project. The facility was built to house hundreds of units, each containing vast arrays of porous barriers.

The plant itself covered a massive area, occupying nearly 1.5 million square feet and consisting of a series of long cylindrical chambers where the gaseous diffusion process took place. Each chamber was designed to separate U-235 from U-238 by using large porous barriers made of materials like nickel or stainless steel. The chambers were separated by complex systems that controlled the temperature, pressure, and flow of gas in order to maximize the separation efficiency of uranium isotopes.

The gaseous diffusion process itself was inefficient by modern standards, requiring multiple stages of separation, with each stage resulting in only a small increase in U-235 concentration. The K-25 Plant's design incorporated thousands of stages, with the gas passing through each stage and becoming progressively enriched in U-235. At its peak, the plant housed over 1,100,000 stages of diffusion, leading to substantial U-235 enrichment.

One of the most significant challenges of gaseous diffusion was the sheer energy consumption required to operate the plant. The separation process demanded large amounts of electrical power to maintain the pressure differential and circulate the gas through the diffusion barriers. To meet the needs of the K-25 plant, the nearby Tennessee Valley Authority (TVA) had to greatly expand its energy production. The TVA, which already operated a series of hydroelectric dams, was tasked with providing electricity for the operation of the K-25 facility. This collaboration between TVA and the Manhattan Project was instrumental in the success of the gaseous diffusion process.

Despite its energy inefficiency and the technological challenges it posed, the K-25 Plant remained a pivotal element of the Manhattan Project. The enriched uranium produced at K-25 was used in the development of the Little Boy atomic bomb, which was dropped on Hiroshima in August 1945.

3. Electromagnetic Separation: The Development and Success of the Calutron at Y-12-

The second major method of uranium enrichment developed at Oak Ridge was electromagnetic separation, based on the use of calutrons, an invention of physicist Ernest O. Lawrence. The calutron worked on the principle of mass spectrometry, utilizing a magnetic field to separate charged uranium ions based on their mass-to-charge ratio. The key difference between U-235 and U-238 was their mass, with U-235 being slightly lighter, which allowed them to be separated by applying an electromagnetic force.

The calutron device consisted of a vacuum chamber where uranium was ionized, and the resulting ions were accelerated through an electric field and passed through a magnetic field. The magnetic field caused the ions to follow curved paths, with the lighter U-235 ions following a tighter curve and the heavier U-238 ions following a broader curve. By placing detectors along the path of the ions, scientists could collect the separated isotopes.

The Y-12 Plant:-

The electromagnetic separation technique was implemented at the Y-12 Plant in Oak Ridge, where hundreds of calutrons were used to separate uranium isotopes. The Y-12 facility, established in 1943, became a critical part of the uranium enrichment process, alongside the gaseous diffusion efforts at K-25.

The Y-12 Plant's main feature was its large number of calutrons—approximately 1,500 units—each of which was used to separate U-235 from U-238. The calutrons themselves were large, complex machines that required highly skilled technicians to operate. They consisted of a series of magnets, electrical coils, and vacuum chambers, all of which had to be carefully tuned to produce the desired separation of uranium isotopes.

The process at Y-12 was highly labor-intensive. Workers, many of whom were women, operated the calutrons, adjusted settings, monitored equipment, and handled the delicate process of collecting the enriched uranium. The separation of uranium was achieved by passing the ionized uranium through a magnetic field and then directing the resulting isotopes to separate collectors based on their mass.

Although electromagnetic separation was less efficient than gaseous diffusion, it was valuable for producing high-purity uranium-235, which was necessary for the development of the Fat Man bomb, which was dropped on Nagasaki. The Y-12 Plant played a crucial role in producing the enriched uranium needed for this second atomic bomb.

Despite the challenges posed by the electromagnetic separation method, the work carried out at Y-12 demonstrated the resilience and ingenuity of the scientists and workers involved. The calutrons produced high-quality uranium-235, which, combined with the gaseous diffusion efforts at K-25, ensured that the United States had the enriched uranium it needed to complete the Manhattan Project.

4. Technological and Engineering Challenges in Oak Ridge-

Both the gaseous diffusion and electromagnetic separation methods faced significant engineering challenges, and much of the success of the Manhattan Project can be attributed to the remarkable ingenuity and dedication of the scientists and engineers working at Oak Ridge. The complexities of uranium enrichment were not solely limited to the science of isotope separation but extended to the construction of the facilities, maintenance of the machines, and secrecy surrounding the entire operation.

Challenges of Scale and Efficiency:-

One of the largest challenges faced by the Manhattan Project was scaling up the uranium enrichment process to industrial levels. The need for large-scale production meant that vast quantities of uranium hexafluoride gas had to be processed, and the engineering infrastructure had to be adapted to handle these large quantities efficiently.

The gaseous diffusion process was particularly energy-intensive, requiring enormous amounts of electricity to maintain pressure differentials across the porous barriers. This created a logistical problem in providing enough power to the K-25 Plant. Engineers at Oak Ridge overcame this challenge by expanding the power infrastructure through partnerships with the TVA.

In the case of the calutrons, one of the major issues was the precision required to separate uranium isotopes. Each calutron had to be carefully calibrated to ensure it was correctly tuned to separate U-235 from U-238. The continuous monitoring, maintenance, and fine-tuning of thousands of individual calutrons required a workforce of technicians and engineers working around the clock.

Security and Secrecy:-

The Oak Ridge facilities were highly secretive, and many of the workers at K-25 and Y-12 did not know the full purpose of their work. Compartmentalization of knowledge was a key element of the Manhattan Project's security protocols. Each worker was aware of only a small portion of the overall project. As a result, the workers at Oak Ridge were unaware that they were contributing to the development of atomic bombs until after the war had ended.

Oak Ridge was also home to a highly skilled workforce, many of whom were recruited from various parts of the country. These workers were brought in to perform the labor-intensive tasks associated with running the calutrons and managing the gaseous diffusion plant. Workers were often trained on-site in order to meet the demand for a large labor force, and many women contributed significantly to the workforce during this period.

5. Legacy of Oak Ridge and the Manhattan Project-

The work done at Oak Ridge during the Manhattan Project not only played a pivotal role in the creation of the atomic bomb but also laid the foundation for the United States' nuclear energy industry. Both gaseous diffusion and electromagnetic separation techniques would influence the development of civilian nuclear energy, with the K-25 Plant later being adapted for peaceful applications such as uranium enrichment for nuclear reactors.

The legacy of Oak Ridge's contributions extends well beyond the immediate aftermath of World War II. The research conducted at Oak Ridge helped establish the United States as a leader in nuclear energy and nuclear weaponry. The development of enrichment technologies at Oak Ridge also provided the scientific and technical foundation for future nuclear research and power generation.

Today, Oak Ridge remains a center of cutting-edge nuclear research and development, hosting a variety of national laboratories that continue to advance the understanding and application of nuclear energy and science. Its role in the Manhattan Project has left an indelible mark on the history of science and engineering, serving as a testament to the power of technological innovation in times of great global need.

Hanford Site: Plutonium production reactors-

Introduction: The Crucial Role of Hanford in the Manhattan Project-

The Hanford Site, a sprawling nuclear production facility located in the Columbia River Basin of southeastern Washington State, holds a place of paramount importance in the history of nuclear energy and weapons development. Initially conceived as a strategic location for plutonium production during the Manhattan Project, Hanford became a cornerstone of the United States' efforts to develop nuclear weapons during World War II. It housed the world's first large-scale plutonium production reactors, which were critical for the creation of plutonium-239

(Pu-239) — the isotope needed for the construction of the "Fat Man" atomic bomb. This bomb would later be dropped on Nagasaki, Japan, in August 1945, marking the first and only use of nuclear weapons in warfare.

The Manhattan Project, a massive, top-secret research and development initiative, aimed to harness the power of atomic energy to develop a weapon of unprecedented destructive power before Nazi Germany or Imperial Japan could achieve the same goal. While significant attention has been paid to the uranium enrichment efforts at Oak Ridge and the assembly of the bombs at Los Alamos, Hanford's role as the central hub for plutonium production was equally vital to the success of the project. The reactors built at Hanford were specifically designed to irradiate uranium fuel, thereby producing the plutonium-239 necessary for bomb-making. This process would go on to form the backbone of nuclear weapons development in the early Cold War years.

Although the site played an essential role in the Allied victory, Hanford's legacy is far from singularly celebratory. The site remains one of the most contaminated places on earth, with a complex history of environmental degradation and health risks associated with the production and disposal of plutonium. Over the decades, cleanup efforts have been ongoing, and the environmental and ethical challenges of nuclear weapons production continue to resonate. This article delves deep into the history of Hanford, its contributions to the Manhattan Project, the reactors it housed, and the enduring legacy it left on nuclear weapons and policy.

2. The Need for Plutonium: Uranium-235 and the Discovery of Plutonium-

Before the dawn of the Manhattan Project, scientists were already experimenting with atomic energy. The discovery of uranium-235 (U-235) as the key fissile material for nuclear reactions marked a breakthrough in understanding nuclear fission. Uranium-235 undergoes fission when bombarded by neutrons, splitting into smaller fragments while releasing substantial amounts of energy. However, natural uranium is composed mostly of uranium-238 (U-238), which is not directly fissile. To use uranium-235 effectively, it had to be separated from the non-fissile uranium-238, a challenging and resource-intensive task.

As research continued, scientists discovered a new method of creating fissile material through the transmutation of uranium-238 into plutonium-239 (Pu-239). This discovery, made by physicists Glenn T. Seaborg, Arthur C. Wahl, and Joseph W. Kennedy at the University of California, Berkeley, opened up a new avenue for nuclear weapons development. The production of plutonium-239, however, was not a straightforward process. It required an industrial-scale nuclear reactor to bombard uranium with neutrons, converting it into plutonium over time.

In the early 1940s, this transmutation process was realized to be the key to supplying plutonium for the atomic bomb. The next step was building a reactor capable of carrying out this process on a large enough scale to produce the material in the quantities required for weaponization. The Manhattan Project would soon turn to the Hanford Site in Washington State, where the first large-scale plutonium production reactors would be built.

3. The Strategic Importance of the Hanford Site-

The location of the Hanford Site was chosen for its combination of strategic and practical advantages. Geographically, the site was located in the remote Columbia River Basin, far from population centers and military targets. This isolation provided both security and secrecy, which were paramount for the Manhattan Project. In addition, the Columbia River, one of the largest rivers in the United States, provided an ample and reliable source of cooling water, essential for the operation of the nuclear reactors. The site's proximity to transportation routes, particularly by rail and river, also ensured that materials, equipment, and personnel could be easily transported to and from the site.

In terms of security, Hanford's location was critical. The U.S. military was deeply concerned about the possibility of espionage and sabotage. Its distance from the coast and major urban centers made it less likely to attract unwanted attention. The sheer remoteness of the area also meant that it would be difficult for the Axis powers to detect and strike the facility, ensuring its protection. The idea of building large-scale reactors in such an isolated location was, in many ways, a logistical and engineering triumph.

However, despite the advantages of the site's remote location, the challenges of constructing and operating a nuclear facility in a barren, largely undeveloped area were immense. Workers needed to construct the necessary infrastructure, including roads, housing, power generation, and waste management systems, from the ground up. The project required vast amounts of labor, materials, and resources, and the timeline for construction was compressed as military leaders pushed for rapid progress.

4. Building the Plutonium Production Reactors-

At the heart of the Hanford Site were its plutonium production reactors, the world's first reactors capable of producing plutonium on an industrial scale. The reactors were designed with an eye toward high-efficiency production, using uranium-238 as the fuel source and graphite as a neutron moderator. These reactors were built to operate under conditions of continuous neutron irradiation, with the uranium fuel being bombarded by neutrons to produce plutonium-239.

The development of these reactors was spearheaded by General Leslie R. Groves, who oversaw the Manhattan Project's construction efforts, and J. Robert Oppenheimer, the project's scientific director. The project team worked under extreme pressure, with the knowledge that the success of the atomic bomb depended on their ability to create these reactors and meet the growing demand for plutonium. The reactors were designed to be graphite-moderated and water-cooled, a configuration that enabled the reactors to generate the necessary energy to produce significant quantities of plutonium.

Among the most notable reactors built at Hanford were the B Reactor, the D Reactor, and the F Reactor. Each reactor had its unique design and specifications, but they all served the same purpose of generating plutonium for the Manhattan Project.

The B Reactor: Completed in 1944, the B Reactor was the first industrial-scale nuclear reactor ever built. It had a thermal power output of 250 megawatts and housed uranium fuel and graphite moderator in a design that maximized neutron absorption and plutonium production. Its successful operation marked a significant milestone in nuclear technology, and it would serve as the model for the subsequent reactors built at Hanford.

The D Reactor: Larger and more efficient than the B Reactor, the D Reactor was completed in 1945. Its design allowed for greater amounts of uranium to be irradiated, resulting in higher plutonium output. The D Reactor's increased production capacity made it an essential component of the plutonium manufacturing process.

The F Reactor: As the largest and most advanced of the reactors at Hanford, the F Reactor was capable of producing even more plutonium than the D Reactor. Built in 1945, it was designed to handle larger quantities of uranium and produce more plutonium per cycle.

In the context of the Manhattan Project, these reactors were critical in the race to produce enough plutonium to build a functional atomic bomb. The success of the reactors depended not only on their design but also on the expertise of the engineers, physicists, and laborers who constructed and operated them under the direction of military and civilian leaders.

5. Reactor Operations: Producing Plutonium-

The operation of the reactors at Hanford was complex and dangerous. Uranium fuel rods were placed into the reactor cores, where they were bombarded by neutrons produced by the reactor's fission process. As the uranium absorbed neutrons, it underwent a nuclear reaction, creating plutonium-239. The goal was to maximize the amount of plutonium produced per cycle while maintaining the reactor's stability and safety.

One of the most challenging aspects of reactor operations was the cooling process. Reactors produce vast amounts of heat as they generate energy. In order to maintain safe operating conditions, the reactors were equipped with sophisticated cooling systems that circulated water from the Columbia River to absorb the heat produced by the reactors. The water was then pumped back into the river, where it was cooled before being used again. This system was essential for ensuring the reactors did not overheat and that the nuclear reaction could be sustained.

As the uranium fuel rods were irradiated, they began to accumulate radioactive byproducts, including fission products and plutonium-239. After a certain period of time, the spent fuel rods were removed from the reactors and transported to a processing facility for the extraction of plutonium.

6. The T-Plant: Extracting the Plutonium-

Once the uranium fuel had been irradiated and transformed into plutonium-239, it was transported to the T-Plant (Plutonium Recovery Plant) for chemical processing. The T-Plant was equipped with a complex chemical processing system designed to separate plutonium from the other materials in the spent fuel. The extraction process was known as the redox extraction process, which utilized a series of chemical reactions to separate the plutonium from uranium and other fission products.

The extraction process was a highly dangerous task, as it involved working with radioactive materials under extreme conditions. However, the success of this operation was crucial to the war effort, as plutonium-239 was the fissile material needed for the atomic bomb. Once purified, the plutonium was processed into a form suitable for weaponization. This marked the final step in producing the fissile material that would be used in the construction of the "Fat Man" atomic bomb.

7. The Legacy of Hanford: Environmental Impact and Cleanup Efforts-

While the plutonium reactors at Hanford played a vital role in the development of the atomic bomb and the Allied victory in World War II, the long-term environmental legacy of the site is a major concern. The production of plutonium at Hanford generated vast amounts of radioactive waste, including spent fuel, contaminated equipment, and polluted groundwater. The risks associated with this contamination continue to affect the site and the surrounding area.

Hanford has become one of the most contaminated sites in the United States. The radioactive waste produced by the reactors, the cooling water used to maintain the reactors' temperature, and the various byproducts of plutonium production created long-lasting environmental hazards. The cleanup of Hanford has been an ongoing project for decades, requiring careful management and advanced technology to ensure that the site does not continue to pose a threat to public health and the environment.

Hanford's Role in the Manhattan Project and Beyond-

The Hanford Site played an indispensable role in the Manhattan Project by producing the plutonium necessary for the development of nuclear weapons. Its reactors—especially the B Reactor, D Reactor, and F Reactor—were essential for irradiating uranium and producing plutonium on a scale never before seen. However, the success of the project came with significant environmental and health costs, and Hanford's legacy remains tied to the challenges of managing nuclear waste and contamination. Today, the Hanford Site serves as a reminder of both the scientific and ethical implications of nuclear technology, and the lessons learned from its history continue to shape global discussions on nuclear energy, weapons, and environmental management.

Challenges of secrecy and logistics-

The Manhattan Project stands as one of the most remarkable and complex scientific and engineering feats in history. The project was not only a monumental achievement in nuclear science but also an unparalleled test of secrecy, logistical coordination, and scientific innovation. The endeavor required an unprecedented degree of confidentiality, as the U.S. government and military feared that if Nazi Germany or Imperial Japan developed nuclear weapons first, they could shift the balance of the war. Simultaneously, the project necessitated the construction of vast industrial facilities, the rapid development of new technologies, and the creation of intricate supply chains to manage resources and materials that were highly sensitive and challenging to obtain. The challenges of secrecy and logistics were intertwined and often compounded by the scale and complexity of the task. This aspect of the project remains a subject of deep interest in both historical and logistical studies, highlighting the difficulty of managing such an expansive and groundbreaking undertaking.

1. The Need for Secrecy-

From the very outset of the Manhattan Project, secrecy was paramount. As the project had the potential to alter the course of the war and shift global power structures, the U.S. government took extreme measures to prevent knowledge of the bomb's existence from leaking to enemy powers. The project was not only secretive in terms of its research and design but also in terms of its implementation and logistical support. Hundreds of thousands of workers were involved, but most had no idea of the true purpose of their labor. To protect the integrity of the project, strict compartmentalization was implemented, and many workers and scientists were only informed about their individual tasks rather than the broader goals.

Challenges in Maintaining Secrecy:-

Compartmentalization of Knowledge: One of the key strategies to maintain secrecy was the compartmentalization of knowledge. This practice meant that people working on the project were only given access to the information necessary for their specific role. For example, engineers at the Oak Ridge National Laboratory worked on uranium enrichment but were unaware that plutonium was being produced at Hanford. Similarly, workers at Los Alamos focused solely on the design and testing of the bomb, without understanding the full process or how the uranium or plutonium would be obtained. This prevented any one person from having complete knowledge of the entire operation, which would have increased the likelihood of espionage or leaks.

The Role of Espionage: Despite the rigorous measures taken, the Manhattan Project was still vulnerable to espionage. The presence of spies within the United States, particularly Soviet agents, was a constant concern. Many spies, such as Klaus Fuchs and Theodore Hall, were able to infiltrate critical areas of the project and pass information back to the Soviet Union. Their actions jeopardized the secrecy of the bomb's development and had far-reaching implications for the Cold War that followed. The discovery of espionage within the ranks of the Manhattan Project made clear how difficult it was to maintain absolute secrecy, even in the face of extraordinary efforts. The betrayal of trusted individuals illustrated the vulnerability of such a highly secretive and complex operation.

Secrecy and Public Life: The strict nature of secrecy extended to the personal lives of the project's workers. Those involved in the Manhattan Project were forbidden from discussing their work with family members, friends, or acquaintances, even though many workers did not fully understand the nature of their jobs. Some workers at the Oak Ridge facility, for instance, were completely in the dark about the purpose of their work, even as they were heavily involved in the construction and operation of reactors designed to produce nuclear materials. This level of secrecy led to a sense of isolation for many involved, with personal lives and professional identities intertwined by the need for confidentiality.

Keeping Secrets from Allies: While secrecy was critical to prevent Nazi Germany or Japan from discovering the project, it also extended to the Allies. The United States did not fully share its nuclear research with other Allied powers, particularly the United Kingdom and the Soviet Union. This was partly due to concerns that the Germans or Soviets might intercept sensitive information and use it for their own benefit. The only exception to this was the United Kingdom, where the Tube Alloys project was already underway. However, British scientists working on the project were kept in the dark about the full scale of the Manhattan Project, and there was little communication between the American and British research efforts.

2. Logistical Challenges: Scaling Up the Science-
While secrecy was an overarching concern, the logistical challenges of the Manhattan Project were equally critical. The project involved the development of new and untested technologies on a massive scale, requiring the construction of highly specialized facilities and the sourcing and transportation of large quantities of raw materials. The sheer scale of the project meant that logistical operations had to be meticulously planned and executed with precision. This included the establishment of production facilities capable of generating fissile materials, developing new infrastructure to house these operations, and managing a supply chain for materials that were both rare and highly sensitive.

Building the Infrastructure:-
Research and Development: The first step in the logistics of the Manhattan Project was to establish research and development labs capable of investigating the fundamental principles of nuclear fission and discovering the best methods for enriching uranium and producing plutonium. Los Alamos was chosen as the site for the main research laboratory, where the

atomic bomb would be designed and tested. The laboratory, led by physicist J. Robert Oppenheimer, became the focal point for the theoretical and practical work on the bomb's development. However, the success of Los Alamos depended heavily on the resources and research generated from other sites.

The Enrichment of Uranium: At Oak Ridge, large-scale uranium enrichment plants were constructed, including the Y-12 Electromagnetic Plant and the K-25 gaseous diffusion plant. These facilities used different methods to separate the fissile isotope uranium-235 from uranium-238. The logistics of building these plants were complex. Materials such as uranium ore had to be transported across vast distances, and the facilities required enormous quantities of electricity and raw materials. These facilities had to be constructed at an expedited pace while maintaining secrecy. As the plants were being built, they were also designed to operate at full capacity almost immediately, requiring careful planning and management.

The Hanford Site: One of the most significant logistical challenges was the construction of the Hanford Site in Washington State, where reactors would be built to produce plutonium. The B Reactor, the world's first large-scale nuclear reactor, was constructed to irradiate uranium and create plutonium-239, which would then be extracted and purified for use in the atomic bomb. The construction of the reactors at Hanford required vast amounts of concrete, steel, and other materials, which had to be sourced and transported to this remote location in the Pacific Northwest. The facility was also built to operate continuously and efficiently, producing large quantities of plutonium within months of its completion. The logistics of keeping the site running smoothly were challenging, as it required precise synchronization of materials, personnel, and resources to meet the demand for plutonium.

Sourcing Materials and Managing Supply Chains: One of the most critical logistical challenges was sourcing and transporting the raw materials required for the project. Uranium, the key material for producing fissile material, had to be sourced from multiple countries and then processed and transported to various facilities. Uranium ore was transported via rail, road, and river to sites like Oak Ridge, where it was enriched to increase the concentration of the fissile isotope uranium-235. The transportation of uranium and other key materials had to be done discreetly, using specially designated routes and methods to prevent any potential interception by enemy forces. Additionally, plutonium and uranium products had to be transported from one facility to another—often over long distances—requiring secure and efficient logistics systems to avoid contamination and damage.

The Transportation of Plutonium: Once plutonium was extracted at the Hanford Site, it had to be transported to Los Alamos for the bomb's assembly. Transporting such radioactive materials presented significant risks, and special protocols had to be developed to ensure the safety of the material, the workers, and the public. The plutonium was transported in specially designed containers that could withstand external impacts and radiation. Throughout the project, safety measures for the transportation of fissile materials were constantly updated and improved as the potential hazards were better understood.

Worker Coordination and Labor Forces: Another aspect of the logistical challenge was coordinating the large labor force required to build and maintain the facilities. Thousands of workers were involved in constructing the reactors, enrichment plants, and other facilities. Many of the workers, especially at Oak Ridge and Hanford, did not know the purpose of their work. Workers at Los Alamos were similarly kept in the dark about the broader objectives of the project. This created difficulties in terms of morale and worker motivation, but it was necessary to prevent leaks of information. The labor force also had to be managed efficiently, with shifts, responsibilities, and security measures carefully planned to ensure that the facilities could operate smoothly and meet deadlines.

3. Coordinating Multiple Sites and Personalities-

Given the vast number of sites involved in the Manhattan Project, one of the most challenging logistical elements was coordinating the activities of the various locations. Each site had its own role, and the success of the overall project depended on how well these roles were synchronized. This required complex management systems and the ability to resolve disputes and conflicts between the different personalities involved in the project.

The Role of General Leslie Groves: General Leslie R. Groves, the military leader of the Manhattan Project, was critical in managing the logistics of the project. Groves oversaw all aspects of the project's construction, including the development of sites like Oak Ridge and Hanford, and worked closely with civilian scientists and military personnel to ensure that the project met its deadlines. His management style was tough and demanding, but it was effective in keeping the project on track. Groves was also responsible for securing the necessary funding for the project, which ran into the billions of dollars—a huge amount at the time.

The Coordination of Scientists: The scientists, led by J. Robert Oppenheimer at Los Alamos, were tasked with designing and testing the atomic bombs. Despite the project's secrecy, these scientists had to work in close collaboration with one another to develop the necessary technology. This meant coordinating the work of scientists from different fields, such as nuclear physics, chemistry, and metallurgy. The scientific team was composed of some of the brightest minds in the world, but this sometimes led to disagreements and personality clashes. Managing these personalities and ensuring that the team could work together was crucial to the project's success.

4. Conclusion: Overcoming Secrecy and Logistical Obstacles-

The Manhattan Project's success in developing nuclear weapons relied on overcoming enormous secrecy and logistical challenges. The project's sheer scale, complexity, and innovation were matched only by the difficulties in keeping its work hidden and ensuring that every component—from raw materials to facilities and labor forces—was carefully coordinated. The results of the project were groundbreaking, but the process was fraught with obstacles that required constant adaptation and strategic management. The legacy of these logistical challenges continues to influence how large-scale scientific and industrial projects are managed today, and the lessons learned from this monumental endeavor are still relevant in contemporary discussions about secrecy, security, and the ethical implications of technological advancements.

Life in the secret cities: The people, security measures, and daily life-

The secret cities that formed the backbone of the Manhattan Project—Oak Ridge, Tennessee; Los Alamos, New Mexico; and Hanford, Washington—were unlike any other communities in the United States during World War II. They were places of intense scientific endeavor, cutting-edge research, and, above all, secrecy. These cities played a critical role in the development of the atomic bomb, but life within them was both extraordinary and constrained by tight security, isolation, and the relentless pressure to complete a world-changing project.

At the heart of these secret cities were the people: highly skilled scientists and engineers, laborers from across the nation, military personnel, and civilians, each working together toward a singular, secretive goal. The workers who were drawn to these sites—from physicists like J. Robert Oppenheimer to construction workers building the facilities—knew they were part of something monumental. Yet most had no idea what they were actually working toward until much later. This blend of knowledge, secrecy, and compartmentalization created an environment that was as much about psychological endurance and moral ambiguity as it was about scientific progress.

1. The People: A Complex, Diverse, and Secretive Workforce-
Recruitment: The Selection Process and Its Secrecy-

The recruitment process for workers at the Manhattan Project sites was deeply shrouded in secrecy, a process designed to ensure that no one knew too much about the project. The first step in recruitment was to identify individuals who possessed the specific skills needed to advance the project's goals. This included scientists, technicians, engineers, and other specialists. However, many of the workers had no idea what they would be doing when they were recruited. In many cases, they were simply told they were working on a crucial military effort, but were not made aware that they were helping to develop the atomic bomb.

The secrecy surrounding recruitment was crucial in preventing leaks to enemy intelligence, especially since the bomb's potential was so profound. Many of the civilian workers, including scientists and engineers, were recruited directly from universities or through professional organizations. Some of the nation's most brilliant minds in physics, chemistry, and engineering were called upon, including Nobel Prize winners and individuals who would go on to become leaders in their fields. However, these recruits had little idea of the scope of the project when they agreed to participate.

For workers in non-scientific roles, such as those at Oak Ridge and Hanford who helped build and maintain the sites, the secrecy was similarly strict. These workers, often from rural backgrounds, were brought in as part of the large workforce required to operate the complex systems of uranium enrichment and plutonium production. Like the scientists, they too were often kept in the dark about the full scope of the project. Many were unaware they were working on processes that would contribute directly to the creation of nuclear weapons.

The Diverse Workforce: A Cross-Section of American Society-

The Manhattan Project attracted a wide range of workers, and the communities that grew around the secret cities became melting pots of American society. Scientists and engineers were joined by workers from different parts of the country, many of whom had little prior experience in scientific fields. Families were relocated to these cities, and the social makeup of the workforce was diverse, with people from urban and rural backgrounds coming together under the intense pressure of wartime secrecy.

Oak Ridge, for instance, was home to many individuals who had never before lived in such a high-pressure, military-like environment. The presence of women in the workforce was notable, as many of them had been brought in to work as clerks, secretaries, technicians, and operators of the uranium-enrichment machinery. As men were drafted into military service, women filled many of these positions, thus expanding the workforce and contributing to the war effort. Despite their vital roles in the project, these women were often kept away from knowing much about the larger purpose of the work they were doing, much as the male workers were.

Moreover, while the majority of the workforce was drawn from the United States, there were also contributions from scientists and experts from other countries, including Great Britain, Canada, and even occupied Europe. This international collaboration brought together the best minds of the time, but it also underscored the secretive nature of the project. Many of the international scientists, like the physicists Leo Szilard and Niels Bohr, were not initially told the full extent of the project's implications.

At Los Alamos, for example, the scientific community became a small, closed society, where even their social lives were intertwined with the work. They lived in homes designed to be isolated and separated from the rest of the community, and personal privacy was rare. This isolation played a crucial role in fostering collaboration but also in ensuring secrecy. The scientists and engineers at Los Alamos were encouraged to live and work as if they were engaged in a common endeavor, with many scientists and their families living on the same campus where the bombs were being developed.

The Challenges of Family Life: Compartmentalization Extended to Loved Ones-

Family life at these secret cities was a constant challenge. While some workers were allowed to bring their families to the sites, they too were kept in the dark about the specifics of the work. Family members were often not told about the dangerous nature of the work their loved ones were engaged in, nor the full implications of the atomic bomb's development. This secrecy extended to the children's experiences as well—parents had to carefully monitor their conversations, ensuring that they did not reveal too much.

At Oak Ridge, families lived in homes surrounded by armed guards and barbed wire. The workers who were assigned to the uranium enrichment plants and other critical facilities often worked long hours, and the town became a place of constant activity. While the families were largely isolated from the outside world, there was still a strong sense of community among them. Social events and family gatherings were common, but they were also marked by an unspoken rule of secrecy. Residents could not talk about the work that was being done, and their conversations often circled around other topics that were safer to discuss, such as the hardships of life in an isolated, rapidly constructed town.

2. Security Measures: Protecting Secrets at All Costs-

The security surrounding the Manhattan Project was absolute, and the stakes were high. The potential for espionage was one of the central concerns, given the value of the bomb to the war effort. The U.S. government took extreme measures to ensure that no information about the project would be leaked to foreign governments, particularly Nazi Germany and the Soviet Union.

Compartmentalization: Keeping Information Within Boundaries-

The concept of "compartmentalization" was fundamental to the security of the Manhattan Project. It meant that workers only knew as much as they needed to know to perform their specific jobs. Workers at Oak Ridge, for example, were unaware of the specifics of the work being done at Los Alamos, and those at Hanford were similarly isolated from those working at Oak Ridge. This was done in order to minimize the risk of leaks. Even the scientists and engineers at Los Alamos, many of whom had some idea of what they were building, were not informed of the larger scope of the project until later.

Additionally, the military played a crucial role in enforcing strict security protocols. Military personnel were stationed at key sites, and armed guards were stationed at the gates of all secret cities. Workers were subject to regular security checks, and anyone found to be talking about the project outside the boundaries of the site faced severe consequences.

At the same time, each worker had their own security clearance, which dictated the level of information they could access. Security clearance levels ranged from the lowest level for laborers, who had no access to classified information, to the highest levels for top scientists and engineers, who were tasked with overseeing the project's most sensitive aspects. In this way, the entire workforce was segregated into different layers of knowledge, with the vast majority of individuals being completely in the dark about the ultimate goal.

Surveillance: Monitoring the Workforce-

Surveillance of the workers was pervasive and constant. In addition to the physical security barriers that surrounded the sites, there were also extensive efforts to monitor the communications of everyone within the cities. Letters were often censored, and phone calls were monitored to ensure that no one leaked sensitive information. Many workers who lived in these secret cities were aware that their correspondence was being read, but the paranoia and fear of breaking security protocols meant that most complied without question.

Espionage was a constant fear, and the U.S. government did everything it could to prevent Soviet spies from infiltrating the project. While most workers were loyal, there were several cases of espionage, such as the famous cases of Klaus Fuchs and Theodore Hall, who passed on information to the Soviet Union. These leaks were not detected until later, underscoring the difficulty of maintaining perfect security in a project of such vast scale.

Security for Family and Visitors-

The restrictions imposed by the government did not just apply to the workers themselves but also to their families and any visitors to the secret cities. Workers were forbidden from revealing anything about the project to their families or friends, and even the families had to live under a constant veil of secrecy. Many workers received letters from friends and family members who were curious about what they were doing, but they had no answers to offer.

Visitors were also heavily restricted. If workers were allowed to leave the facility, they had to undergo strict security checks. If they were allowed to have visitors, those visitors were not permitted to ask any questions about their work. In many cases, workers and their families did not know how long they would be in the secret cities, and they were not allowed to share their experiences with the outside world.

3. Daily Life: A Mix of Work, Isolation, and Compartmentalized Communities-

Living and working in the secret cities meant that daily life was defined by a unique mixture of secrecy, isolation, and pressure. The daily routines of workers and their families were shaped by the demands of the project as well as the limitations imposed by security measures.

Work Hours and the Pressure of the Project-

The work schedule for those involved in the Manhattan Project was grueling. Scientists and technicians often worked long hours—sometimes up to 12 or 16 hours a day—on the various aspects of the atomic bomb's development. In many cases, they worked for days without rest, especially when they were facing imminent deadlines or scientific breakthroughs.

At Los Alamos, the work pace was relentless. Oppenheimer himself was known to push his team hard, sometimes working on projects with little to no sleep. The pressure to succeed was immense because the success of the atomic bomb was seen as the key to winning the war. Workers understood the importance of their efforts, but the intense pressure often took a toll on their mental and physical well-being.

For those working in the uranium-enrichment facilities at Oak Ridge and Hanford, the work was no less grueling. They operated complex machinery and were tasked with processing dangerous materials. Their work was physically demanding, and long shifts in often harsh conditions were the norm. But despite the harsh work environment, many workers reported a strong sense of camaraderie, knowing that they were part of something larger than themselves.

Social Life in the Secret Cities-

The social life in the secret cities was understandably limited by the intense secrecy and isolation. At Los Alamos, for example, workers lived in close quarters and socialized primarily with others who were working on the same scientific tasks. Social events were common, but the content of conversations was always constrained. Even casual discussions about the weather or local news were tightly controlled, and any mention of work outside the facility could be grounds for disciplinary action.

In Oak Ridge and Hanford, social life was similarly constrained. Oak Ridge, as one of the largest of the secret cities, had more developed social structures, including schools, theaters, and community centers. However, most social activities revolved around work and the war effort. Sports teams, social clubs, and other leisure activities were created to give workers a sense of normalcy, but the knowledge that everyone's actions were under constant surveillance prevented people from discussing anything too personal or revealing.

At Hanford, social life was even more limited. The area was remote, with few amenities, and many workers lived in temporary housing. Still, despite these limitations, a sense of community persisted. Shared hardships and the knowledge that they were contributing to a larger goal created bonds that lasted long after the project concluded.

Living in Isolation: A Double-Edged Sword-

For many families, living in one of these secret cities was an experience of both isolation and pride. On the one hand, they were separated from the outside world and had little contact with friends or family outside the project. On the other hand, there was a sense of shared purpose and pride in their role in supporting the war effort and helping to win the war.

Families were often moved to these cities under duress, with little knowledge of what they were getting into. Housing was basic, and the isolation from the rest of society could be stifling. But the work of their loved ones was vital, and many families came to understand that they were living in one of the most significant and secretive places on Earth.

The Legacy of the Manhattan Project Cities-

The secret cities of the Manhattan Project were critical to the success of the atomic bomb, but the lives of the people who lived and worked there were marked by secrecy, isolation, and sacrifice. Workers faced constant pressure and were often kept in the dark about the true nature of their work, while their families had to endure the strain of living in communities defined by secrecy. Despite these challenges, the workers of the Manhattan Project achieved something that had never been done before, and their work changed the course of history. The secret cities became symbols of both the remarkable potential of science and technology and the ethical dilemmas posed by that power. They are a testament to the power of human ingenuity, but also a reminder of the price of secrecy and the costs of progress.

CHAPTER FIVE

SCIENCE UNDER PRESSURE – THE PHYSICS OF THE BOMB

Fission: The science of splitting atoms-

Nuclear fission, the process of splitting atoms, stands as one of the most groundbreaking discoveries in the history of science. It not only unlocked the potential for nuclear energy but also formed the foundation for the development of atomic weaponry, forever altering the course of human history. This discovery has shaped industries, fueled global debates, and introduced both immense opportunities and dangerous risks. Understanding the science behind fission is crucial to grasping its far-reaching implications in various fields, including energy production, warfare, and environmental considerations.

1. The Basics of Fission: What Happens When Atoms Split-

At the most fundamental level, nuclear fission refers to the process by which the nucleus of a heavy atom, typically an isotope of uranium or plutonium, splits into two or more smaller nuclei. During this process, an enormous amount of energy is released, primarily in the form of heat. This heat can then be harnessed to produce electricity in nuclear reactors or, in the case of atomic bombs, it results in a catastrophic explosion. Fission also produces additional neutrons that can, in turn, initiate further fission reactions, creating a chain reaction.

The Structure of an Atom-

To fully understand fission, one must first explore the atomic structure. Atoms consist of a nucleus, composed of positively charged protons and uncharged neutrons, and electrons that orbit the nucleus. The protons determine the atomic number, while neutrons affect the atomic mass. In the case of nuclear fission, it is the nucleus that plays the crucial role. Fission typically occurs in heavy, unstable elements that possess large atomic nuclei, such as uranium-235 or plutonium-239. These nuclei are inherently unstable, meaning they are more likely to break apart when bombarded with neutrons.

The Fission Process-

The fission process begins when a heavy, unstable nucleus captures a free neutron. The addition of this neutron destabilizes the nucleus further, causing it to undergo a split. When the nucleus breaks apart, it produces smaller nuclei, known as fission fragments, as well as additional free neutrons and an immense release of energy. This release of energy is due to the difference in binding energy between the original, larger nucleus and the smaller nuclei resulting from the fission. Essentially, the energy released is a result of the mass lost during the splitting process, which is converted into energy according to Einstein's famous equation, $E=mc2$.

The fission reaction produces two or more lighter nuclei, several free neutrons, and large amounts of energy. The free neutrons that are emitted can go on to trigger further fission reactions in nearby atoms, leading to a self-sustaining chain reaction. This principle is the foundation for both nuclear reactors and nuclear weapons.

2. Discovery of Nuclear Fission: A Pioneering Moment in Science-

The discovery of nuclear fission was not the result of a single eureka moment but rather a series of experiments and observations made by several scientists. The breakthrough came in 1938, a pivotal year in nuclear physics, and is primarily attributed to the work of German chemists Otto Hahn and Fritz Strassmann, with the theoretical explanation provided by Lise Meitner and her nephew Otto Frisch.

The Role of Neutrons in Fission-

Otto Hahn and Fritz Strassmann, who were conducting experiments on uranium, were the first to observe that when uranium was bombarded with neutrons, the product of the reaction was not just a single heavy nucleus but rather a mixture of lighter elements. Their findings suggested that the uranium nucleus had split into smaller fragments, something that had never been observed before. The precise nature of these fragments, however, was unclear at first.

Lise Meitner, a physicist who had been forced to flee Nazi Germany due to her Jewish heritage, and her nephew Otto Frisch, working separately from Hahn and Strassmann, were the ones to offer a theoretical explanation for the observed results. Meitner and Frisch proposed that the uranium nucleus had undergone fission, breaking apart into two smaller nuclei and releasing a tremendous amount of energy in the process. This groundbreaking theoretical understanding led to the coinage of the term "fission," inspired by the biological process of cell division.

Meitner and Frisch's insight provided the missing piece of the puzzle, explaining the experimental results and helping to establish the theoretical basis for what would become the key to harnessing nuclear energy. Their work, however, was not immediately acknowledged in the scientific community, with Hahn receiving the Nobel Prize in Chemistry in 1944 for the discovery of nuclear fission, while Meitner was excluded from the recognition despite her pivotal role in the discovery.

The Impact of Fission on Nuclear Physics-

The discovery of fission fundamentally transformed nuclear physics and opened up new avenues of research and development. It demonstrated the possibility of splitting the atom, which had long been considered the epitome of indivisibility. This not only changed the course of physics but also held enormous implications for the future of energy production, weapons technology, and scientific innovation. Fission also introduced the concept of a chain reaction, which would later prove to be both an asset and a peril in the development of nuclear energy.

3. The Chain Reaction: Fission's Energy Release-

A critical aspect of nuclear fission is the phenomenon of the chain reaction, where the energy released from one fission event can trigger additional fission events, perpetuating the process. This chain reaction is what allows nuclear reactors to function as continuous power sources and is the principle behind the explosive force of nuclear weapons.

Critical Mass and Self-Sustaining Reactions-

For a chain reaction to sustain itself, a sufficient amount of fissile material must be present. This minimum amount of material is known as the "critical mass." If there is too little fissile material, the neutrons released by one fission event will escape without causing further fission. However, when the critical mass is reached, the neutrons released by each fission event can go on to induce further fissions in nearby atoms, creating a self-sustaining chain reaction.

In a controlled nuclear reactor, the reaction is carefully regulated to avoid an uncontrollable release of energy. The goal is to maintain a steady rate of fission that generates continuous power. This is accomplished by using materials like control rods, which absorb neutrons and reduce the number of neutrons available to sustain the chain reaction.

In contrast, in a nuclear bomb, the goal is to achieve a supercritical mass rapidly, resulting in an uncontrolled, explosive chain reaction. This massive release of energy is what makes nuclear bombs so powerful and devastating.

The Energy Released in Fission-

The amount of energy released by nuclear fission is immense. A single fission event releases several million electron volts (MeV) of energy, far more than the energy released by chemical reactions such as the burning of fossil fuels. In practical terms, this means that a small amount of fissile material, like uranium-235, can release an enormous amount of energy. For example, one kilogram of uranium-235 can release as much energy as 24,000 kilograms of coal.

This energy is primarily released in the form of heat. In a nuclear reactor, this heat is used to produce steam, which drives turbines connected to generators that produce electricity. In an atomic bomb, the heat and pressure from the rapid release of energy cause massive destruction through an explosion.

4. Fission in Nuclear Reactors: Harnessing the Power of the Atom-

Nuclear fission has been harnessed in the form of nuclear reactors to generate electricity for decades. Nuclear power plants around the world rely on fission to produce heat, which is used to generate steam and drive turbines, just like in conventional power plants. However, nuclear reactors have the added benefit of producing large amounts of energy without the carbon emissions associated with fossil fuels.

The Nuclear Fuel Cycle-

The nuclear fuel cycle refers to the process by which uranium is mined, enriched, used as fuel in reactors, and eventually processed or disposed of. The first step in the fuel cycle is the extraction of uranium from the earth. The uranium is then enriched to increase the proportion of uranium-235, the fissile isotope required for fission.

Once enriched, the uranium is fabricated into fuel rods, which are placed in the reactor. When the reactor is active, the uranium-235 undergoes fission, producing heat. This heat is transferred to a coolant, usually water, which circulates through the reactor and carries the heat away. The coolant is then used to produce steam, which drives a turbine and generates electricity.

Control of the Reaction in a Nuclear Reactor-

To maintain a steady and controlled rate of fission, nuclear reactors use control rods made of materials that absorb neutrons, such as boron or cadmium. By inserting or removing the control rods from the reactor core, operators can control the number of neutrons available to sustain the chain reaction. This careful management ensures that the reactor operates safely and efficiently, avoiding the risk of overheating or a dangerous chain reaction.

In addition to control rods, the reactor core is surrounded by a coolant, which helps to dissipate the heat produced by the fission process. The coolant is typically water, but some reactors use gas or liquid metal as a coolant. After the coolant absorbs heat, it is pumped through a heat exchanger, where it transfers heat to a secondary loop, producing steam to drive turbines.

Safety Considerations in Nuclear Power-

Safety is a primary concern in nuclear power plants, as the potential consequences of a reactor malfunction are severe. The most significant risks include the release of radioactive materials, overheating, and potential meltdowns. Several safety systems are in place to mitigate these risks, including redundant cooling systems, pressure relief valves, and containment structures designed to prevent the release of radiation.

Despite the safety measures, accidents like the 1986 Chernobyl disaster and the 2011 Fukushima Daiichi disaster have highlighted the dangers of nuclear power. These incidents have led to increased scrutiny of nuclear safety and raised concerns about the long-term viability of nuclear energy.

Nuclear Waste and Its Management-

One of the most challenging aspects of nuclear power is the management of nuclear waste. After uranium fuel is used in a reactor, it becomes radioactive and must be stored safely for long periods of time. Spent fuel contains a variety of radioactive isotopes, many of which have long half-lives and remain hazardous for thousands of years. As a result, nuclear waste must be stored in specially designed facilities that can isolate it from the environment.

The management of nuclear waste remains a contentious issue, with some advocating for the construction of permanent disposal sites, such as deep geological repositories, while others argue for the recycling of spent nuclear fuel to reduce the amount of waste produced.

5. The Use of Fission in Nuclear Weapons: The Dark Side of Splitting Atoms-

While nuclear fission has many peaceful applications, such as in energy production, it has also been used to create some of the most devastating weapons in human history. The first application of fission in weapons came during World War II with the development of the atomic bomb as part of the Manhattan Project.

The Atomic Bomb: A Weapon of Mass Destruction-

The atomic bombs dropped on Hiroshima and Nagasaki in 1945 were powered by fission. These bombs used uranium-235 and plutonium-239, respectively, as their fissile materials. In both cases, the goal was to achieve a supercritical mass of fissile material, resulting in an uncontrollable chain reaction that would release an enormous amount of energy in the form of an explosion. The bombs produced by the Manhattan Project were the first and only nuclear weapons ever used in war, but they marked the beginning of the nuclear age.

The use of atomic bombs in Hiroshima and Nagasaki brought about the end of World War II but also showcased the terrifying potential of fission as a weapon of mass destruction. The sheer magnitude of destruction caused by the bombs, along with the long-term health consequences due to radiation exposure, raised profound ethical and political questions about the use of nuclear weapons.

Nuclear Arms Race and Global Politics-

The development of nuclear weapons sparked a nuclear arms race between the United States and the Soviet Union during the Cold War. Both superpowers sought to develop more advanced nuclear weapons, leading to the creation of even more powerful bombs, such as the hydrogen bomb, which relies on nuclear fusion but often incorporates fission as a triggering mechanism. This arms race not only led to the stockpiling of nuclear weapons but also created the threat of mutually assured destruction (MAD), wherein any nuclear attack by one superpower would result in a devastating retaliation.

Despite numerous efforts to control the spread of nuclear weapons through arms control agreements and nonproliferation treaties, the existence of nuclear weapons remains a serious global concern. The potential for nuclear conflict, whether intentional or accidental, continues to be one of the greatest risks facing humanity.

6. Fission's Future: Advancements and Ethical Considerations-

The development of nuclear fission technology has come a long way since its discovery in the late 1930s, and its applications in energy production, medicine, and research continue to evolve. However, the challenges associated with nuclear energy, such as radioactive waste management, safety, and the risk of weaponization, remain significant issues that require careful consideration.

Future of Nuclear Power-

In recent years, there has been a push for more sustainable and safe nuclear energy technologies, including the development of small modular reactors (SMRs) and advanced fission reactors. These newer reactors aim to be more efficient, less prone to accidents, and capable of utilizing a wider range of nuclear fuel sources.

At the same time, there are growing efforts to develop nuclear fusion, the process of combining atomic nuclei, as a cleaner and more abundant source of energy. While fusion has yet to become a practical energy source, the potential for virtually limitless, clean energy has generated immense interest and investment in the field.

Ethical Considerations-

As we look toward the future of nuclear fission, we must confront the ethical dilemmas it presents. The dual-use nature of nuclear technology—its potential for both peaceful and destructive purposes—requires careful governance, regulation, and international cooperation. Furthermore, the long-term environmental and health impacts of nuclear waste and the risks associated with nuclear proliferation demand ongoing attention and action.

Fission has undeniably had a profound impact on the world, both positively and negatively. As we continue to explore the possibilities of nuclear energy and technology, we must balance the benefits with the ethical responsibility of ensuring that its power is used wisely and safely. The lessons learned from the history of fission will continue to shape the future of nuclear science, energy, and international relations for generations to come.

Uranium-235 and Plutonium-239: Properties, production, and challenges-

Uranium-235 (U-235) and Plutonium-239 (Pu-239) are two of the most critical fissile materials used in nuclear energy production, nuclear weapons, and scientific research. These two isotopes of uranium and plutonium have a significant role in both peaceful and military applications, from providing electricity in nuclear power plants to fueling the destructive power of nuclear bombs. These isotopes are at the heart of the debate about the future of energy, security, and environmental safety, as they present both unprecedented technological possibilities and grave risks. This article will delve into their properties, production processes, applications, challenges, and the role they play in global nuclear governance.

1. Uranium-235: Properties, Characteristics, and Uses-

Uranium-235 (U-235) is one of the most well-known fissile isotopes in nuclear science. It is the primary fuel used in most nuclear reactors and was central to the early development of nuclear weapons. Below, we examine U-235's properties, how it is used in nuclear energy generation, and its critical role in nuclear weapons development.

A. Fissile Nature and Fundamental Properties-

Uranium-235 is a naturally occurring isotope of uranium. Unlike its more abundant counterpart, Uranium-238 (U-238), which is a fertile isotope, U-235 is fissile, meaning it can sustain a chain reaction of fission when bombarded by neutrons. This property makes U-235 essential in nuclear energy generation and weapons production.

Atomic Structure: Uranium-235 has 92 protons and 143 neutrons, giving it an atomic mass of approximately 235. This makes it relatively heavy compared to lighter elements. The ability of U-235 to undergo nuclear fission when hit with a neutron is what makes it so valuable for both energy generation and weapons development.

Fission Process: When a neutron collides with a U-235 nucleus, it can cause the nucleus to split into smaller nuclei, releasing a considerable amount of energy. Each fission event releases about 200 MeV (million electron volts) of energy, which is harnessed in nuclear reactors to generate heat. This heat is converted into electricity by driving turbines connected to generators. Additionally, the fission process releases several neutrons, which can then go on to induce fission in other U-235 nuclei, creating a self-sustaining chain reaction.

Half-life: Uranium-235 has a half-life of about 703.8 million years. This long-lived isotope decays slowly, making it a relatively stable source of energy over extended periods. Its longevity is also a factor in why nuclear reactors can operate efficiently for long periods without needing to replace fuel.

Radioactivity: Although U-235 itself is radioactive, it is much less radioactive than some of its fission products. However, when U-235 is used in nuclear reactors, the fission products can be highly radioactive and pose significant risks in terms of radiation exposure and environmental contamination. Therefore, handling U-235 and its fission products requires significant precautions and safety measures.

B. Role of Uranium-235 in Nuclear Energy Production-

Uranium-235 is the most common fissile material used in nuclear reactors. It provides the energy necessary to sustain the chain reaction that produces heat for electricity generation. However, the natural occurrence of U-235 is not sufficient for effective use in most nuclear reactors, so enrichment is necessary.

Natural Uranium and Enrichment: Natural uranium consists of about 99.3% U-238 and only about 0.7% U-235. The concentration of U-235 in natural uranium is too low to support a practical chain reaction in most types of nuclear reactors. To increase the proportion of U-235, uranium is subjected to enrichment processes. Enrichment involves separating U-235 from U-238 by methods such as gas diffusion or gas centrifugation, allowing for the production of uranium with a higher percentage of U-235. Enriched uranium typically contains between 3% and 5% U-235, which is suitable for most commercial nuclear reactors.

Fission Chain Reaction and Control: In nuclear reactors, the rate of the fission chain reaction must be carefully controlled to ensure safe and efficient operation. This is achieved through the use of control rods made of materials like boron or cadmium, which absorb excess neutrons and slow down the chain reaction when necessary. Reactors also employ coolant systems to remove heat generated by the fission reaction and maintain the reactor's optimal temperature.

Reactors Using U-235: Nuclear reactors that use U-235 as fuel operate under principles of controlled fission. The energy produced by U-235 is harnessed to produce steam, which drives turbines connected to electrical generators. Some reactors, such as pressurized water reactors (PWRs) and boiling water reactors (BWRs), are designed to operate using enriched uranium fuel. Advanced reactor types, such as fast breeder reactors, use U-235 in combination with U-238 to produce more fissile material during operation.

C. Uranium-235 in Nuclear Weapons Development-

The discovery of U-235's ability to undergo fission led to the development of nuclear weapons, starting with the Manhattan Project during World War II. The Hiroshima bombing in 1945, which employed a uranium-based weapon, marked the first time in history that nuclear weapons were used in warfare.

The Little Boy Bomb: The first atomic bomb used in combat was "Little Boy," which was dropped on Hiroshima, Japan, in 1945. It used U-235 as its fissile material and employed a "gun-type" design in which two sub-critical masses of U-235 were combined by conventional explosives to form a supercritical mass, initiating a rapid chain reaction. This resulted in an explosion with the force of approximately 15 kilotons of TNT.

Challenges with Uranium-235 in Weapons: One of the challenges with U-235 in nuclear weapons is the need for highly enriched uranium. Weapons-grade uranium contains at least 90% U-235, which is far higher than the typical enrichment level used in nuclear reactors (3-5%). Enriching uranium to weapons-grade levels requires sophisticated and costly technology, such as gas centrifuges or gaseous diffusion. This presents significant barriers to nuclear weapons proliferation, though some nations have pursued these capabilities for military purposes.

2. Plutonium-239: Production, Properties, and Uses-

Plutonium-239 is another vital fissile material, with both nuclear energy and weapons applications. Unlike U-235, which is found naturally in the Earth, Pu-239 is produced through nuclear reactions and is an essential element in the modern nuclear fuel cycle.

A. Production of Plutonium-239-

Plutonium-239 is not found in significant amounts in nature. Instead, it is produced in nuclear reactors through the irradiation of Uranium-238 (U-238). Here's how the process works:

Neutron Capture: Uranium-238, the most abundant isotope in natural uranium, is not directly fissile under normal conditions. However, when U-238 absorbs a neutron, it becomes U-239. U-239 decays into Neptunium-239 (Np-239) and then into Plutonium-239 (Pu-239) through beta decay. This process occurs naturally in nuclear reactors, where U-238 absorbs neutrons generated during the fission of U-235.

Reactor Production: Plutonium-239 is produced in large quantities in reactors designed to use uranium as fuel. As U-238 absorbs neutrons, it is converted into plutonium, which accumulates in spent nuclear fuel. Once extracted from spent fuel, plutonium can be chemically purified for use in new fuel assemblies or in nuclear weapons.

Breeder Reactors: Breeder reactors are designed to convert non-fissile U-238 into fissile Pu-239 while simultaneously generating energy. This breeding process makes breeder reactors an important part of nuclear power production, particularly in systems aimed at maximizing the use of available uranium resources.

B. Properties of Plutonium-239-

Plutonium-239 shares many characteristics with Uranium-235, particularly its ability to sustain a chain reaction of fission. Below are its key properties:

Fissile Nature: Plutonium-239 is also a fissile isotope, meaning it can undergo fission when bombarded with neutrons. This property makes it an efficient nuclear fuel for reactors and a potent material for nuclear weapons.

Energy Release: Like U-235, Pu-239 releases about 200 MeV of energy per fission event. The energy release from Pu-239 is comparable to that of U-235, making it highly effective for energy generation and weaponry.

Half-life and Radioactivity: The half-life of Plutonium-239 is about 24,100 years, which is much shorter than Uranium-235's half-life. This means that Plutonium-239 decays at a faster rate, releasing radiation for a shorter period compared to U-235. However, the radioactivity of Pu-239 remains a concern for environmental and human health.

C. Plutonium-239 in Nuclear Energy-

Plutonium-239 can be used as a fuel in nuclear reactors, either in mixed oxide (MOX) fuel, which combines plutonium with natural or depleted uranium, or as a pure plutonium fuel. MOX fuel is used in some advanced nuclear reactors as a way to utilize surplus plutonium, particularly from nuclear weapons disarmament efforts.

MOX Fuel: Mixed oxide fuel is used in certain reactors as an alternative to uranium fuel. It is made by mixing plutonium with uranium oxide. MOX fuel provides a solution to the problem of excess plutonium, which could otherwise be a proliferation risk. The use of MOX fuel helps to reduce plutonium stockpiles and is considered a step toward more sustainable nuclear fuel cycles.

Fast Breeder Reactors: Fast breeder reactors, which can use plutonium as fuel, play a role in sustaining nuclear energy generation over the long term. These reactors not only produce energy but also breed more fissile material (plutonium) than they consume, thus offering a potential long-term solution for nuclear energy sustainability.

D. Plutonium-239 in Nuclear Weapons-

Plutonium-239 is a critical material for nuclear weapons, particularly in implosion-type designs. Unlike uranium bombs, which require the use of highly enriched uranium, plutonium bombs typically use a more compact form of fissile material.

The Fat Man Bomb: The "Fat Man" bomb, which was dropped on Nagasaki in 1945, was based on plutonium-239. It used a spherical core of plutonium-239 that was compressed by explosives in an implosion-type design. This design was more efficient than the "Little Boy" uranium bomb used on Hiroshima, as plutonium is easier to compress and can achieve greater yields in a smaller size.

Nuclear Proliferation and Security: The potential for the use of plutonium-239 in nuclear weapons is a major security concern. Due to its high efficiency and availability in nuclear reactors, plutonium-239 is a key material for nations pursuing nuclear weapons programs. Tight international controls, such as the Nuclear Non-Proliferation Treaty (NPT), are in place to prevent the spread of plutonium and other fissile materials to non-nuclear states.

3. Challenges in Uranium-235 and Plutonium-239 Use-

While Uranium-235 and Plutonium-239 have revolutionized energy production and military technology, their use presents significant challenges, particularly related to safety, waste management, and security.

A. Environmental and Health Risks-

Both Uranium-235 and Plutonium-239 present significant environmental and health risks. Their radioactivity can have long-lasting effects on human health and the environment, particularly in the case of contamination from nuclear accidents, waste disposal issues, and improper handling.

Waste Management: The long-lived radioactive waste produced from U-235 and Pu-239 fission remains a significant challenge. Handling, storing, and disposing of this waste requires advanced technology and long-term planning, as radioactive materials can remain hazardous for thousands of years. Strategies for dealing with nuclear waste include geological disposal, reprocessing, and recycling.

Health Concerns: The exposure to radiation from U-235 and Pu-239, even at low levels, can lead to long-term health effects, including cancer and genetic mutations. Occupational exposure in nuclear facilities, accidents such as the Chernobyl disaster, and radioactive contamination from weapons tests have resulted in widespread public health concerns.

B. Security Concerns and Non-Proliferation-

The potential for both U-235 and Pu-239 to be used in nuclear weapons is a central issue in global security. The proliferation of nuclear weapons and materials is a serious international concern, leading to efforts to curb the spread of nuclear technology through treaties and international agreements.

International Non-Proliferation Efforts: The Nuclear Non-Proliferation Treaty (NPT), which was first adopted in 1968, aims to prevent the spread of nuclear weapons and to promote the peaceful use of nuclear energy. It encourages nuclear disarmament, non-proliferation of nuclear weapons, and the peaceful use of nuclear technology. The treaty is a key framework for controlling the production and movement of fissile materials like U-235 and Pu-239.

Plutonium for Dirty Bombs: Beyond nuclear weapons, there are concerns that plutonium-239 could be used in "dirty bombs." These bombs would not have the massive destructive power of a nuclear weapon but would spread radioactive material over a wide area, causing contamination and panic. The security of plutonium-239 and other fissile materials remains a priority for global counterterrorism efforts.

C. Technical and Economic Challenges-

Producing and enriching Uranium-235, or extracting and purifying Plutonium-239, is a highly technical and costly process. The equipment, infrastructure, and security required to handle these materials come with substantial financial and logistical challenges.

Enrichment Facilities: Enriching uranium to weapons-grade levels or processing plutonium requires sophisticated technologies such as gas centrifuges or laser isotope separation. These processes are energy-intensive and expensive, requiring highly controlled environments to prevent mishaps and unauthorized access.

Cost of Reprocessing: Reprocessing plutonium from spent nuclear fuel to create new fuel or for disposal purposes involves complex chemical processes. It is costly to extract plutonium safely, and the infrastructure for such reprocessing plants is extremely expensive to build and maintain. Furthermore, political and security concerns often hinder the widespread implementation of reprocessing technologies.

,Uranium-235 and Plutonium-239 are at the forefront of nuclear science and technology, powering everything from peaceful nuclear reactors to the most destructive weapons ever created by humanity. Their properties as fissile materials have revolutionized energy production and military technologies, but they have also created formidable challenges. The environmental, health, security, and logistical issues surrounding their use and disposal are significant, and the global community continues to struggle with finding sustainable and safe solutions to these challenges.

The future of nuclear energy and nuclear weapons will depend heavily on the responsible management of these powerful materials. Whether through improved reactor designs, advances in waste reprocessing, or strengthened non-proliferation measures, the role of Uranium-235 and Plutonium-239 in global affairs will remain as critical as ever. As we continue to evolve in our use of these elements, we must carefully balance the benefits they provide with the profound risks they pose to ensure a safer, more sustainable future.

Engineering the bomb: Implosion vs. gun-type design-

1. Introduction to Nuclear Bomb Design-

The atomic bomb is arguably the most complex and transformative invention of the 20th century. It is a product of the Manhattan Project, a covert American project during World War

II aimed at developing nuclear weapons before the Axis powers. The project, which spanned from 1942 to 1945, culminated in the creation of two distinct types of bombs: the gun-type and the implosion-type nuclear bombs. Both of these designs are based on the principle of nuclear fission, the splitting of heavy atomic nuclei to release vast amounts of energy, but they employ radically different methods to achieve a chain reaction.

This exploration will delve into the scientific principles that underlie the gun-type and implosion-type bombs, their historical context, and their profound impact on the development of nuclear weapons. By examining the design, engineering, and challenges behind each, we can better understand the legacy of these weapons in both military and civilian contexts.

2. The Gun-Type Design: Simplicity and Directness-

The gun-type design represents the earliest and most basic method of achieving a nuclear explosion. It is often considered the "first generation" of atomic bomb design and was used in the bomb dropped on Hiroshima (known as Little Boy) on August 6, 1945. The design itself is relatively simple, relying on the principle of bringing two sub-critical masses of fissile material together to form a supercritical mass that will undergo a chain reaction.

2.1 The Fundamental Concept: Achieving Supercriticality-

At the core of the gun-type bomb is the concept of supercriticality. A sub-critical mass of fissile material, such as uranium-235, will not spontaneously undergo a nuclear chain reaction. However, if two pieces of this material are combined in a sufficiently rapid and efficient manner, the resulting mass will become supercritical, initiating the chain reaction. In a gun-type design, this process is achieved by using conventional explosives to fire one sub-critical mass of uranium into another.

The Geometry of the Design: The uranium is shaped in cylindrical or cylindrical-like forms. One piece is positioned at the rear end of a long tube, and the other is placed at the front. A high-explosive charge is situated behind the rear piece of uranium, and when detonated, the explosion forces the uranium pieces together, creating a supercritical mass.

Effect of the Explosion: Once the uranium masses combine, they undergo a rapid chain reaction. Each fission event produces energy and releases neutrons, which, in turn, initiate more fission reactions. The result is a massive release of energy in the form of heat and radiation, equivalent to the destructive force of thousands of tons of TNT.

2.2 Engineering Challenges and Innovations-

Although the basic concept was simple, the engineering behind the gun-type bomb required overcoming significant challenges:

Efficient Use of Uranium: One of the key challenges was the enrichment of uranium-235, which makes up only a small fraction of natural uranium. The amount of enriched uranium needed for the bomb was substantial and involved a complex and resource-intensive enrichment process. To produce enough fissile material, the Uranium Enrichment Program utilized various methods, such as gaseous diffusion and electromagnetic separation, to isolate the uranium-235 isotope.

Safety Considerations: Due to the simplicity of the gun-type mechanism, ensuring that the fissile material would not undergo premature fission was a critical concern. Unlike plutonium, uranium-235 has a relatively low spontaneous fission rate, which made it more manageable in a gun-type design. However, the engineers still had to account for the possibility of a pre-detonation before the masses could come together.

Precision Timing: Despite its relatively simple nature, the design required precise control over timing to ensure that the fission process occurred at the right moment. The conventional explosives had to be detonated simultaneously and with high precision to avoid any premature failure in initiating the chain reaction.

2.3 The Little Boy Bomb: A Historical Milestone-

The first practical use of the gun-type bomb was in the Little Boy bomb, which was dropped on Hiroshima, Japan, on August 6, 1945. It was the first nuclear weapon to be used in warfare, and its devastating power changed the course of history. Little Boy contained about 64 kg (141 lbs) of uranium-235 and used the gun-type design to bring together two sub-critical masses of uranium. Upon detonation, the bomb unleashed an explosion with an energy equivalent to around 15 kilotons of TNT, causing massive destruction and loss of life.

The successful detonation of Little Boy marked the first practical application of nuclear fission as a weapon. The bomb's use in Hiroshima not only led to the end of World War II but also ushered in the atomic age and set the stage for the Cold War and nuclear proliferation in the decades that followed.

2.4 Limitations and the Decline of the Gun-Type Design-

While the gun-type bomb was a crucial stepping stone in the development of nuclear weapons, it had several limitations:

Inefficiency: The gun-type bomb required a relatively large amount of uranium-235 to achieve critical mass. This made it inefficient in terms of both the quantity of fissile material and the resulting size of the bomb. The bomb was large, unwieldy, and less efficient than later designs.

Limited Application: The gun-type design was only effective with uranium-235. Its limitations made it unsuitable for use with plutonium-239, which would become the basis for future nuclear bombs.

Resource Intensive: The process of enriching uranium to obtain the necessary quantity of uranium-235 was resource-intensive and involved massive facilities for isotope separation, such as the Oak Ridge facility in Tennessee.

These limitations ultimately led to the development of the more efficient implosion-type bomb, which would replace the gun-type design in most future nuclear weapons.

3. The Implosion-Type Design: Efficiency and Precision-

The implosion-type nuclear bomb, which was used in the Fat Man bomb dropped on Nagasaki on August 9, 1945, represented a more sophisticated and efficient approach to nuclear weapon design. Unlike the gun-type design, which relied on firing two pieces of fissile material together, the implosion-type bomb used a spherical configuration of explosives to compress a sub-critical mass of fissile material into a supercritical state.

3.1 Basic Concept: Spherical Compression of Plutonium

In the implosion-type bomb, the fissile material—typically plutonium-239—is placed at the center of a sphere of high-explosive material. Surrounding this core is a set of explosive lenses, which are shaped charges designed to direct the explosive force inward in a highly controlled and symmetrical manner.

Compression: When the explosives are detonated, the resulting shockwave compresses the plutonium core from all directions simultaneously. This compression increases the density of the plutonium, making it reach supercriticality and initiating the rapid nuclear chain reaction that produces an immense amount of energy.

Symmetry and Precision: The key to the success of the implosion-type design is achieving perfect symmetry in the compression. Any deviation from symmetry could result in a failed detonation. The explosive lenses must be carefully shaped and arranged to ensure the shockwave is evenly distributed across the plutonium core.

3.2 The Development of the Implosion-Type Bomb-

The development of the implosion-type bomb was a monumental scientific and engineering challenge. The Manhattan Project team, led by J. Robert Oppenheimer, faced numerous hurdles in developing the technology needed for the bomb's success. The use of plutonium-239 was a necessity because it was more readily produced than uranium-235, but plutonium posed several unique challenges:

Spontaneous Fission: Plutonium-239 undergoes spontaneous fission at a higher rate than uranium-235, making it more difficult to handle. The scientists needed to design a system that could safely bring the plutonium to critical mass without initiating a premature detonation.

Implosion Mechanism: The creation of the explosive lenses was a major engineering challenge. These lenses had to be carefully designed to ensure that the shockwave created by the conventional explosives would compress the plutonium core evenly and symmetrically.

The implosion-type design required extensive experimentation with various materials and configurations. The scientists at Los Alamos conducted numerous tests and calculations, and after months of trial and error, they perfected the design.

3.3 The Fat Man Bomb: The First Successful Implosion-

The Fat Man bomb, dropped on Nagasaki, represented the culmination of the implosion-type design. Weighing 4,670 kg (10,300 pounds), Fat Man used around 6.2 kg (14 lbs) of plutonium-239. It was significantly smaller than the Little Boy bomb and was able to release a far more powerful explosion, equivalent to about 21 kilotons of TNT.

Unlike Little Boy, which was relatively simple, the Fat Man bomb was a marvel of precision engineering. The bomb's spherical core was surrounded by 32 explosive lenses, arranged in a precisely calculated configuration to compress the plutonium core and initiate a chain reaction. The success of this bomb marked a turning point in the development of nuclear weapons, providing a much more efficient design.

3.4 Challenges and Innovations in the Implosion Design-

Developing the implosion-type bomb involved numerous scientific and technological challenges:

Explosive Lenses: One of the most significant innovations was the creation of the explosive lenses. These lenses had to be made from materials that could focus the shockwave from the conventional explosives precisely onto the plutonium core. This required the precise calculation of the speed and direction of the shockwaves, which was no small feat given the complexity of the physics involved.

Timing and Detonation: The bomb's detonation was controlled by a series of highly accurate timing mechanisms that ensured all the explosive lenses were triggered simultaneously. Any variation in timing could have resulted in a failed detonation or incomplete compression, rendering the bomb ineffective.

Plutonium Purity: The success of the implosion-type bomb also depended on the purity of the plutonium used. The material had to be refined to a very high degree to ensure that it would behave as expected under compression.

3.5 Legacy of the Implosion-Type Design-

The success of the implosion-type bomb not only marked the end of World War II but also ushered in the atomic age. The design became the foundation for subsequent nuclear weapons, including hydrogen bombs (thermonuclear weapons). The implosion mechanism and the principles of spherical compression continue to be used in modern nuclear weapons designs.

4. A World Transformed-

The gun-type and implosion-type designs represent two critical phases in the evolution of nuclear weapons. The gun-type bomb, though relatively simple, paved the way for the implosion-type bomb, which was a quantum leap in terms of power, precision, and efficiency. The legacy of these designs continues to shape the world, influencing everything from military strategy to global diplomacy and arms control.

The development of nuclear weapons not only changed the nature of warfare but also brought with it profound ethical and political challenges. As the world grapples with the implications of these powerful tools of destruction, the history of nuclear bomb design serves as both a cautionary tale and a testament to human ingenuity.

Breakthroughs in theoretical physics and practical engineering-

Breakthroughs in Theoretical Physics and Practical Engineering: A Deep Dive into Their Interplay and Impact

The 20th and 21st centuries have witnessed a remarkable transformation in the fields of theoretical physics and practical engineering, both of which have reshaped the course of human history. The interconnection between these two fields is deeply intertwined—each breakthrough in theoretical physics often leads to new engineering feats, and advancements in engineering provide the tools and resources required to test, apply, and refine theoretical concepts. This complex relationship has driven profound changes in technology, society, and our understanding of the universe. This article explores key breakthroughs in both fields, the ongoing interaction between them, and the wide-ranging implications of their achievements.

1. The Role of Theoretical Physics in Engineering-

Theoretical physics, at its core, is concerned with understanding the fundamental principles of nature. The profound insights into the universe provided by theoretical physics have not only revolutionized our understanding of the natural world but have also provided the framework for creating a wealth of practical technologies that have transformed industries and daily life.

1.1 Classical Mechanics: Foundations of Early Engineering-

At the dawn of modern science, Isaac Newton's classical mechanics provided the foundation for much of modern engineering. Newton's three laws of motion and his law of universal gravitation formed the bedrock upon which engineers built designs for structures, machines, and transportation systems. Classical mechanics, which deals with the behavior of macroscopic objects in motion, provided engineers with the tools they needed to understand the forces acting on objects, how they respond to these forces, and how they can be manipulated for practical purposes.

The use of Newtonian mechanics in the design of steam engines in the 18th and 19th centuries marked one of the earliest and most influential applications of theoretical physics to practical engineering. The steam engine revolutionized transportation, manufacturing, and energy production. James Watt, building on earlier developments, improved steam engine efficiency, incorporating principles of thermodynamics into practical systems for driving mechanical work. By applying Newtonian physics, Watt could create engines that could power trains, ships, and factories, leading to the Industrial Revolution, which reshaped the global economy.

1.2 The Rise of Electromagnetism and Electrical Engineering-

One of the most significant breakthroughs in theoretical physics came with the work of James Clerk Maxwell in the 19th century, who unified the study of electricity and magnetism into the theory of electromagnetism. Maxwell's equations, which describe the behavior of electric and magnetic fields, proved essential for the development of electrical engineering. These equations not only demonstrated that electricity and magnetism were interconnected but also explained how electromagnetic waves propagate through space.

This theoretical framework paved the way for numerous practical applications, including the electric motor, the telegraph, and electrical power generation. Nikola Tesla, for example, applied Maxwell's work to develop the alternating current (AC) system for efficiently transmitting electrical power over long distances. The use of AC for electrical power distribution became the standard, providing the foundation for the modern electric grid.

Moreover, the application of electromagnetism led to technologies that have become integral to modern life, including telecommunications (radio, television, and later, the internet) and electronics. Engineers used Maxwell's equations to design circuits and devices that could manipulate electromagnetic fields, ultimately leading to the invention of technologies such as radios, television sets, and computers.

2. The Quantum Leap: From Theoretical Physics to Practical Engineering-

The early 20th century marked a revolutionary shift in our understanding of the universe with the development of quantum mechanics and relativity. These fields fundamentally altered how scientists and engineers approach problems, providing new insights into the behavior of matter and energy on microscopic and cosmological scales.

2.1 Quantum Mechanics: A New Paradigm for Technology-

Quantum mechanics, developed through the contributions of Max Planck, Albert Einstein, Werner Heisenberg, and others, introduced a radically different view of the microscopic world. Quantum theory proposes that matter and energy are quantized, existing in discrete units rather than continuous forms. The behavior of particles like electrons is probabilistic, governed by wave functions rather than deterministic trajectories.

While quantum mechanics was initially seen as a purely theoretical discipline, it soon became evident that its implications were profoundly practical. One of the first major technological innovations based on quantum theory was the transistor, developed in 1947 by John Bardeen, Walter Brattain, and William Shockley. The transistor revolutionized electronics by allowing engineers to build smaller, more efficient circuits that could amplify electrical signals. Transistors became the building blocks for modern computers, telecommunications, and countless other technologies.

The development of semiconductor physics led to the miniaturization of electronic devices, enabling the creation of devices like smartphones, laptops, and digital cameras. These technologies, built on the principles of quantum mechanics, are now ubiquitous in daily life.

2.2 Quantum Computing: The Next Frontier-

One of the most exciting frontiers of modern engineering and theoretical physics is quantum computing. While classical computers store and process information in binary form, quantum computers use quantum bits (qubits), which can represent multiple states simultaneously due to a phenomenon known as superposition. This allows quantum computers to solve certain types of problems exponentially faster than classical computers.

Quantum computers hold the potential to revolutionize fields such as cryptography, optimization, artificial intelligence, and materials science. However, the practical realization of quantum computing has proven difficult, as qubits are highly sensitive to their environment and require complex systems to manipulate and stabilize them. Nevertheless, progress in quantum error correction, quantum entanglement, and quantum algorithms continues to accelerate, bringing us closer to building large-scale quantum computers that could outperform classical computers in solving certain problems.

2.3 Lasers: Harnessing Quantum Mechanics for Everyday Use-

Another critical application of quantum mechanics is the laser, first demonstrated in 1960 by Theodore Maiman. The laser relies on the principle of stimulated emission, where atoms or molecules are excited to higher energy levels and then release photons in a coherent, focused beam when they return to lower energy levels. Lasers have become integral in fields ranging from medicine (e.g., in laser surgeries) to telecommunications (e.g., in optical fiber networks) and entertainment (e.g., in laser light shows).

The use of lasers has expanded beyond these applications, with laser cooling technologies enabling researchers to study matter at extremely low temperatures, and laser radar (LIDAR) systems helping with autonomous vehicles' navigation. Engineers continue to develop new types of lasers, including fiber lasers, semiconductor lasers, and quantum dot lasers, to push the boundaries of technology further.

3. Relativity and the Engineering Challenges It Created-

Albert Einstein's theories of special relativity and general relativity reshaped our understanding of the universe, not only in theoretical terms but also in practical engineering applications. The theory of relativity introduced the idea that time and space are not absolute but relative, dependent on the observer's velocity and gravitational field.

3.1 GPS: Navigating with Relativity-

The development of Global Positioning System (GPS) technology provides one of the most prominent examples of how the theory of relativity has influenced engineering. GPS satellites orbit the Earth at high altitudes, and due to the difference in the gravitational field experienced by the satellites and the ground-based receivers, time passes at slightly different rates. If engineers had not accounted for these relativistic effects, the GPS system would accumulate errors of several kilometers per day, rendering it useless.

Thus, the design of GPS technology required collaboration between physicists and engineers, using the principles of relativity to ensure that the satellites' clocks were synchronized with ground-based clocks. This interplay of theoretical physics and practical engineering made it possible for GPS to become the global navigation tool we rely on today.

3.2 Nuclear Engineering: Harnessing the Power of $E=mc^2$-

One of the most important and controversial applications of Einstein's mass-energy equivalence equation ($E=mc^2$) is in the field of nuclear energy. The realization that mass could be converted into energy underpins the processes that occur in both nuclear reactors and nuclear weapons. Nuclear engineering, which involves harnessing the energy released from atomic nuclei, has been transformative for both energy production and military technology.

While nuclear reactors have been critical in generating large-scale electricity, nuclear fusion—the process that powers the Sun—remains a major challenge for engineers. Fusion promises to provide an abundant, clean energy source if it can be realized on Earth, and scientists and engineers are working on tokamaks and laser fusion to contain and control the reaction. These efforts to develop fusion power represent the pinnacle of engineering challenges rooted in the theories of relativity and quantum mechanics.

4. The Symbiotic Relationship Between Theory and Engineering-

The relationship between theoretical physics and practical engineering is an ongoing, dynamic cycle. Each field informs the other, driving progress and innovation. As engineers push the limits of technology, they encounter new challenges that demand theoretical insights, while breakthroughs in theory often require new engineering solutions to be realized.

4.1 Particle Accelerators and Their Role in Advancing Physics-

One of the most visible examples of the relationship between theoretical physics and engineering is the development of particle accelerators. The Large Hadron Collider (LHC) at CERN is a marvel of modern engineering, designed to accelerate protons and other particles to near-light speeds before smashing them together to reveal the fundamental particles and forces that make up the universe.

The design and construction of the LHC required an intimate understanding of quantum mechanics, special relativity, and electromagnetism. Engineers had to build the accelerator using superconducting magnets to generate the high magnetic fields needed to steer particles, along with cryogenic systems to keep the magnets at near absolute zero temperatures. The LHC provides a direct example of how engineering is crucial to testing and validating the theories of particle physics.

5. The Future of Theoretical Physics and Practical Engineering-

The ongoing advances in theoretical physics and engineering suggest an exciting future where the boundaries between theory and application continue to blur. Emerging technologies, such as quantum computing, nanotechnology, and artificial intelligence, rely on an ever-deepening partnership between theoretical physics and engineering to unlock new possibilities.

As we look ahead, the challenges humanity faces—ranging from climate change to space exploration—will require innovations that emerge from the interplay between these two fields. Understanding and exploiting the fundamental laws of nature will be key to tackling issues such as energy production, environmental sustainability, and the exploration of distant planets.

, the breakthroughs in theoretical physics and practical engineering of the past century have had a profound and lasting impact on society. By combining theory with practical engineering, we have developed technologies that have reshaped the world. The future holds immense promise, driven by the ongoing collaboration between theoretical insights and engineering innovation. As we move forward, it is clear that this symbiotic relationship will continue to be a driving force behind the scientific and technological progress that shapes our future.

The Trinity Test: Preparations and scientific milestones-

Historical Context: The Birth of Nuclear Science-
The development of nuclear weapons, and the events leading up to the Trinity Test, were grounded in the broader context of scientific breakthroughs in nuclear physics and the geopolitical environment of the early 20th century. The discovery of the atom's structure and the realization that its nucleus could be split into smaller components sparked profound interest in the scientific community. While the first notable findings were more theoretical, the realization that atomic fission could release vast amounts of energy began to take root by the 1930s.

The first documented scientific breakthrough came in 1938, when German scientists Otto Hahn and Fritz Strassmann discovered nuclear fission while working with uranium. Their findings were soon confirmed by Lise Meitner and Otto Frisch, and it was they who recognized that splitting the uranium atom released a tremendous amount of energy. Their discoveries were revolutionary, as they showed that controlled fission reactions could potentially produce enormous amounts of energy. This idea would later form the theoretical foundation of nuclear weapons.

The world was soon thrown into turmoil with the rise of Nazi Germany and the outbreak of World War II. The threat of an enemy nation developing nuclear weapons became a concern for the Allied powers. In response, physicist Albert Einstein and physicist Leo Szilard, among others, alerted President Franklin D. Roosevelt to the potential dangers and the possibility of a race to build an atomic bomb. This letter, delivered in 1939, led to the establishment of the Manhattan Project in 1942, which aimed to harness the power of nuclear fission for military purposes.

The Manhattan Project: Genesis and Growth-

The Manhattan Project was a highly secretive research and development project, its aim singular and its stakes high: to develop a nuclear weapon before Nazi Germany or any other power could do so. The project was led by General Leslie R. Groves, a U.S. Army Corps of Engineers officer, and J. Robert Oppenheimer, a theoretical physicist who was appointed the scientific director. Under their leadership, the project rapidly expanded across multiple sites in the United States, with primary laboratories at Los Alamos, New Mexico; uranium enrichment facilities at Oak Ridge, Tennessee; and the plutonium production reactors at Hanford, Washington.

The selection of Los Alamos as the central research and development site for the bomb was strategic. It provided isolation for secret work and could accommodate the large scientific team that would contribute to the project. Oppenheimer's leadership was instrumental in bringing together some of the greatest minds of the era, including Enrico Fermi, Niels Bohr, and Richard Feynman, to work on the theoretical and experimental challenges of building a nuclear bomb.

The Science of Nuclear Fission and Fusion-

Understanding the science behind the bomb's construction was essential to its success. The key to building the first nuclear weapon was mastering the process of nuclear fission, in which the nucleus of a heavy atom like uranium-235 or plutonium-239 is split into smaller nuclei, releasing vast amounts of energy. Scientists needed to find a way to achieve a chain reaction, where the splitting of one atom causes others to split, creating an exponentially increasing reaction.

This principle of nuclear chain reactions was critical to bomb design. Two distinct approaches were pursued in the Manhattan Project: the implosion method and the gun-type method.

The Gun-Type Design-

The gun-type design, which was used in the Hiroshima bomb (Little Boy), involved two sub-critical masses of uranium-235, which were brought together by conventional explosives. The uranium was enriched so that its fissionable material had a high percentage of uranium-235. The sub-critical masses were positioned at opposite ends of a barrel, and when detonated, the explosives would force the uranium into a single supercritical mass, initiating a rapid fission chain reaction. This design was relatively simple but required high precision to ensure the critical mass was achieved effectively.

The Implosion Design-

The more complex implosion-type design, which was used for the Nagasaki bomb (Fat Man), involved the use of plutonium-239. In this design, a sub-critical mass of plutonium was surrounded by a shell of high explosives arranged in a precise configuration. The explosives were detonated simultaneously, compressing the plutonium into a supercritical mass. This design was far more efficient than the gun-type design and was selected for the plutonium bomb because of the difficulties in obtaining enough uranium-235 for a gun-type weapon.

The development of the implosion design was much more challenging. Early designs suffered from problems with symmetry and the failure of conventional explosives to compress the plutonium core effectively. It was only through significant breakthroughs in materials science, engineering, and explosive physics that the Trinity Test became possible.

The Site of the Trinity Test: The Desert of New Mexico

The Trinity Test itself was conducted on July 16, 1945, in the remote desert of New Mexico, on the Alamogordo Bombing and Gunnery Range. The site was chosen for its isolation, which was crucial for both security and safety concerns. The location was about 35 miles southeast of Alamogordo and far from any major population centers. It was a site that had been used for military testing for several years, making it an ideal, secure location for the test.

The Trinity Test site, an area known as Ground Zero, was a vast and desolate space where thousands of scientists, engineers, military personnel, and support staff gathered to witness the first atomic detonation. Despite the tremendous significance of the event, only a select few were present for the actual detonation, and the details of what happened in the hours leading up to the test were kept under wraps.

Preparation for the Trinity Test: A Monumental Undertaking

The preparations for the Trinity Test involved more than just the scientific efforts to build the bomb; it required meticulous planning, coordination, and careful consideration of the security, logistics, and technical issues surrounding the event. The scientific community had already made major breakthroughs in theoretical nuclear physics and engineering, but translating these breakthroughs into an actual, functioning weapon was a monumental challenge.

Securing the Test Site

One of the most important logistical challenges was ensuring the security of the test site. The project was highly classified, and any leaks of information could jeopardize the entire endeavor.

Security measures at the test site were stringent, with armed guards patrolling the area and access tightly controlled. Only a handful of scientists and military personnel were authorized to be on-site during the test.

The Construction of the Test Device

As the date for the Trinity Test approached, the bomb itself was carefully assembled. The implosion-type bomb was more sophisticated, and many of the final stages of assembly were conducted under extreme secrecy. The device was loaded onto a specially designed tower, called the "Jumbo", which was used to hold the bomb in place for the detonation. The bomb was surrounded by sophisticated instruments designed to record data on the explosion, including seismographs, radiation detectors, and thermal sensors.

The Countdown to Detonation-

On the day of the Trinity Test, a highly orchestrated countdown took place. While many members of the Manhattan Project had known about the test for some time, there was still a sense of unease and uncertainty about how the test would unfold. No one knew exactly what to expect—there was even the possibility that the bomb might ignite the atmosphere, potentially destroying the world in a chain reaction. Fortunately, this was not the case, but the anxiety surrounding the test was palpable.

The moment of detonation occurred at precisely 5:29 a.m. on July 16, 1945. The explosion was felt miles away, and the light produced by the explosion was brighter than the sun itself. It created a fireball that reached temperatures exceeding those at the core of the sun and a mushroom cloud that rose to a height of over 40,000 feet. The bomb's power was far greater than anyone had anticipated, with the explosion producing an equivalent force of 20 kilotons of TNT.

The Aftermath: The World Changes Forever-

The successful detonation of the bomb at Trinity was a major milestone, marking the first time that humankind had harnessed the power of the atom for destructive purposes. The test proved the viability of nuclear weapons and demonstrated that atomic warfare was no longer a theoretical concept but a reality. The immediate reaction to the Trinity Test was one of astonishment and awe, mixed with apprehension about what this newfound power meant for the future of warfare and international relations.

Within weeks of the test, the United States would go on to drop two atomic bombs on Japan—first on Hiroshima on August 6, 1945, and then on Nagasaki three days later. These bombings led to Japan's surrender and the official end of World War II. However, the consequences of the Trinity Test and the use of nuclear weapons would resonate far beyond the end of the war.

The success of the Trinity Test set the stage for the Cold War, as the United States and the Soviet Union began an arms race to develop more advanced nuclear weapons. The test also sparked significant debates about the ethical implications of nuclear weapons and the moral responsibility of scientists who had helped develop the bomb.

In the decades following the test, the global geopolitical landscape would be forever shaped by the specter of nuclear war. The legacy of the Trinity Test and the advent of nuclear weapons would continue to influence military strategy, diplomacy, and international relations for generations.

A World Changed by the Trinity Test-

The Trinity Test was a moment of profound historical significance. It marked the first detonation of an atomic bomb and represented a major scientific and technological achievement. However, it also marked the beginning of a new era of nuclear warfare and global tensions. The test itself, along with the development of the nuclear bomb, altered the trajectory of history in ways that are still being felt today. It is a moment in time that continues to shape the world's political, ethical, and scientific landscapes.

Through the Trinity Test, humanity unlocked a new, terrifying power. This event, a symbol of both scientific achievement and the destructive potential of modern technology, changed the course of human history forever.

CHAPTER SIX

THE MATHEMATICS OF DESTRUCTION – NUCLEAR PHYSICS IN ACTION

Introduction to Nuclear Physics Calculations-

Introduction: The Role of Nuclear Physics in Atomic Bomb Development-

The development of the atomic bomb during the Manhattan Project in the 1940s marked an unprecedented scientific and technological achievement. At its core, this monumental project relied heavily on nuclear physics, a field of science that explores the interactions and behavior of atomic nuclei and their constituent particles. The bomb's creation was predicated on a deep understanding of nuclear fission, a process that releases tremendous amounts of energy when the nucleus of a heavy atom is split into smaller parts.

The core scientific problem that needed to be addressed was how to create a controlled chain reaction in which nuclear fission could be sustained long enough to produce a massive release of energy. This challenge required extensive calculations, including determining the necessary amounts of fissile material, the geometry of the bomb, the method of initiating the reaction, and the rate of energy release. Central to these calculations were a variety of mathematical models and key equations drawn from quantum mechanics, thermodynamics, and statistical physics, which were applied to the processes of nuclear fission and its use in bomb design.

This section will explore the key equations and mathematical concepts that underpinned the theoretical and practical aspects of nuclear physics calculations used to develop the atomic bomb. It will focus on nuclear fission, chain reactions, critical mass, bomb design, and the principles behind the gun-type and implosion designs. Furthermore, it will delve into the mathematics of neutron multiplication, energy release, and the efficiency of the explosive reaction.

Nuclear Fission and Chain Reactions: The Physics of Splitting Atoms-

The discovery of nuclear fission in the 1930s was pivotal in the development of nuclear weapons. Fission involves the splitting of the nucleus of a heavy atom, such as uranium-235 or plutonium-239, into two smaller nuclei, accompanied by the release of energy in the form of kinetic energy of the fission products and the emission of neutrons. These neutrons, in turn, can induce further fission reactions, initiating a self-propagating chain reaction.

The ability to create a controlled and sustained chain reaction was crucial for the bomb's development. This required precise calculations to understand the probability of fission events and the behavior of neutrons. The chain reaction's efficiency and the yield of the bomb depended on the interplay between several factors, including the type of fissile material, the number of neutrons produced per fission, the material's geometry, and the density of the material. Understanding the nuclear physics involved required mathematical formulations that were grounded in these parameters.

Energy Released per Fission Event: The Basis of Nuclear Power

The energy released in a fission event is governed by Einstein's equation, $E = mc^2$, where:

E is the energy released,

m is the mass defect (the difference between the mass of the original atom and the sum of the masses of the fission fragments and released neutrons),

c is the speed of light in a vacuum (approximately 3×10^8 m/s).

In practice, a fission event in uranium-235 typically releases about 200 MeV (million electron volts) of energy. A practical understanding of this quantity of energy, when multiplied by the enormous number of atoms undergoing fission, helps conceptualize the scale of the bomb's destructive power.

For example, when uranium-235 undergoes fission, the total energy released is approximately:

$$E\_fission = 200\ MeV \times (1.602 \times 10^{-13}\ J\ /\ MeV) = 3.204 \times 10^{-11}\ J$$

Thus, a single fission event releases around 3.204×10^{-11} J of energy. The sheer scale of the energy release becomes evident when one considers the number of fission reactions involved in a bomb's detonation, typically involving billions of fission events in a fraction of a second.

Neutron Multiplication Factor (k): The Heart of the Chain Reaction

The key to achieving a sustained chain reaction lies in the neutron multiplication factor (k). The multiplication factor represents the number of neutrons produced per fission that causes subsequent fission reactions. If k is greater than 1, the chain reaction accelerates exponentially, and if k is less than 1, the reaction will subside.

To determine whether a chain reaction will sustain itself, the average number of neutrons produced per fission, which we denote as v, is a critical factor. For instance, uranium-235 typically produces about 2.5 neutrons per fission. If the number of neutrons that escape the material is less than the number that causes further fission, the reaction can go on indefinitely.

The multiplication factor k is given by the equation

$$k = n\_fission \, / \, n\_neutrons$$

Where:

n_fission is the number of fission events per time unit,

n_neutrons is the number of neutrons produced by these events.

For the reaction to be sustained, k must be greater than or equal to 1. In practical terms, for k = 1, the system is said to be critical, where the number of neutrons that initiate further fission events is balanced by those that escape.

Critical Mass and Critical Radius: Determining the Size of the Chain Reaction

The critical mass of a fissile material is the minimum amount of material required to sustain a chain reaction. Below this mass, too many neutrons escape from the material, and the reaction does not continue. Above this critical mass, the reaction becomes self-sustaining.

The critical mass is influenced by several factors, including the geometry of the fissile material, its purity, and its isotopic composition. For example, uranium-235 requires about 50 kg of material to achieve critical mass, while plutonium-239, being more reactive, needs less material.

To calculate the critical mass, the relationship can be expressed as:

$$M\_critical = (1 / \rho) * (4\pi r\_critical^3 / 3)$$

Where:

M_critical is the critical mass,

ρ is the density of the fissile material,

r_critical is the critical radius of the material.

Using the density of uranium-235 (18,950 kg/m³) and its critical radius, which is typically around 10 cm, the mass required to achieve criticality can be determined.

For plutonium-239, which has a higher v (approximately 3.2 neutrons per fission), the critical mass is smaller compared to uranium-235. The exact critical mass can be calculated using a combination of empirical measurements and theoretical models based on neutron behavior.

Bomb Design: Gun-Type vs. Implosion-Type

Once the theoretical understanding of fission and chain reactions was established, the challenge shifted to designing the bomb itself. There were two primary designs for achieving a supercritical mass of fissile material: the gun-type design and the implosion-type design.

Gun-Type Design

The gun-type design was used for the uranium-235 bomb dropped on Hiroshima. The concept behind this design is relatively simple: it involves shooting two subcritical masses of uranium-235 together using conventional explosives to form a supercritical mass. Once the two pieces are joined, they undergo a rapid chain reaction, releasing massive amounts of energy.

Gun-Type Design:

The key to the gun-type design is achieving the right velocity to bring the uranium masses together before too many neutrons escape, thus preventing a premature detonation. The velocity is calculated using the equation:

$$v = sqrt((2 * Egun) / muranium)$$

Where:

v is the velocity needed to bring the uranium masses together,

Egun is the energy provided by the conventional explosives,

muranium is the mass of the uranium.

To achieve a reliable detonation, the uranium pieces need to come together with sufficient speed to create a supercritical mass before the material can expand or disperse.

Implosion-Type Design:

The implosion-type design was more complex and was used for the plutonium-239 bomb dropped on Nagasaki. This design involved using a shell of high explosives to symmetrically compress a subcritical sphere of plutonium-239 into a supercritical mass. The goal was to compress the plutonium uniformly, triggering a chain reaction throughout the entire material.

The implosion process was governed by complex equations in hydrodynamics. The force from the explosive shell must be balanced so that the plutonium sphere achieves uniform compression, resulting in a rapid increase in density and initiating fission.

The pressure exerted on the plutonium sphere during the implosion can be calculated by:

$$P = (3 * Eexplosive) / (4 * \pi * rimplosion\char`\^3)$$

Where:

P is the pressure on the plutonium,

Eexplosive is the total energy released by the explosives,

rimplosion is the radius of the plutonium sphere.

This equation helps designers optimize the explosive charge and its distribution to achieve the necessary compression of the plutonium core.

Yield Calculations and Energy Release:

The final aspect of the bomb's design involved determining the expected yield—the amount of energy released during detonation. This yield is typically measured in kilotons of TNT, where 1 kiloton is equal to 1,000 tons of TNT.

The energy released in the bomb's explosion depends on the efficiency of the chain reaction, the geometry of the fissile material, and the type of material used. The energy yield Y can be approximated by:

$$Y = Efficiency * Mfissile * Efission$$

Where:

Y is the yield in joules,

Efficiency is the fraction of the fissile material that undergoes fission,

Mfissile is the mass of the fissile material,

Efission is the energy released per fission event.

For example, in the case of a uranium-235 bomb with an efficiency of 20% (a typical value), and a mass of 50 kg of uranium, the energy yield would be:

$$Y = 0.20 * 50 * 3.204 * 10^{(-11)}$$

This energy is then converted to kilotons of TNT to provide a measure of the bomb's explosive power.

Conclusion: The Mathematical Foundations of the Atomic Bomb

The development of the atomic bomb was made possible by a combination of theoretical nuclear physics, practical engineering, and extensive mathematical calculations. These calculations were instrumental in understanding the complex interactions within nuclear fission reactions, the behavior of neutrons, and the precise configurations needed to achieve a controlled chain reaction. The theoretical groundwork laid by scientists like J. Robert Oppenheimer, Enrico Fermi, and others, combined with the practical ingenuity of engineers, culminated in the creation of one of the most powerful and devastating weapons ever devised. The bomb's design, efficiency, and destructive yield were all products of the careful application of nuclear physics equations, each critical to its success.

Critical Mass and Chain Reactions-

Critical Mass and Chain Reactions: Mathematical Derivations for Sustaining a Chain Reaction in Uranium and Plutonium

The development of nuclear weapons hinges on the fundamental principles of nuclear physics, particularly the chain reaction that occurs when a fissile material like uranium-235 or plutonium-239 undergoes fission. For a chain reaction to be sustained, several key factors must be considered, including the critical mass of the fissile material, the multiplication factor (k), and the dynamics of neutron interactions.

1. Multiplication Factor (k)

The multiplication factor kkk is a critical parameter in understanding the dynamics of a nuclear chain reaction. It represents the ratio of the number of neutrons produced by fission to the number of neutrons available to sustain the reaction. If $k>1k > 1k>1$, the chain reaction will accelerate, while if $k<1k < 1k<1$, it will eventually die out. For a stable chain reaction, $k=1k = 1k=1$.

The equation for kkk is given by:

$$k = n\_fission \,/\, n\_neutrons$$

Where:
n_fission is the number of fission events caused by neutrons.

n_neutrons is the number of neutrons available to sustain the reaction.

To ensure a self-sustaining chain reaction, it's essential to have a sufficient number of neutrons available for each fission event. Achieving the right balance between the production of neutrons and the loss of neutrons is crucial in maintaining a controlled reaction.

2. Critical Mass (M_critical)

Critical mass refers to the minimum amount of fissile material needed to maintain a sustained chain reaction. It is influenced by factors such as the material's density and the size of the system. The critical mass depends on the density of the fissile material and the critical radius at which the material must be confined for the chain reaction to occur.

The equation for critical mass is:

$$M\_critical = (1 \, / \, rho) * (4 * pi * r\_critical^3 \, / \, 3)$$

Where:

Mcritical is the critical mass,

ρ\rho$\rho$ is the density of the fissile material,

rcritical is the critical radius of the material.

For a given fissile material, the density and the geometry of the material play a pivotal role in determining the critical mass. If the amount of material is less than the critical mass, the chain reaction will not sustain itself.

3. Velocity for Gun-Type Design

The gun-type design is one of the methods used to assemble the critical mass in a nuclear weapon. In this design, two subcritical masses of uranium-235 are brought together rapidly by conventional explosives. The key to this design is achieving the right velocity to bring the uranium masses together before too many neutrons escape, preventing a premature detonation.

The velocity required for this process is calculated using the equation:

$$v = sqrt(2 * E\_gun \, / \, m\_uranium)$$

Where:

vis the velocity needed to bring the uranium masses together,

Egun is the energy provided by the conventional explosives,

muranium is the mass of the uranium.

This calculation helps in determining the proper explosive charge required to ensure the uranium masses achieve a supercritical state before any significant loss of neutrons can occur.

4. Pressure during Implosion-Type Design

The implosion-type design is a more sophisticated method used for plutonium-239 bombs, such as the one dropped on Nagasaki. In this design, a shell of high explosives is used to symmetrically compress a subcritical sphere of plutonium-239 into a supercritical mass. The process is governed by complex principles of hydrodynamics, with the goal of uniformly compressing the plutonium sphere to initiate a chain reaction.

The pressure exerted on the plutonium sphere during implosion is calculated by the equation:

$$P = (3 * E\_explosive) / (4 * pi * r\_implosion^3)$$

Where:
P is the pressure on the plutonium,
Eexplosive is the total energy released by the explosives,
rimplosion is the radius of the plutonium sphere.

This equation helps in determining the optimal distribution of explosives around the plutonium core to achieve the required compression and initiation of the chain reaction.

5. Energy Yield Calculation

The yield of a nuclear explosion is a measure of the energy released during detonation. It is typically measured in kilotons of TNT, where 1 kiloton equals 1,000 tons of TNT. The energy released in the explosion depends on the efficiency of the chain reaction, the type of fissile material used, and the geometry of the system.

The energy yield can be approximated by the equation:

$Y = Efficiency * M\_fissile * E\_fission$

Where:

Y is the yield in joules,

Efficiency is the fraction of the fissile material that undergoes fission,

Mfissile is the mass of the fissile material,

Efission is the energy released per fission event.

For example, if the efficiency is 20%, and the mass of uranium-235 is 50 kg, the energy yield would be:

$Y = 0.20 * 50 * 3.204 * 10^{-11}$

This energy is then converted to kilotons of TNT for understanding the explosive power of the weapon.

Conclusion: The Mathematical Foundations of the Atomic Bomb

The development of the atomic bomb relied on a deep understanding of nuclear physics and mathematics. Through a combination of theoretical knowledge and practical engineering, scientists were able to design a weapon of unprecedented power. The key equations derived in this section, such as the multiplication factor, critical mass, velocity for gun-type design, implosion pressure, and yield calculations, all contributed to the successful creation of the atomic bomb.

The atomic bomb's design required meticulous mathematical calculations and understanding of nuclear fission dynamics. The collaboration of physicists, engineers, and mathematicians was instrumental in transforming theoretical knowledge into a practical weapon. These calculations not only helped scientists to understand how to achieve critical mass and sustain a chain reaction but also guided the design of the explosive devices that would trigger this immense release of energy.

In conclusion, the creation of the atomic bomb was the result of intense scientific and mathematical research, leading to the most powerful weapon ever created by mankind. The detailed equations and calculations discussed here were crucial in determining the proper conditions for initiating and sustaining the nuclear chain reaction that led to the bomb's catastrophic detonatio.

Fission Cross-Section: Calculations determining the probability of fission reactions-

The fission cross-section is a key concept in nuclear physics that quantifies the likelihood of a fission event occurring when a nucleus interacts with a neutron. In the context of nuclear reactors, nuclear weapons, and other nuclear applications, understanding and calculating the fission cross-section is essential to understanding the behavior of fissile materials and the efficiency of nuclear reactions. This in-depth analysis will explore the fission cross-section, its calculation, and its significance in nuclear fission processes.

1. Introduction to Nuclear Fission

Nuclear fission is the process by which a heavy nucleus, typically uranium-235 (235U) or plutonium-239 (239Pu), absorbs a neutron and becomes unstable, splitting into two smaller nuclei (fission fragments) and releasing a large amount of energy. During this process, additional neutrons are also released, which can potentially induce further fission reactions, resulting in a chain reaction.

The probability of a neutron causing fission depends on several factors, including the energy of the neutron, the type of fissile material, and the physical properties of the material. The likelihood of fission occurring when a neutron interacts with a nucleus is measured by the fission cross-section (σ_f\sigma_fσ_f).

2. Understanding Cross-Section

In nuclear physics, a cross-section is a measure of the probability that a specific interaction will occur between a particle (such as a neutron) and a target nucleus (such as $235^{235}235U$). The cross-section is expressed in units of area, typically barns (1 barn = $10{-28}10^{-28}10{-28}$ m²). The cross-section provides insight into the likelihood of an interaction, with a larger cross-section corresponding to a higher probability of the interaction occurring.

The fission cross-section specifically refers to the likelihood that a neutron will cause fission when it interacts with a fissile nucleus. It is crucial for determining the efficiency of nuclear reactors and weapons. The fission cross-section depends on the energy of the incoming neutrons, as well as the type of nucleus being irradiated.

3. Mathematical Formulation of the Fission Cross-Section

The fission cross-section is related to the probability of a fission event occurring upon the interaction of a neutron with a nucleus. The fission cross-section σ_f can be expressed as:

$$\sigma\_f = (1 \, / \, N) * (\Delta N\_fission \, / \, \Delta t)$$

Where:

σ_f is the fission cross-section.

N is the number of target nuclei (atoms of the fissile material).

$\Delta N_{fission}$ is the change in the number of fission events.

Δt is the time interval during which the change is observed.

This formulation represents the probability per unit time for a neutron to cause a fission event within a given amount of fissile material. The fission cross-section is essential for understanding the behavior of neutrons as they interact with nuclear fuel in reactors or nuclear bombs.

4. Energy Dependence of the Fission Cross-Section

The fission cross-section is strongly dependent on the energy of the incoming neutron. Neutrons can be classified into different categories based on their energy levels:

Thermal neutrons: These are low-energy neutrons in thermal equilibrium with the surrounding environment, typically in the range of 0.025 eV. They have the highest likelihood of inducing fission in certain fissile materials such as uranium-235.

Fast neutrons: These are high-energy neutrons, typically with energies ranging from 1 eV to several MeV.

Epithermal neutrons: These neutrons have energies between thermal and fast neutrons, typically ranging from 0.025 eV to 1 eV.

For many fissile materials, such as uranium-235, the fission cross-section is large for thermal neutrons, but it decreases for fast neutrons. This is because the probability of a neutron-induced fission event is influenced by the resonance absorption characteristics of the material, which are most favorable for thermal neutrons.

The energy dependence of the fission cross-section is typically described using the following equation:

$$\sigma\_f(E) = \sigma\_0 * E^{\wedge}\text{-}\alpha$$

Where:

f(E) is the fission cross-section as a function of neutron energy EEE,

σ0 is a constant that represents the fission cross-section at a reference energy,

E is the energy of the incoming neutron,

α is an energy-dependent parameter that characterizes the decrease in the cross-section with increasing energy.

For thermal neutrons, the fission cross-section can be relatively large, while for fast neutrons, the cross-section decreases rapidly.

5. Resonance Region and the Fission Cross-Section

In the case of uranium-235, there is a region of neutron energies known as the "resonance region" where the fission cross-section increases significantly due to resonant absorption. This occurs because the energy of the incoming neutron matches the energy levels of the target nucleus, causing an enhanced probability of absorption and subsequent fission.

The resonance region is typically observed in the energy range of a few eV to a few hundred eV, and the fission cross-section can be described by a Breit-Wigner distribution:

$$\sigma\_f(E) = (\pi * \Gamma\_f * \Gamma\_n) / ((E - E\_res)^2 + (\Gamma\_n)^2)$$

Where:

f(E) is the fission cross-section at a specific energy EEE,

Γf is the fission width (a measure of the likelihood of fission occurring),

Γn is the neutron width (a measure of the likelihood of neutron absorption),

Eres is the resonance energy,

E is the energy of the incoming neutron.

The resonance effect leads to a significant increase in the fission cross-section for neutrons with energies in the resonance region. This effect is particularly important for uranium-235, which has a large fission cross-section at certain resonance energies.

6. Neutron Flux and the Rate of Fission Reactions

The rate of fission reactions in a nuclear system is determined by the neutron flux, which is a measure of the number of neutrons passing through a unit area per unit time. The neutron flux is critical in determining how often fission events occur within a given material.

The rate of fission reactions per unit volume is given by:

$$R\_fission = \varphi * \sigma\_f * N$$

Where:

Rfission is the rate of fission reactions per unit volume,

φ is the neutron flux,

σf is the fission cross-section,

N is the number of target nuclei per unit volume.

The neutron flux φ\phi$\varphi$ is often expressed as:

$$\varphi = N\_neutrons\,/\,A$$

Where:

Nneutrons is the number of neutrons passing through a given area,

A is the area through which the neutrons are passing.

In nuclear reactors, maintaining an optimal neutron flux is essential for sustaining a controlled chain reaction. The fission rate depends on both the neutron flux and the fission cross-section, with higher flux and cross-section values leading to a greater rate of fission reactions.

7. Calculation of Fission Cross-Section for Uranium-235

To illustrate the practical calculation of the fission cross-section, we can consider uranium-235, which is a commonly used fissile material in nuclear reactors and weapons.

The fission cross-section for thermal neutrons in uranium-235 is approximately 585 barns at a neutron energy of 0.025 eV. This value corresponds to the large probability of fission occurring when thermal neutrons interact with uranium-235. For fast neutrons, the fission cross-section is much smaller, typically on the order of 1–2 barns.

8. Importance of the Fission Cross-Section in Reactor Design

The fission cross-section plays a critical role in the design and operation of nuclear reactors. Reactor designers need to carefully consider the energy spectrum of neutrons, the types of fuel used, and the geometry of the reactor to optimize the fission process. Materials with high fission cross-sections for thermal neutrons, such as uranium-235, are commonly used in nuclear reactors because they efficiently sustain a chain reaction at low neutron energies.

The design of the reactor's fuel assemblies, control rods, and moderator materials is heavily influenced by the fission cross-section. Moderators, such as graphite or heavy water, are used to slow down fast neutrons to thermal energies, thereby increasing the likelihood of fission events by increasing the number of thermal neutrons.

,The fission cross-section is an essential parameter for understanding nuclear fission reactions. It quantifies the probability that a neutron will cause a fission event when interacting with a nucleus, and it varies depending on the energy of the neutron and the type of fissile material. The calculation of the fission cross-section is crucial for reactor design, nuclear weapons, and other nuclear applications, as it determines the rate of fission reactions and the efficiency of energy production.

Through a detailed understanding of the fission cross-section, scientists and engineers can optimize nuclear reactors for energy production, improve the safety and efficiency of nuclear power plants, and develop advanced nuclear technologies for various applications. The ongoing research into nuclear physics and the fission cross-section continues to enhance our understanding of nuclear processes and their applications in modern society.

Neutron Transport Theory-

Neutron transport theory describes the behavior of neutrons within a nuclear system. It helps in understanding how neutrons interact with materials, propagate, and eventually trigger fission reactions. The mathematical model for neutron transport is governed by the following equation:

Neutron Diffusion Equation:

$$\partial\varphi/\partial t = D\,\nabla^2\varphi + \Sigma a\varphi - \Sigma s \int (4\pi)\, \varphi(\Omega)\, d\Omega$$

Where:

φ is the neutron flux, representing the number of neutrons per unit volume per unit time.

D is the diffusion coefficient, which dictates the rate of diffusion of neutrons in the material.

Σa is the absorption cross-section, indicating the probability of neutrons being absorbed by the material.

Σs is the scattering cross-section, representing the probability of neutrons being scattered by the material.

Ω is the direction of the neutron's movement, where $\varphi(\Omega)$ is the angular dependence of the neutron flux.

This equation is essential for determining the distribution of neutrons in nuclear reactors, weapons, and other nuclear systems. It governs how neutrons move through different materials and how they interact with them, either by being absorbed, scattered, or leading to fission.

Chain Reaction Multiplication Factor (k):

$$k = n\_fission / n\_neutrons$$

Where:

n_fission is the number of neutrons produced by fission events.

n_neutrons is the total number of neutrons available for reactions.

The multiplication factor k represents the ratio of the number of neutrons produced in one generation to the number of neutrons in the previous generation. If k > 1, the chain reaction will continue to grow, while if k < 1, the reaction will subside.

Implosion Design Calculations:

In the implosion design used for plutonium bombs, the plutonium core is compressed symmetrically using high explosives. This compression increases the density of the material, leading to a supercritical state, where a chain reaction can begin.

Pressure on the Plutonium Core:

$$P = (3 * E\_explosive) / (4\pi * r\_implosion^3)$$

Where:

P is the pressure on the plutonium core during the implosion.

E_explosive is the total energy released by the explosives.

r_implosion is the radius of the plutonium sphere.

This equation is used to determine the pressure needed to compress the plutonium sphere to a supercritical state. The energy from the high explosives must be distributed evenly around the sphere to achieve uniform compression.

Velocity of Implosion:

$$v = \sqrt{(2 * E\_implosive / m\_plutonium)}$$

Where:

v is the velocity of the implosion front, which is the speed at which the compression wave moves toward the plutonium core.

E_implosive is the energy released by the explosive charge.

m_plutonium is the mass of the plutonium core.

This equation determines the velocity at which the uranium or plutonium core must compress to initiate a supercritical chain reaction. The speed of the implosion is critical in ensuring that enough compression is achieved before the material can disperse.

Modeling the Trinity Test:

The Trinity Test, conducted on July 16, 1945, was the first detonation of a nuclear weapon. To model the explosion and understand its effects, scientists used several mathematical equations to estimate energy release, blast radius, and other factors.

Energy Release and Yield:

$$Y = Efficiency * M\_fissile * E\_fission$$

Where:

Y is the yield of the explosion, measured in joules.

Efficiency is the fraction of fissile material that undergoes fission.

M_fissile is the mass of the fissile material used in the bomb (in kilograms).

E_fission is the energy released per fission event.

This equation estimates the total energy released during detonation by taking into account the efficiency of the chain reaction, the mass of fissile material, and the energy produced per fission event.

Blast Radius Calculation:

$$r = (Y / (4\pi * P0))^{(1/3)}$$

Where:

r is the blast radius, which measures the distance from the explosion where significant damage occurs.

Y is the energy yield of the explosion.

P0 is the standard atmospheric pressure.

This equation is used to calculate the radius of the blast. It takes into account the energy released and the pressure exerted by the explosion.

Real-World Examples:

The principles and equations used in the development of nuclear bombs were not just theoretical; they were applied in the real-world design of the bombs dropped on Hiroshima and Nagasaki. These equations helped guide scientists in achieving a functioning and powerful weapon.

Critical Mass Calculation:

$$Critical\ Mass = f(M\_fissile, Density, Geometry)$$

Where:

Critical Mass is the minimum mass of fissile material required to sustain a chain reaction.

f(M_fissile, Density, Geometry) is a function that depends on the mass of the fissile material, the density of the material, and its geometric configuration.

The critical mass depends on various factors, including the shape and density of the fissile material, as well as the type of material used. For example, uranium-235 and plutonium-239 have different critical masses based on these factors.

Energy Yield in Hiroshima and Nagasaki:

$$Y = Efficiency * M\_fissile * E\_fission$$

Where:

Y is the yield of the explosion.

M_fissile is the mass of the fissile material.

E_fission is the energy released per fission event.

This equation was used to determine the energy output of the bombs dropped on Hiroshima and Nagasaki. For example, "Little Boy," the uranium-based bomb dropped on Hiroshima, had a yield of around 15 kilotons of TNT, while "Fat Man," the plutonium-based bomb dropped on Nagasaki, had a yield of around 21 kilotons of TNT.

Legacy of Nuclear Physics Calculations:

The mathematical calculations used to design the first nuclear bombs were groundbreaking and paved the way for future advancements in nuclear physics, both for peaceful applications (such as nuclear power) and for the development of more advanced weaponry.

Impact on Modern Nuclear Research:

The equations and principles developed for the atomic bomb continue to influence modern nuclear research. For example:

Nuclear Power Generation: Many of the same equations used to model fission reactions in bombs are also applied in nuclear reactors to produce energy.

Nuclear Medicine: The understanding of neutron interactions and radiation transport has led to innovations in medical imaging and cancer treatment.

Nuclear Weapons Technology: The development of thermonuclear weapons (hydrogen bombs) relies on the same principles of fission, though with much more complexity involving fusion.

Continuing Research and Development:

As nuclear technology continues to evolve, research is ongoing to better understand the physics of fission and fusion. Advances in computational modeling, materials science, and particle physics continue to improve the precision of nuclear calculations and the effectiveness of nuclear technologies.

The legacy of these equations and the knowledge gained from the early nuclear tests has shaped the trajectory of modern nuclear research and continues to have a profound impact on both scientific and political arenas.

CHAPTER SEVEN

ETHICAL DILEMMAS AND INTERNAL CONFLICTS

The debates among scientists over whether or not to build the atomic bomb were profound, complex, and fraught with moral, ethical, and political dilemmas. The story of the atomic bomb's development is not just one of scientific discovery but one that raises deep philosophical and humanitarian questions. While the end result—the successful detonation of the first atomic bomb—marked a significant moment in world history, it also left many scientists grappling with the consequences of their contributions to the project. The creation of the atomic bomb not only reshaped the course of World War II but also changed the very fabric of the scientific community, introducing debates that continue to this day.

The decision to build the atomic bomb was made under the shadow of World War II, as the Allied nations feared that Nazi Germany might be the first to develop such a weapon. The German scientific community, led by figures like Werner Heisenberg, had made significant advancements in nuclear physics, though they ultimately failed to create a functional bomb. The Allied effort, codenamed the Manhattan Project, was spearheaded by the United States with support from the United Kingdom and Canada. It brought together some of the greatest scientific minds of the time, including J. Robert Oppenheimer, Enrico Fermi, Niels Bohr, and many others. However, as the project unfolded, the scientific community was divided on whether it was right to build such a weapon and, if so, what the consequences of its use would be.

The Early Decision to Build the Bomb-

The debate over whether the bomb should be built began in the 1930s when scientists first realized the potential for nuclear fission to release enormous amounts of energy. In 1938, Otto Hahn and Fritz Strassmann discovered nuclear fission in uranium, a discovery that would lay the groundwork for the development of the atomic bomb. At the time, many scientists, particularly those working in Europe, recognized the potential for a nuclear chain reaction to be harnessed for military purposes. The physics behind nuclear fission was both awe-inspiring and terrifying, as the release of immense amounts of energy from a small amount of matter seemed to hold the power of unimaginable destruction.

The situation became even more pressing when physicists such as Leo Szilard, a Hungarian-born physicist, learned that the Nazis were working on their own atomic bomb program. Szilard, along with Albert Einstein, sent a letter to President Franklin D. Roosevelt in 1939, warning of the potential for Germany to build a nuclear weapon. This letter, which was signed by several prominent scientists, marked the beginning of the U.S. government's involvement in nuclear weapons research. Although Einstein's name on the letter was well-known, it was Szilard who was the driving force behind the letter, and he was also the one who first envisioned the possibility of using uranium for a chain reaction.

In the early stages of the Manhattan Project, many scientists who participated were motivated by a desire to prevent Nazi Germany from acquiring the bomb. They feared that the Axis powers, particularly Nazi Germany, could win the war and change the course of history if they succeeded in developing such a devastating weapon. The idea that the Allies could lose the war to a nuclear-armed Nazi regime was terrifying and provided much of the initial impetus for the project. In these early days, the project's goal was clear: develop the bomb before Germany could. There was a shared sense of urgency among the scientists, who were both motivated by the war effort and by the intellectual challenge posed by the new physics of nuclear fission.

As the project progressed, however, the focus began to shift. The initial sense of fear and urgency began to be replaced by more complicated considerations. The knowledge that the United States was on the verge of developing such a powerful weapon raised significant ethical and moral questions, ones that had never been posed to the scientific community on this scale before. Would such a weapon, if developed, ultimately be used in warfare? Should it be used? And if so, how could the scientists and engineers involved reconcile their work with the devastating potential consequences?

The Involvement of Prominent Scientists-

The Manhattan Project brought together a diverse group of scientists, including some of the most famous and accomplished physicists of the time. J. Robert Oppenheimer, who was appointed as the scientific director of the project, played a central role in organizing and leading the efforts of the research teams. Oppenheimer had a unique blend of scientific brilliance and organizational skills, and he was able to manage the various components of the project. However, as the project progressed, Oppenheimer and many of his colleagues began to struggle with the moral implications of their work.

Oppenheimer himself was deeply conflicted about the atomic bomb. He was a man of immense intellectual curiosity and had a genuine passion for scientific discovery, but he was also a person who deeply understood the implications of his work. According to some accounts, Oppenheimer's feelings about the bomb began to shift after he attended a meeting with President Roosevelt and General Leslie Groves, the military head of the project. During the meeting, Oppenheimer learned that the primary goal of the project was not just to create a bomb to defeat Nazi Germany, but to create a weapon that would have a decisive impact on the war with Japan. This shift in focus from merely stopping the Nazis to creating a weapon of immense destructive power for use against the Japanese led Oppenheimer to question the ultimate purpose of the bomb.

Oppenheimer's internal conflict grew as he became more deeply involved in the development process. The successful test of the first atomic bomb in July 1945, in the desert of New Mexico, was a moment of triumph for the scientists involved in the Manhattan Project. Yet, for Oppenheimer, the achievement was bittersweet. He had seen firsthand the devastating potential of the weapon, and he became increasingly troubled by the consequences of its use. According to some accounts, Oppenheimer's reflection on the test was summed up in his famous quote from the Bhagavad Gita: "Now I am become Death, the destroyer of worlds." This quote, while poetic, encapsulated the profound moral and ethical dilemma that Oppenheimer and many of his colleagues faced. The successful detonation of the bomb marked the culmination of years of intense work, but it also represented the unleashing of a power that could potentially endanger humanity itself.

The Debate Over the Bomb's Use-

While the scientific community was deeply involved in the development of the atomic bomb, there was significant disagreement about whether or not the bomb should be used once it was completed. Some scientists, including Leo Szilard, continued to press for the bomb to be used only as a last resort, in the hopes that it would never have to be deployed in warfare. Szilard believed that the weapon could be used as a deterrent but should be kept in reserve to avoid using it against civilians. He feared that the bomb could be used indiscriminately, leading to massive loss of life and setting a dangerous precedent for future conflict.

Szilard's concerns were not limited to the potential destruction caused by the bomb itself, but also the aftermath of its use. He and others believed that the use of such a weapon would be morally indefensible, as it would result in the deaths of hundreds of thousands of civilians. Szilard even went so far as to attempt to organize a petition among scientists involved in the project to prevent the use of the bomb on Japan unless they were first warned of its power. He believed that the Japanese government could be made aware of the bomb's capabilities, which might prompt them to surrender without the need for its deployment.

However, many other scientists involved in the Manhattan Project believed that the bomb should be used immediately to end the war. They argued that the bomb's deployment would save lives in the long term by shortening the war and preventing a costly invasion of Japan. The decision to use the bomb was also framed as a way to demonstrate U.S. technological superiority to the Soviet Union, which had been gaining ground in Europe. Some scientists, including physicist Niels Bohr, had become concerned about the political ramifications of nuclear weapons and the potential for the Soviet Union to develop their own atomic bomb.

In the months leading up to the bombing of Hiroshima and Nagasaki, discussions among policymakers and military officials about the bomb's use were often clouded by a mixture of strategic, military, and political considerations. The decision was made to drop the bombs on Japan to hasten the end of the war, with the belief that it would ultimately save lives by avoiding a prolonged conflict. The military justification for using the bomb was based on the assumption that Japan would not surrender unconditionally and that an invasion of Japan would result in even greater casualties. However, this assumption was not universally accepted, and many historians and scholars continue to debate whether the bombings were necessary to achieve Japan's surrender.

The Bombing of Hiroshima and Nagasaki-

The dropping of the atomic bombs on Hiroshima and Nagasaki in August 1945 remains one of the most controversial decisions in history. While the bombs played a role in bringing about the end of World War II, they also unleashed a level of destruction that shocked the world. The bombing of Hiroshima on August 6, 1945, followed by the bombing of Nagasaki on August 9, led to the deaths of an estimated 200,000 people, most of them civilians. The immediate effects of the bombs were catastrophic. The blast and subsequent fires destroyed much of both cities, while the long-term effects of radiation exposure caused severe illness, death, and lasting genetic damage.

The bombings also had a profound psychological impact on both the Japanese people and the world at large. The sheer scale of destruction caused by the bombs and the realization that such a weapon could be used in warfare led to widespread horror and shock. In the aftermath of the bombings, many scientists involved in the Manhattan Project expressed their horror and regret over the bomb's use. Some, like Szilard, felt a sense of responsibility for the deaths caused by their work and believed that the U.S. government had acted irresponsibly by using the bombs on civilian populations.

In contrast, others argued that the bombings were justified by the need to bring a swift end to the war and to avoid the immense casualties that would have resulted from a land invasion of Japan. The United States had already suffered heavy casualties in the Pacific theater, and military leaders believed that the bombings would hasten Japan's surrender. Despite the bomb's devastating power, many scientists believed that its use had been necessary to defeat an implacable enemy. The ethical debate surrounding the bomb's use, however, would continue for years after the war ended, as scientists, ethicists, and politicians grappled with the implications of atomic warfare.

Post-War Reflections and Ethical Dilemmas-

After the war, the debate about the bomb's use continued to stir strong emotions among the scientific community. For some, the development and use of the atomic bomb marked the dawn of a new era in human history, one where the destructive power of science could be wielded for both good and ill. For others, the bomb represented an alarming precedent for the future, where the pursuit of scientific discovery could lead to catastrophic consequences if unchecked.

Many scientists who had worked on the Manhattan Project became outspoken advocates for international arms control and the peaceful use of nuclear technology. The atomic bomb had shown them the power that science could wield, and they understood the need for global cooperation to prevent the spread of such destructive technologies. Some, like Niels Bohr, advocated for openness and transparency in international relations, arguing that only through mutual understanding and cooperation could humanity prevent nuclear war.

The creation of the atomic bomb and its use during World War II fundamentally changed the way scientists viewed their role in society. No longer could they simply focus on the pursuit of knowledge for knowledge's sake; the implications of their work had become far too great. The ethical dilemmas raised by the development of the bomb continue to inform debates about scientific responsibility, the regulation of powerful technologies, and the broader impact of scientific discovery on society.

The legacy of the atomic bomb's creation and use has made it clear that science, particularly when it comes to powerful technologies, must be tempered with an understanding of the broader social, ethical, and political implications. The responsibility of scientists extends beyond the laboratory or research facility—it extends to the wider world and the consequences their work may have on humanity. The debates that raged among scientists during and after the Manhattan Project provide valuable lessons for future generations of scientists, policymakers, and citizens alike.

The legacy of these debates serves as a stark reminder of the immense responsibility that comes with the power of modern science. Scientists today continue to confront complex ethical dilemmas in fields such as genetics, artificial intelligence, and climate change. As the world moves further into an age of unprecedented technological advancement, the need for careful, thoughtful consideration of the ethical implications of scientific progress becomes more urgent than ever. The debates over the atomic bomb are a testament to the complexity of this challenge, and their lessons are more relevant today than ever before.

Voices of dissent, including Leo Szilard and others-

The development of nuclear weapons during World War II is one of the most consequential and controversial episodes in the history of science and technology. Central to the story of the atomic bomb is the debate among scientists, political leaders, and military officials regarding whether the bomb should be built in the first place, whether it should be used, and what the moral and ethical implications of its use were. While the creation of the bomb was seen as necessary by many to end the war and defeat Japan, others, including prominent scientists who had contributed to the Manhattan Project, were deeply conflicted about its development and use. The voices of dissent, including those of Leo Szilard and others, raised important questions about the role of science in warfare, the responsibilities of scientists, and the long-term consequences of developing such destructive weapons. These voices, though often overshadowed by the political and military forces behind the bomb's deployment, played a significant role in shaping postwar discussions on nuclear weapons, arms control, and the ethics of scientific discovery.

Leo Szilard: The Scientist Who Warned Against the Bomb-

Among the most vocal and persistent critics of the atomic bomb during its development was Leo Szilard, a Hungarian physicist who was a key figure in the early discovery of nuclear fission. Szilard's opposition to the bomb, however, was not an outright rejection of scientific progress or the importance of defeating Nazi Germany in World War II. Rather, it was a cautionary stance based on his profound understanding of the potential dangers of atomic energy and his belief that the bomb could lead to a new, terrifying era of warfare and political instability.

Szilard's initial involvement in nuclear weapons research began with his co-authorship of the famous "Einstein-Szilard Letter" in 1939. This letter, sent to President Franklin D. Roosevelt, warned that Nazi Germany might be attempting to develop nuclear weapons and urged the U.S. government to take steps to counter this threat. The letter was instrumental in the creation of the Advisory Committee on Uranium, which would eventually evolve into the Manhattan Project.

Despite his role in alerting the U.S. government to the potential dangers of nuclear weapons, Szilard grew increasingly uncomfortable with the direction the project was taking. As the atomic bomb neared completion, Szilard began to worry not just about the bomb's destructive power but also about its use in warfare. He was particularly concerned about the morality of using such a weapon against civilians, and he feared that the bomb would only be the beginning of an arms race that could destroy civilization.

Szilard was one of the first to realize that the power of nuclear weapons could not be confined to a single country or even a single generation. He saw that atomic weapons would have global consequences, and that once the genie was out of the bottle, there would be no way to contain the threat they posed. His foresight about the dangers of nuclear proliferation and the need for international control of nuclear weapons proved to be prescient, as the Cold War and the nuclear arms race soon became defining features of the postwar geopolitical landscape.

Szilard's dissent became particularly evident as the U.S. military approached the decision to use the atomic bomb on Japan. He was adamantly opposed to the bombing of civilian populations, and he argued that Japan was already on the brink of surrender, meaning that the use of the bomb was not necessary to bring an end to the war. Szilard's objections were rooted in his deeply held belief that scientists had a responsibility to prevent the use of the bomb in such a manner.

In 1945, as the bomb's completion drew near, Szilard sought to mobilize a group of Manhattan Project scientists to pressure the U.S. government to refrain from using the bomb on Japan. He drafted a petition, known as the "Szilard Petition," calling for the U.S. to demonstrate the power of the bomb to Japan before actually using it in combat. The petition argued that Japan could be persuaded to surrender if it were warned of the bomb's power. Szilard's efforts were ultimately unsuccessful, as most of the other scientists involved in the Manhattan Project believed that Japan would not surrender without a show of force. Nevertheless, Szilard's petition was an important early attempt to raise ethical concerns about the bomb's use.

Szilard's opposition to the bomb did not end with the bombings of Hiroshima and Nagasaki. After the war, he continued to advocate for arms control and the peaceful use of atomic energy. He became an outspoken critic of the U.S. government's nuclear weapons policy and worked tirelessly to promote disarmament and prevent the further proliferation of nuclear weapons. Szilard's postwar efforts to warn against the dangers of nuclear war and advocate for international cooperation on nuclear issues have had a lasting impact on the discourse surrounding nuclear weapons and their role in global security.

The Opposition of Niels Bohr: A Voice of Wisdom and Warnings-

Another prominent scientist who voiced dissent during the development of the atomic bomb was Niels Bohr, the Danish physicist who was one of the founding figures of quantum mechanics. Bohr's involvement in the Manhattan Project was limited, but he played an important role in shaping the postwar conversation about nuclear weapons. Like Szilard, Bohr was initially supportive of the Allied effort to develop nuclear weapons, believing that the United States needed to secure atomic technology to prevent Nazi Germany from gaining access to it. However, as the war ended and the reality of nuclear weapons' destructive power became clearer, Bohr's stance shifted.

Bohr's opposition to the use of the bomb was rooted in his belief that nuclear weapons represented a profound new chapter in human history, one that demanded new forms of international cooperation and transparency. Bohr was one of the first scientists to recognize that nuclear weapons could not be controlled by any single nation. He believed that their power was so great that no country, regardless of its military or political influence, would be able to control their use without global cooperation.

Bohr's advocacy for international cooperation in the control of nuclear weapons led him to attempt to open a dialogue with the Soviet Union and the United States about the peaceful use of atomic energy and the need for international safeguards. He proposed that all nations share their knowledge of nuclear physics in the hope that transparency and collaboration would prevent the outbreak of nuclear war. Bohr's proposals, however, were largely rejected by both the U.S. and the Soviet Union, who were more focused on securing their own national interests than on achieving global nuclear disarmament.

Despite his failure to secure international cooperation, Bohr's advocacy for a global approach to nuclear weapons and his warnings about the dangers of secrecy and isolation in the nuclear age were prescient. His belief that the atomic bomb marked a new phase in human civilization, one in which the survival of humanity itself was at risk, continues to resonate in the debates about nuclear weapons today.

J. Robert Oppenheimer: The Conscience of the Manhattan Project-

J. Robert Oppenheimer, the scientific director of the Manhattan Project, is perhaps one of the most famous figures associated with the atomic bomb. While he was deeply involved in the development of the bomb and played a key role in overseeing its successful detonation, Oppenheimer's feelings about the bomb and its use were complex and conflicted.

Oppenheimer was initially enthusiastic about the project and believed that the atomic bomb was necessary to end the war with Japan. He recognized the devastating potential of the bomb but viewed its development as a necessary evil in the context of the larger conflict with the Axis powers. However, after the successful detonation of the first atomic bomb in July 1945, Oppenheimer's perspective shifted dramatically. He famously quoted from the Bhagavad Gita: "Now I am become Death, the destroyer of worlds," reflecting the profound emotional and moral toll the development of the bomb had on him.

Following the bombings of Hiroshima and Nagasaki, Oppenheimer's feelings of guilt and regret deepened. Although he had played a central role in the development of the bomb, he became one of its most prominent critics, advocating for international control of nuclear weapons and warning about the dangers of an arms race between the United States and the Soviet Union. Oppenheimer's dissent, however, was more complicated than Szilard's. He remained a strong advocate for U.S. military and political interests, even as he grew more concerned about the ethical implications of nuclear weapons.

In the years following the war, Oppenheimer's dissent became more public. He became a strong proponent of arms control and was a key figure in the development of the U.S. policy on nuclear disarmament. His opposition to the arms race and his calls for international cooperation made him a target of suspicion during the McCarthy era, and he was eventually stripped of his security clearance in 1954. Despite the personal and professional costs of his dissent, Oppenheimer remained steadfast in his belief that nuclear weapons were a threat to humanity and needed to be controlled.

The Impact of Dissent on Nuclear Policy-

The voices of dissent from figures like Leo Szilard, Niels Bohr, and J. Robert Oppenheimer had a profound impact on the development of nuclear policy in the postwar period. While their opposition to the atomic bomb did not prevent its use, their efforts to raise ethical and moral concerns about the bomb played a significant role in shaping postwar discussions about nuclear weapons and arms control.

After the war, the U.S. and the Soviet Union engaged in a nuclear arms race, each nation seeking to build more powerful and more numerous nuclear weapons. The danger of nuclear war and the possibility of global annihilation led to the establishment of arms control treaties, such as the Partial Nuclear Test Ban Treaty (1963) and the Nuclear Non-Proliferation Treaty (1968), both of which sought to limit the spread of nuclear weapons and encourage disarmament.

The voices of dissent also influenced the rise of the anti-nuclear movement, which became increasingly active during the Cold War. Scientists, politicians, and activists who shared the concerns of Szilard, Bohr, and Oppenheimer worked together to promote nuclear disarmament and to ensure that the horrors of Hiroshima and Nagasaki were never repeated.

Legacy of the Dissenters: Ethical Responsibility in Science-

The legacy of Leo Szilard, Niels Bohr, and J. Robert Oppenheimer is a testament to the profound ethical responsibility that scientists bear in the development and application of new technologies. These figures understood that the power of science could be wielded for both good and ill, and they worked tirelessly to ensure that the destructive potential of nuclear weapons was acknowledged and addressed. Their efforts continue to inspire scientists and policymakers today, reminding us that scientific discovery must always be accompanied by careful ethical consideration.

The voices of dissent from the atomic age are an essential part of the history of nuclear weapons and their use. As we continue to confront new challenges in science and technology, it is essential that we remember the lessons of the past and the importance of considering the broader implications of scientific progress. The struggle to balance technological advancement with ethical responsibility is ongoing, and the legacy of those who spoke out against the atomic bomb remains a powerful reminder of the need for vigilance and moral clarity in the pursuit of knowledge and innovation.

In the end, the story of Leo Szilard, Niels Bohr, and J. Robert Oppenheimer is not just about their opposition to the atomic bomb. It is about the enduring moral questions that arise whenever humanity creates new technologies with the potential to destroy or fundamentally alter life as we know it. Their voices remind us that science is never neutral and that the path we choose in the application of new discoveries will determine not only the future of science but the future of humanity itself.

Oppenheimer's moral struggles and leadership challenges-

J. Robert Oppenheimer's role in the development of the atomic bomb is one of the most complex and multifaceted narratives in the history of modern science and warfare. Oppenheimer, known as the "father of the atomic bomb," was a brilliant physicist who led the scientific effort that created the most destructive weapon ever conceived by humankind. However, as the architect of the Manhattan Project, Oppenheimer's moral struggles and leadership challenges were not only a significant part of his personal life but also played a crucial role in shaping the trajectory of global history in the 20th century. His involvement in the creation of nuclear weapons marked a pivotal turning point for humanity, both in terms of scientific progress and ethical consideration, leading to an inescapable moral reckoning that Oppenheimer himself would wrestle with for the rest of his life.

The duality of Oppenheimer's legacy — that of a brilliant scientist and a deeply conflicted human being — is shaped by his initial dedication to winning the Second World War, followed by his increasing realization of the horrors that the weapon he had helped create could unleash. His leadership of the Manhattan Project, which produced the atomic bomb that was later used to end the war, presented not only scientific challenges but immense moral and philosophical dilemmas that would haunt him long after the war had ended. In this extended reflection, we will explore the intricate layers of Oppenheimer's moral struggles, leadership challenges, and his attempts to come to terms with the weapon he had helped bring into being. These themes are essential to understanding the complexities of his character and the broader implications of the nuclear age.

The Intellectual Background and Philosophical Foundations of Oppenheimer-

Before delving into the moral conflicts and leadership challenges that Oppenheimer faced during and after the Manhattan Project, it is essential to first examine the intellectual and philosophical foundations upon which Oppenheimer's moral reasoning was built. From a young age, Oppenheimer was intellectually gifted, excelling in mathematics, chemistry, and physics. His academic journey took him to prestigious institutions such as Harvard University and the University of Göttingen, where he worked alongside some of the most prominent physicists of the time. Oppenheimer's academic success led him to specialize in theoretical physics, and he soon established himself as a prominent figure in the field.

While Oppenheimer's scientific prowess was indisputable, his personal interests extended far beyond the realm of physics. He was deeply interested in literature, philosophy, and the humanities. This intellectual diversity set him apart from many of his contemporaries and helped shape his worldview. Oppenheimer's reading of the Bhagavad Gita, a Hindu scripture, is especially notable. The text profoundly influenced his moral reflections during the development of the atomic bomb. The Bhagavad Gita, which centers on the moral duties of a warrior, offered Oppenheimer a framework for understanding his own role as a scientist in a world at war. In particular, the text's teachings on duty and the nature of destruction resonated with Oppenheimer as he grappled with the ethical implications of his work on the bomb.

Oppenheimer's philosophical reflections were not merely academic exercises. They had practical significance during his involvement in the Manhattan Project, where the responsibility of building a weapon capable of mass destruction weighed heavily on him. His engagement with philosophy, particularly with Eastern thought, revealed his deep concern about the potential consequences of scientific advancements when they are wielded by political forces for military purposes. This concern would become central to Oppenheimer's ethical struggles once the bomb was completed and its use was considered.

The Manhattan Project: The Intersection of Science and Morality-

The Manhattan Project, the secret U.S. government program to develop nuclear weapons, was launched in response to the growing fear that Nazi Germany was developing its own atomic bomb. At the time, the potential of nuclear energy was not fully understood, but the possibility that the Nazis might harness the power of the atom for military purposes spurred the U.S. government into action. The project, which began in 1942, brought together scientists, engineers, and military personnel under the leadership of General Leslie Groves and scientific director J. Robert Oppenheimer.

Oppenheimer's appointment as the scientific leader of the project was based on his expertise in nuclear physics and his ability to organize and lead a team of brilliant minds. Under Oppenheimer's direction, a diverse group of scientists, including Enrico Fermi, Niels Bohr, and Richard Feynman, worked at the Los Alamos Laboratory in New Mexico to develop the atomic bomb. Although Oppenheimer was deeply invested in the success of the project, his leadership role required him to make difficult decisions that would have far-reaching consequences, not only for the outcome of the war but for the future of humanity.

Oppenheimer's initial focus was on achieving victory in World War II. He understood that the development of the atomic bomb would potentially shorten the war and save countless lives. The military urgency of the project was clear: the Allies needed to build the bomb before the Axis powers, particularly Germany, could harness nuclear energy for destructive purposes. However, as the bomb neared completion, Oppenheimer's moral and ethical concerns began to intensify. His awareness of the unprecedented power of the weapon he had helped create raised questions about the morality of its potential use.

The Trinity Test: A Moment of Moral Reckoning-

The culmination of the Manhattan Project came in July 1945 with the successful detonation of the first atomic bomb in the desert of New Mexico, known as the Trinity Test. Oppenheimer, who had overseen the design and construction of the bomb, witnessed the explosion along with his scientific team and military personnel. The test was a resounding success, and the implications of the event were immediate and far-reaching.

In the aftermath of the Trinity Test, Oppenheimer famously quoted the Bhagavad Gita: "Now I am become Death, the destroyer of worlds." This quote is often seen as a reflection of Oppenheimer's internal moral turmoil following the detonation of the atomic bomb. Although the success of the test was a monumental scientific achievement, Oppenheimer's reaction revealed his recognition of the devastating power of the weapon and the profound consequences it would have for humanity. The detonation of the bomb marked the dawn of the nuclear age, and Oppenheimer's recognition of the destructive potential of his creation was a moment of moral reckoning.

Oppenheimer's leadership during the Manhattan Project was characterized by his ability to manage a diverse and often contentious team of scientists and military personnel. However, the aftermath of the Trinity Test forced him to confront the broader implications of the project. Oppenheimer had worked tirelessly to ensure the success of the bomb, but now he was faced with the realization that the weapon could be used to wipe out entire cities and cause untold human suffering. The success of the Trinity Test, while a triumph of scientific achievement, also forced Oppenheimer to reckon with the ethical and moral dilemmas that came with the bomb's use.

The Decision to Use the Bomb: Ethical Dilemmas and Leadership in Crisis-

The decision to use the atomic bomb on Japan was one of the most controversial and consequential decisions in the history of warfare. After the successful detonation of the Trinity bomb, the U.S. government faced a choice: whether to use the weapon to bring about the end of the war or to pursue other diplomatic options. The decision was made by President Harry S. Truman, who, in consultation with his military advisors, authorized the use of the bomb on Japan. The bombs were dropped on the cities of Hiroshima and Nagasaki in August 1945, leading to the deaths of over 200,000 people, most of them civilians.

For Oppenheimer, the decision to use the bomb was fraught with moral and ethical conflicts. While he had long believed that the development of the atomic bomb was a necessary measure to end the war, the reality of its deployment left him conflicted. Oppenheimer's scientific team, many of whom had worked on the project with the hope that the bomb would be used as a deterrent to end the war, were now faced with the knowledge that the weapon they had created had been used to destroy entire cities.

Oppenheimer's reaction to the bombings of Hiroshima and Nagasaki was not one of triumph but one of deep sorrow. His growing moral concerns about the bomb were compounded by the devastating human cost of its use. While the bomb may have hastened the end of the war, it also introduced a new era of destruction and fear that would shape international relations for decades to come. Oppenheimer, a man who had once been driven by a sense of duty to his country, now found himself questioning the morality of his own actions.

The Fallout: Oppenheimer's Moral Struggles in the Postwar Era-

In the years following the bombings, Oppenheimer's moral struggles became even more pronounced. He became increasingly concerned about the potential for a nuclear arms race between the United States and the Soviet Union, which was beginning to take shape after the end of World War II. The threat of nuclear war became a central focus of Cold War politics, and Oppenheimer became a vocal advocate for arms control and the peaceful use of nuclear energy.

However, Oppenheimer's calls for arms control and his moral objections to the further development of nuclear weapons were met with resistance from the U.S. government and the military. In the early 1950s, with the advent of the hydrogen bomb, Oppenheimer's position became even more contentious. His opposition to the development of the hydrogen bomb, which was far more powerful than the atomic bomb, put him at odds with many of his colleagues and the military leadership.

The McCarthy Era and the Loss of Oppenheimer's Security Clearance-

In 1954, during the height of the McCarthy era, Oppenheimer was subjected to a security clearance hearing, which ultimately resulted in the revocation of his security clearance. The hearing was politically motivated and was fueled by suspicions about Oppenheimer's past associations with left-wing individuals and organizations. The revocation of his security clearance marked a dramatic fall from grace for Oppenheimer, who had once been regarded as one of the most respected scientists in the world.

The loss of his security clearance was a devastating blow to Oppenheimer, both professionally and personally. It effectively ended his career as a government advisor on nuclear policy and placed him in the crosshairs of political scrutiny. However, Oppenheimer's moral struggles and leadership challenges did not end with the revocation of his security clearance. Instead, they became a defining feature of his later life.

Oppenheimer's Legacy and the Continued Relevance of His Moral Struggles-

J. Robert Oppenheimer's moral struggles and leadership challenges were inextricably linked to the profound ethical dilemmas posed by the development and use of the atomic bomb. His role in the Manhattan Project and his subsequent reflections on the bomb's use and the potential consequences of nuclear weapons raised fundamental questions about the relationship between science, politics, and morality. Oppenheimer's legacy is one of a man who, despite his brilliant scientific contributions, was deeply aware of the destructive potential of his work and the responsibility that came with it.

As the world continues to grapple with the implications of nuclear weapons, Oppenheimer's moral struggles remain relevant today. The ethical questions he faced — about the responsibility of scientists, the consequences of technological progress, and the role of politics in shaping the future of warfare — continue to resonate in the modern world. Oppenheimer's story serves as a reminder that the pursuit of scientific knowledge and the development of powerful technologies come with significant moral and ethical responsibilities. His legacy challenges us to reflect on the potential consequences of our actions and the role that science plays in shaping the future of humanity.

Oppenheimer's experiences highlight the tension between the pursuit of knowledge and the need to consider the moral consequences of that knowledge. His life and work offer an enduring lesson in the ethical complexities that arise when science and technology intersect with politics and war.

The ethical implications of targeting civilian populations-

The ethical implications of targeting civilian populations in warfare are deeply entwined with broader questions about justice, morality, and the sanctity of human life. In the modern era, as technological advancements have introduced new forms of warfare, the debate surrounding the intentional targeting of civilians has become increasingly complex. Although there are many historical instances of civilian targeting, the atomic bombings of Hiroshima and Nagasaki during World War II remain the most prominent and controversial example of such practices. This issue, however, is not confined to the events of World War II and continues to influence modern-day conflicts and debates regarding military ethics.

This extended discussion aims to expand on the moral and ethical challenges posed by the intentional targeting of civilians, particularly through nuclear warfare, while also drawing connections to contemporary forms of warfare, such as drone strikes and cyber warfare. By examining these topics in greater depth, we can better understand the evolving nature of warfare and the ethical issues that arise as military technology continues to advance.

The Historical Context of Targeting Civilians in Warfare-

The practice of targeting civilians in warfare has a long and complicated history. While the idea of avoiding civilian casualties has always been a central tenet of the just war tradition, it has not always been upheld in practice. Historically, civilians have been caught in the crossfire of military conflicts, especially during sieges and battles, but the deliberate targeting of civilians as part of a strategy to weaken an enemy has been a more recent development.

The roots of modern warfare's approach to civilian targeting can be traced back to the early 20th century, particularly during World War I. During the war, both sides employed bombing campaigns aimed at civilian centers, although the technology of the time was limited, and most bombings were inaccurate and caused unintended damage. The use of chemical weapons also targeted civilian populations, albeit indirectly, by contaminating food, water, and agricultural land.

World War II marked a significant turning point in the scale and purpose of civilian targeting. The bombings of Dresden, Berlin, and other German cities by the Allies, as well as the strategic bombing campaigns against Japan, were explicitly aimed at demoralizing the civilian population and disrupting enemy war production. However, it was the atomic bombings of Hiroshima and Nagasaki that fundamentally altered the ethical calculus of warfare. The bombings raised a host of moral and philosophical questions that continue to shape the ethics of war to this day.

The Decision to Drop the Atomic Bombs: The Context of War-

The decision to drop atomic bombs on Hiroshima and Nagasaki was made in the context of a war that had already claimed millions of lives. The leaders of the United States, led by President Harry Truman, believed that using the atomic bomb would end the war quickly and avoid a costly invasion of Japan that could have resulted in even greater casualties. This was the justification given by the U.S. government at the time, which argued that the bombings were necessary to save lives in the long run. However, the use of atomic bombs, with their immense destructive power, raised serious questions about whether such an action was morally justifiable, especially when it resulted in the deaths of over 200,000 civilians.

The philosophical and ethical justification for the bombings has been a subject of intense debate among scholars, historians, and ethicists. Proponents of the bombings argue that Japan's leaders were unwilling to surrender, and that the bombings forced them to capitulate, thus preventing a protracted and bloody invasion. They argue that the bombings ultimately saved lives, as the number of casualties from a prolonged war would have been much higher than the immediate death toll from the bombs.

On the other hand, critics of the bombings argue that Japan was already on the brink of surrender and that the bombings were unnecessary. They contend that the use of atomic bombs was a morally indefensible act, as it intentionally targeted civilian populations in a manner that was disproportionate to the military objectives. Many critics also point to the racial motivations behind the bombings, arguing that the decision to use atomic bombs on Japan was partly influenced by racist attitudes toward the Japanese population. This argument emphasizes the inhumanity of using a weapon of mass destruction on an already weakened enemy, especially when there were other ways to end the war.

Military Necessity vs. Moral Justification-

At the heart of the debate over the ethics of targeting civilians is the principle of military necessity. The concept of military necessity holds that actions in war are justified if they are necessary to achieve a legitimate military objective and are proportionate to the military gain. This principle has long been a cornerstone of just war theory, but it is increasingly contested in the context of modern warfare. The argument for military necessity is most often invoked by those who support the use of nuclear weapons, as it seeks to justify extreme measures for the sake of achieving victory and ending the war quickly.

In the case of the atomic bombings, the U.S. government argued that the bombings were necessary to achieve Japan's surrender, thereby bringing the war to an end and saving lives in the process. However, the principle of military necessity is difficult to apply to such a catastrophic event. The sheer scale of destruction caused by the atomic bombs on Hiroshima and Nagasaki, as well as the long-term effects of radiation exposure, make it difficult to argue that the bombings were proportionate to the goal of forcing Japan's surrender. The fact that the bombings resulted in the deaths of tens of thousands of innocent civilians raises serious questions about the morality of using such a weapon in the first place.

Additionally, the concept of proportionality must also be considered when evaluating military necessity. The bombings of Hiroshima and Nagasaki did not target specific military objectives or military personnel; instead, they sought to inflict massive damage on civilian populations. The destruction was so overwhelming that it obliterated entire cities and killed tens of thousands of civilians instantly, with many more dying in the aftermath from radiation sickness and injuries. In light of these consequences, it is difficult to justify the bombings under the principle of proportionality, as the cost in civilian lives seems far too high relative to the potential military benefits.

The Principle of Distinction and Its Application-

One of the key principles of modern warfare ethics is the principle of distinction, which dictates that military forces should distinguish between combatants and non-combatants. Under this principle, civilians should not be targeted intentionally, and military attacks should only be directed at legitimate military targets. The bombings of Hiroshima and Nagasaki, however, fundamentally violated this principle. The use of atomic bombs did not distinguish between soldiers and civilians; it killed indiscriminately, inflicting devastating harm on non-combatants who had no role in the conflict. The fact that the bombs targeted entire cities, with little regard for the distinction between military and civilian targets, underscores the ethical failure of the bombings.

Furthermore, the principle of distinction is further reinforced by the concept of proportionality, which asserts that military force should not be excessive in relation to the military objective. In the case of the atomic bombings, the scale of destruction caused by the bombs was far beyond what could be justified by the strategic objectives of the war. The bombings killed large numbers of civilians and caused immense suffering, making it difficult to argue that the use of atomic bombs was in any way proportionate to the goal of bringing about Japan's surrender.

The violation of the principle of distinction also raises concerns about the broader ethical implications of using weapons of mass destruction in warfare. Nuclear weapons, by their very nature, are indiscriminate and cause widespread death and destruction. Unlike conventional weapons, which can be aimed at specific military targets, nuclear weapons obliterate everything within their blast radius, killing both combatants and civilians. The use of such weapons fundamentally challenges the ethical framework that underpins modern warfare, which seeks to protect civilian lives and minimize harm to non-combatants.

The Human Cost of War and the Ethics of Civilian Suffering-

The human cost of war is another important consideration when evaluating the ethics of targeting civilians. The bombings of Hiroshima and Nagasaki, as well as other instances of civilian targeting, caused immense physical, emotional, and psychological suffering. The survivors of the bombings, known as hibakusha, endured horrific injuries, radiation sickness, and long-term health effects. Many of them suffered from cancer, genetic mutations, and other radiation-induced illnesses, with the effects passed down to future generations.

In addition to the physical suffering, the bombings also caused deep psychological trauma. The survivors of the atomic bombings lived with the memories of the devastation they witnessed and experienced, and many struggled with feelings of guilt, shame, and survivor's remorse. The emotional scars left by such events can last a lifetime, affecting not only the survivors but also their families and communities.

The suffering caused by the bombings highlights the broader moral implications of targeting civilians. In modern warfare, the protection of civilians is a central concern of international law and humanitarian efforts. The Geneva Conventions and other international agreements are designed to limit the harm done to civilians during conflict, and to ensure that military forces respect the rights of non-combatants. The deliberate targeting of civilians, whether through aerial bombardment or the use of nuclear weapons, violates these principles and results in immeasurable harm to innocent people.

The Ongoing Debate: Nuclear Weapons, Drone Strikes, and Contemporary Warfare-

As the nature of warfare continues to evolve, the ethical questions surrounding the targeting of civilians remain relevant. In recent years, the rise of drone warfare has introduced new challenges to the ethical framework governing armed conflict. Drones, which allow military forces to conduct strikes remotely, have made it easier to target individuals with precision, but they have also raised concerns about accountability and the potential for civilian casualties.

One of the main ethical issues surrounding drone strikes is the lack of transparency and oversight. In many cases, drone strikes are conducted without public knowledge, and the identities of those targeted are often unknown. The use of drones also raises concerns about the "signature strike" approach, in which individuals are targeted based on patterns of behavior rather than confirmed identification. This practice has led to accusations that drone strikes have killed civilians who were mistakenly identified as combatants.

Moreover, drone warfare has made it possible to conduct military operations without risking the lives of soldiers, which has raised concerns about the psychological impact on drone operators. Drones are often operated from thousands of miles away from the battlefield, which can create a sense of detachment and disconnection from the consequences of military actions. This detachment raises questions about the morality of conducting warfare in a manner that allows military personnel to kill without fully experiencing the human cost of their actions.

Finally, the rise of autonomous weapons systems, which can make decisions about targeting and firing without human intervention, introduces even greater ethical challenges. As technology advances, the question of who is responsible for the actions of autonomous weapons becomes more pressing. If an autonomous weapon were to mistakenly target civilians, who would be held accountable for the consequences? These questions illustrate the ongoing complexity of the ethical issues surrounding the use of advanced technology in warfare.

The Need for Strong Ethical Frameworks in Warfare-

The ethical implications of targeting civilian populations in warfare are profound and multifaceted. The bombings of Hiroshima and Nagasaki serve as a tragic reminder of the potential consequences of targeting civilians in war, and the moral dilemmas associated with such actions continue to influence military ethics today. As warfare evolves with the advent of new technologies, it is essential that the principles of international humanitarian law, such as distinction, proportionality, and necessity, continue to guide military decision-making.

Ultimately, the deliberate targeting of civilians in warfare poses significant ethical challenges that cannot be easily resolved. As the world grapples with the legacy of past conflicts and the ethical implications of modern warfare, it is vital that we strive for a future where the protection of civilian lives remains paramount. The ethical framework governing warfare must adapt to the challenges posed by new technologies, ensuring that military actions are conducted with the utmost consideration for human life and dignity. Only by upholding these ethical principles can we hope to avoid the mistakes of the past and ensure that future conflicts do not come at the expense of innocent lives.

Tensions between military objectives and scientific curiosity-

The tension between military objectives and scientific curiosity has long been a subject of debate and controversy, particularly in the context of technological advancements in warfare. Throughout history, many scientific innovations have been borne out of military necessity, while others have been driven by scientific curiosity. The relationship between these two forces is often complex and fraught with ethical, moral, and practical challenges. In particular, the development of nuclear weapons during World War II exemplifies the intersection of military objectives and scientific inquiry, illustrating the immense power and peril inherent in the fusion of these two spheres.

Historical Context: Science and Warfare-

Historically, the relationship between science and warfare has been one of symbiosis and sometimes tension. On one hand, military conflicts have often driven scientific advancements, particularly in the fields of engineering, medicine, and physics. The development of new technologies for military use has been one of the primary catalysts for scientific innovation. On the other hand, scientific curiosity has frequently led researchers to explore ideas and technologies without fully considering their potential military applications or consequences.

During the Renaissance and into the Industrial Revolution, warfare drove many technological innovations. The development of gunpowder in China, which spread across Europe and Asia, revolutionized military strategy and led to the creation of firearms, cannons, and explosives. Similarly, the invention of the airplane, initially conceived for military purposes, paved the way for civilian air travel.

However, as the world entered the 20th century, a new kind of scientific curiosity emerged—one that sought to explore the very nature of the universe itself. Physicists began to probe the mysteries of the atom, not necessarily with military intentions, but with an overarching desire to understand the fundamental forces of nature. Yet, the path of scientific discovery during this time was inexorably intertwined with military objectives, culminating in the creation of atomic bombs.

World War II: The Manhattan Project and the Birth of the Atomic Bomb-

The Manhattan Project, which developed the first nuclear weapons during World War II, is perhaps the clearest example of how military objectives and scientific curiosity can converge. On the one hand, the United States was motivated by military concerns—the desire to end the war quickly and decisively, and to prevent Nazi Germany from developing nuclear weapons first. On the other hand, the scientific community was deeply invested in understanding the process of nuclear fission, a discovery that had significant potential for peaceful applications but was also recognized for its military implications.

Physicists like J. Robert Oppenheimer, Enrico Fermi, and Niels Bohr were part of a new generation of scientists who were profoundly influenced by both the scientific curiosity that propelled their research and the urgency of the war. The development of nuclear weapons, though born out of wartime necessity, relied on deep scientific principles that had nothing to do with military concerns. The discovery of nuclear fission by Lise Meitner and Otto Hahn in 1938 sparked an intellectual curiosity about the structure of the atom and the possibility of harnessing the energy released during fission. This curiosity, however, soon intersected with the realization that such a discovery could lead to a devastating weapon of war.

The decision to develop the atomic bomb, under the leadership of Oppenheimer and the U.S. government, raised profound ethical questions. The scientific curiosity behind the development of atomic theory clashed with the military imperative to use the bomb to end the war. While the scientists involved in the Manhattan Project were focused on the intellectual challenges of splitting the atom, the military and political leaders involved were concerned with the strategic implications of the bomb. The decision to use the bomb on Hiroshima and Nagasaki was influenced not only by the military goals of ending the war, but also by the desire to demonstrate the overwhelming power of the new weapon, which could change the course of history.

The Ethical Dilemma: Civilian Casualties and the Role of Scientists-

The development and use of nuclear weapons raised immediate ethical concerns about the targeting of civilians. The bombings of Hiroshima and Nagasaki killed an estimated 200,000 people, most of them civilians. The scientific community, which had been so focused on the technical aspects of fission and the potential for peaceful uses of nuclear energy, was confronted with the realization that their curiosity had led to the creation of a weapon that could annihilate entire populations.

Many scientists involved in the Manhattan Project struggled with the moral implications of their work. Oppenheimer, in particular, became a figure symbolizing the moral burden of scientific discovery in the context of war. His famous quote, "Now I am become Death, the destroyer of worlds," reflects the profound internal conflict he felt as a scientist who had contributed to a weapon capable of unprecedented destruction. Oppenheimer's moral struggle encapsulated the broader ethical dilemma faced by scientists who had contributed to the creation of nuclear weapons without fully considering the consequences of their work.

The moral quandary of scientists working on military projects is not unique to the atomic bomb. Throughout history, many technological innovations intended for peaceful purposes have been diverted toward military applications, leading to unintended consequences. The tension between scientific curiosity and military objectives has led to numerous ethical debates, as scientists often find themselves in a position where their research may be used for destructive ends.

In the aftermath of World War II, many scientists began to advocate for international cooperation in the peaceful use of atomic energy, recognizing the catastrophic potential of nuclear weapons. Yet, even as the U.S. and the Soviet Union entered into a Cold War arms race, the tension between scientific progress and military competition remained a central issue. The development of hydrogen bombs, intercontinental ballistic missiles, and other advanced weaponry in the years following World War II further fueled the debate about the proper role of scientists in military research and the ethical responsibilities they carried.

The Arms Race: A Struggle Between Military Strategy and Scientific Innovation-

The Cold War era saw the acceleration of the arms race, with both the United States and the Soviet Union developing increasingly powerful nuclear weapons. The military objective, at least from the perspective of the superpowers, was clear: to deter the enemy from attacking by ensuring that the destruction would be mutual, a doctrine known as mutually assured destruction (MAD). For military planners, the logic was that a strong nuclear arsenal would prevent war by making it too costly for any nation to engage in direct conflict. However, the growth of nuclear arsenals was driven by technological advancements in science, with new designs and delivery systems emerging at a rapid pace.

The scientific community found itself once again in the uncomfortable position of contributing to the development of technologies designed to ensure the destruction of humanity. Physicists and engineers were caught between their commitment to advancing human knowledge and the military demands for more effective weapons systems. The tension between military objectives and scientific curiosity reached new heights as the technology behind the hydrogen bomb, thermonuclear weapons, and missile defense systems pushed the boundaries of scientific innovation.

The emergence of more advanced weapons systems, such as the hydrogen bomb, escalated the stakes of the Cold War. The hydrogen bomb, which harnesses the power of nuclear fusion, was far more powerful than the fission-based atomic bombs. Its development relied on the scientific principles of quantum mechanics, thermodynamics, and nuclear physics. Yet, its purpose was unequivocally military. The bomb was not meant to advance scientific understanding, but rather to ensure that the United States and the Soviet Union maintained their global influence through the threat of annihilation. The stark contrast between the military objectives and scientific discovery highlighted the ethical challenges faced by the scientific community.

Nuclear Proliferation and the Global Impact-

As nuclear weapons spread across the globe, the tension between military and scientific interests became even more pronounced. The nuclear proliferation that followed the end of the Cold War, with countries like India, Pakistan, and North Korea developing nuclear weapons, raised concerns about the destabilizing effects of these weapons on global security. The scientific community, once again, found itself grappling with the consequences of its contributions to military technology.

The scientific curiosity that drove the early development of nuclear physics was overshadowed by the military applications of that knowledge. The desire to explore the atom and unlock its potential for energy production was inevitably bound to the development of weapons that could destroy entire cities. This tension between the desire for scientific understanding and the military applications of that knowledge is central to the ongoing debate about nuclear proliferation and disarmament.

The Ethical Considerations in Modern Warfare: Drones and Cyberwarfare

In the 21st century, new forms of warfare, such as drone strikes and cyberwarfare, have introduced new ethical concerns regarding the relationship between military objectives and scientific curiosity. Drones, which were originally developed for reconnaissance and surveillance, have been adapted for targeted killings and other military operations. The scientific community, particularly in the fields of robotics and artificial intelligence, has contributed to the development of drones, but the military objectives for which they are used—such as targeted assassinations and covert operations—raise questions about the ethical implications of these technologies.

Similarly, cyberwarfare, which involves the use of computers and networks to conduct sabotage, espionage, and attacks, is another area where scientific curiosity and military objectives intersect. The development of cyberweapons, such as the Stuxnet virus, reflects the fusion of scientific innovation and military strategy. While these technologies are designed for military purposes, they also raise concerns about their unintended consequences, particularly in terms of civilian infrastructure and global stability.

The relationship between scientific curiosity and military objectives in the context of drones and cyberwarfare underscores the ongoing ethical dilemma of modern warfare. As technology continues to advance, the potential for new forms of conflict—many of which have far-reaching consequences—presents even greater moral challenges for the scientific and military communities.

The Tension Remains-
The tension between military objectives and scientific curiosity remains one of the most complex and controversial aspects of modern warfare. The development of nuclear weapons during World War II and the subsequent Cold War arms race exemplify the challenges scientists face when their discoveries are diverted to military ends. While scientific curiosity has led to many advancements that benefit humanity, the military

applications of these technologies raise profound ethical questions.

As warfare continues to evolve with the development of new technologies like drones and cyberweapons, the tension between military objectives and scientific curiosity will only grow more pronounced. The challenge for the scientific community will be to navigate this tension, ensuring that technological advancements are used responsibly and ethically while still pushing the boundaries of human knowledge.

Ultimately, the relationship between science and warfare underscores the need for strong ethical frameworks to guide the development and use of military technologies. As history has shown, the pursuit of scientific understanding must be tempered by an awareness of its potential consequences. The legacy of the atomic bomb and the ongoing debates over the use of nuclear weapons serve as a reminder of the moral responsibilities that accompany scientific discovery and its military applications.

CHAPTER EIGHT

THE FINAL ACT – DEPLOYMENT AND DESTRUCTION

The bombings of Hiroshima and Nagasaki remain deeply etched in the collective memory of humanity as one of the most devastating events in the history of warfare. They represent the first and only use of nuclear weapons in a conflict, marking a turning point in global history. The decision to drop these bombs not only shaped the outcome of World War II but also left an indelible mark on the global consciousness, raising profound moral and ethical questions. While the bombings of Hiroshima and Nagasaki hastened the end of the war, they also unleashed horrors on civilian populations, leaving survivors with physical, psychological, and emotional scars that would last a lifetime. Today, many people reflect on those events with deep sympathy for the suffering experienced by the Japanese people, acknowledging the immense human cost of such actions.

The Context of World War II and the Development of the Atomic Bomb-

The Strategic Situation-

By 1945, the Allied forces had achieved significant victories in Europe, culminating in the unconditional surrender of Nazi

Germany. Yet, in the Pacific, Japan remained resolute in its refusal to surrender. The United States, along with its allies, had been engaged in an increasingly fierce and costly campaign against Japan. The war in the Pacific had already exacted a heavy toll on both sides, with millions of lives lost. The prospect of a final invasion of Japan, dubbed "Operation Downfall," promised to cost countless more lives. This created immense pressure on the U.S. government to find a way to bring the war to a swift conclusion.

The scientists working on the Manhattan Project, which was responsible for the development of the atomic bomb, understood that they were creating a weapon of unprecedented destructive power. Yet, few could have fully comprehended the immense suffering their work would cause when it was used on human populations. At the time, the primary goal of the Manhattan Project was to produce a weapon that could force Japan's surrender, thereby ending the war and preventing further loss of life.

The military leadership of the United States, including President Harry S. Truman, faced an agonizing dilemma. While Japan's military and civilian infrastructure were being destroyed through conventional bombings and naval blockades, the Japanese government still refused to surrender. Thus, the idea of using the atomic bomb—an option that promised to end the war quickly—gained traction among military strategists and political leaders. However, the human consequences of using such a weapon weighed heavily on some of the very people who developed it.

The Manhattan Project and the Development of Nuclear Weapons-

The Manhattan Project was a colossal undertaking, involving thousands of scientists, engineers, and military personnel, and it carried with it the weight of history. Initially spurred by fears that Nazi Germany was attempting to develop its own atomic bomb, the United States, the United Kingdom, and Canada joined forces to create a weapon that could change the course of the war. The project, led by General Leslie Groves, brought together some of the most brilliant minds of the time, including physicist J. Robert Oppenheimer, who served as the scientific director.

The project's ultimate success, culminating in the Trinity Test on July 16, 1945, marked a new era of warfare. For the first time, humans had unlocked the power of the atom, and with it, the power to destroy entire cities in the blink of an eye. The test, conducted in the deserts of New Mexico, was a monumental achievement in science and engineering. Yet, it also marked the beginning of a new, terrible chapter in human history. The development of nuclear weapons raised crucial moral questions that the scientists, military leaders, and policymakers would later have to confront.

J. Robert Oppenheimer, in particular, was tormented by the implications of what he had helped create. A brilliant physicist, Oppenheimer was no stranger to the potential for science to shape the course of human history. However, when the atomic bomb was finally used, he grappled with the ethical implications of unleashing such devastating power on civilian populations. His famous quote, "Now I am become Death, the destroyer of worlds," reflects the inner turmoil he faced after witnessing the destructive potential of the bomb that he had worked to create.

The moral consequences of the Manhattan Project would become more apparent as the bombs were prepared for use against Japan. By this time, the race to end the war had reached a fever pitch. The atomic bomb was not just a military tool; it was a symbol of the immense power that had been unleashed upon the world. The decision to use it would shape not only the outcome of the war but also the future of international relations, scientific responsibility, and human suffering.

The Decision to Use the Bomb-

The decision to use the atomic bomb was not taken lightly. President Truman, having inherited the weighty responsibility of leading the country during the final stages of the war, was faced with a range of difficult choices. On one hand, the U.S. military had suffered heavy casualties in the Pacific campaign, and the invasion of Japan promised to be even more costly. On the other hand, the atomic bomb's potential for destruction was beyond anything humanity had ever seen.

In meetings with his military advisors, Truman was told that the atomic bomb could potentially bring Japan to its knees, forcing a quick surrender and avoiding the need for a bloody invasion. Some of Truman's advisors, such as General Leslie Groves and General Curtis LeMay, supported the use of the bomb, believing that it would save lives in the long run by shortening the war. However, there were others, including military leaders like General Dwight D. Eisenhower, who expressed reservations about using such a powerful weapon.

The decision was also influenced by considerations beyond military strategy. The U.S. was entering a new geopolitical landscape, with tensions already emerging between the United States and the Soviet Union. The use of the atomic bomb was seen by some as a means of demonstrating American technological and military superiority, particularly to the Soviets.

However, the bomb was also a symbol of great moral weight. The U.S. government was not just unleashing a weapon; it was dropping a weapon that would result in the suffering of countless civilians. Though it was argued that Japan's refusal to surrender made the use of the bomb necessary, the immense human cost of this decision remains a deeply contested issue to this day.

The U.S. government faced no easy choice. However, on July 25, 1945, Truman authorized the use of the bomb, with the primary goal of forcing Japan to surrender unconditionally. In this decision, there was no consideration of the horrific consequences that would follow.

The Bombings of Hiroshima and Nagasaki-

Hiroshima: The First Atomic Bombing-

On August 6, 1945, the United States dropped the first atomic bomb, codenamed "Little Boy," on the city of Hiroshima. The bomb, a uranium-235-based weapon, exploded with a force of approximately 15 kilotons of TNT, instantly killing an estimated 70,000 to 80,000 people. Tens of thousands more would die in the ensuing weeks and months from radiation sickness and burns. Hiroshima was a military target, housing factories and troop concentrations. However, the city also contained countless civilians who were caught in the devastation of the blast.

The consequences of the bombing of Hiroshima were unimaginable. The sheer magnitude of destruction left survivors with lifelong physical and psychological scars. The survivors, known as hibakusha, were subjected to radiation that caused debilitating illnesses, and the psychological trauma of witnessing their families and friends perish in a matter of moments haunted them for the rest of their lives. The bomb created a landscape of horror, with entire neighborhoods reduced to rubble and a sky filled with choking smoke.

In the years following the bombing, the survivors were often stigmatized and marginalized. Many of them were unable to receive proper medical care, and their experiences were often overlooked by the Japanese government and the international community. Today, there is a deep sense of sympathy and sorrow for those who suffered in Hiroshima, as well as a recognition that the bombings were not just acts of war but were deeply human tragedies that left a lasting legacy of pain and loss.

Nagasaki: The Second Atomic Bombing-

Just three days after the bombing of Hiroshima, the United States dropped a second atomic bomb on the city of Nagasaki on August 9, 1945. This bomb, named "Fat Man," was a plutonium-239-based weapon, and it had a yield of approximately 21 kilotons of TNT. Nagasaki was an important industrial city, and its destruction was aimed at further compelling Japan to surrender. However, the decision to bomb Nagasaki was also influenced by weather conditions, as the primary target, Kokura, had been obscured by clouds.

The bomb exploded with devastating force, killing an estimated 40,000 to 75,000 people instantly. The survivors of Nagasaki, much like those in Hiroshima, endured the effects of radiation, and many lived with the lasting effects of the bomb's destructive power for the rest of their lives. The impact of the Nagasaki bombing, like Hiroshima, was not just physical—it was psychological, emotional, and cultural. The people of Nagasaki, like those of Hiroshima, struggled with loss, guilt, and the burden of being forever marked by their survival.

While the bombing of Hiroshima had already demonstrated the power of the atomic bomb, the second bombing raised further questions about the necessity and morality of using such a weapon. In Nagasaki, too, the city was devastated, and innocent civilians bore the brunt of the destruction. The people of both cities had already suffered from years of war, and the bombings only deepened their suffering.

The Aftermath and Japan's Surrender-

Despite the devastation caused by the bombings, Japan did not immediately surrender. However, the use of atomic weapons, coupled with the Soviet Union's entry into the war against Japan on August 8, 1945, placed immense pressure on Japan's leadership. On August 15, 1945, Japan announced its unconditional surrender, bringing an end to World War II. The formal surrender took place on September 2, 1945, aboard the USS Missouri in Tokyo Bay.

The bombings of Hiroshima and Nagasaki played a key role in forcing Japan's surrender, but the full scope of their impact was felt far beyond the battlefield. The human toll of the bombings was staggering, and the long-term effects on the survivors—both physical and psychological—continue to reverberate. The bombings left deep scars on the collective psyche of the Japanese people, and the survivors have spent decades grappling with the trauma of their experiences.

For many, the bombings were a tragic and unnecessary loss of life. While the bombings may have hastened Japan's surrender, the question remains: at what cost? The moral implications of using atomic bombs on civilian populations continue to spark debate, as it is impossible to ignore the human suffering that resulted from the bombings. Many still mourn the loss of life, not just in the immediate aftermath of the bombings, but in the long-term health consequences that continue to affect survivors today.

Controversy and Debate: The Ethics of Using the Atomic Bomb-

The decision to use the atomic bomb on Hiroshima and Nagasaki has remained one of the most controversial actions in the history of warfare. The bombings are often justified as necessary to end the war quickly and save lives that would have been lost in a prolonged conflict or an invasion of Japan. However, critics of the bombings argue that Japan was already on the verge of surrender, and the use of such devastating weapons was not only unnecessary but morally indefensible.

Some have also argued that the bombings were motivated by a desire to demonstrate the United States' newfound power to the Soviet Union, which was emerging as a rival in the postwar world. This raises uncomfortable questions about whether the bombings were used as much for political and strategic purposes as they were for military reasons.

Despite the various justifications put forth by those who support the bombings, it is impossible to ignore the human suffering that occurred as a result. For many, the bombings are an example of how scientific advancements, when wielded without regard for human life and dignity, can lead to catastrophic consequences.

Sympathy and Reflection on the Suffering of Hiroshima and Nagasaki-

As we reflect on the bombings of Hiroshima and Nagasaki, it is impossible not to feel deep sympathy for the millions of lives lost or forever altered by these events. The survivors of the bombings, the hibakusha, lived through unimaginable horrors, and their stories of loss, pain, and resilience serve as a poignant reminder of the human cost of war. It is a sorrow that transcends national boundaries, for the victims of the bombings were human beings, not just citizens of Japan. Their suffering calls for empathy, understanding, and a commitment to ensuring that such a tragedy is never repeated.

The bombings of Hiroshima and Nagasaki were not merely acts of war; they were acts of violence that inflicted irreparable harm on individuals and families. The scars of these events remain, and the world must continue to grapple with their legacy. While history cannot be undone, we can, as a global community, commit ourselves to a future where the horrors of nuclear warfare are never repeated. The bombings remind us of the need to respect human life and dignity, and to seek peaceful solutions to conflict—no matter how dire the circumstances may seem.

The lessons of Hiroshima and Nagasaki urge us to reflect on the choices we make and the consequences they carry. May we never forget the suffering of those who lived through the bombings, and may their voices continue to guide us toward a more compassionate and just world.

The roles of Little Boy (Hiroshima) and Fat Man (Nagasaki)-

The Roles of Little Boy (Hiroshima) and Fat Man (Nagasaki)-
1. Introduction-
The atomic bombings of Hiroshima and Nagasaki remain among the most significant events in the history of warfare. These bombings, carried out by the United States on August 6 and August 9, 1945, marked the first and only use of nuclear weapons in combat. The two bombs, Little Boy and Fat Man, not only ended the war with Japan but also ushered in the nuclear age, changing global politics, military strategies, and international relations forever. While the bombings were seen by many as a decisive means to bring an end to World War II, they also sparked a wide-ranging moral and ethical debate

regarding the justification of targeting civilian populations with such a devastating weapon. This essay explores the roles of Little Boy and Fat Man, analyzing their development, design, deployment, and the far-reaching consequences they had on the course of the war and on future generations.

2. Little Boy: The First Atomic Bomb-

Development and Design-

The design of Little Boy, the first atomic bomb, was simpler than that of its successor, Fat Man. Little Boy was a uranium-based bomb using Uranium-235 as its fissile material. The weapon was designed based on a relatively straightforward "gun-type" mechanism. In this design, two sub-critical masses of uranium-235 were brought together using conventional explosives to form a supercritical mass, initiating a rapid chain reaction.

One of the challenges of working with uranium-235 was obtaining enough of it in pure form, as the isotope is rare and difficult to separate. However, the Manhattan Project succeeded in creating a large enough quantity of enriched uranium to design the bomb. Unlike later plutonium-based bombs, which required more complex designs and precise engineering, Little Boy relied on the more rudimentary concept of simply firing one piece of uranium into another at high speed, triggering a chain reaction.

The bomb was designed by a team of physicists led by Robert Oppenheimer and scientists such as Norris Bradbury and Kenneth Bainbridge. They worked tirelessly in laboratories and secret facilities to develop a working nuclear weapon, not knowing the exact outcome but understanding the profound implications of their work. Despite the simplicity of its design, Little Boy represented a breakthrough in understanding nuclear reactions and the potential for energy release from atomic fission.

The Bombing of Hiroshima-

On August 6, 1945, Little Boy was dropped on the city of Hiroshima, a significant military hub located in southern Japan. The mission was carried out by the B-29 bomber Enola Gay, piloted by Colonel Paul Tibbets. The bomb exploded about 600 meters above the city, creating a massive fireball and shockwave that obliterated everything within a one-mile radius.

The immediate effects of the bombing were catastrophic. The bomb caused the deaths of an estimated 70,000 to 80,000 people, most of them civilians. The city's infrastructure was completely destroyed, and countless buildings were reduced to rubble. Additionally, thousands of people died from radiation exposure in the weeks and months that followed, with many more suffering from burns, injuries, and illnesses caused by the blast.

The bombing of Hiroshima not only caused immense loss of life but also left the survivors, known as the hibakusha, with permanent physical and emotional scars. Radiation exposure led to a spike in cancer rates and other chronic health conditions among the survivors. The psychological toll was also significant, with many people suffering from post-traumatic stress and enduring social stigma due to their radiation-related illnesses.

Despite the scale of destruction, the Japanese government, led by Emperor Hirohito, initially refused to surrender. The military leadership, particularly the hawkish faction within the Japanese Imperial Army, continued to advocate for resistance. The hope was that Japan could endure an Allied invasion or force a negotiated peace, but the bombings would continue to weaken their resolve.

The Strategic Significance of Hiroshima-

The decision to target Hiroshima was strategic as well as symbolic. The city was an important military and industrial center, with military command centers, supply depots, and factories that supported Japan's war effort. It was also home to a significant portion of Japan's industrial capacity, contributing to the war machine. The choice of Hiroshima was made partly to demonstrate the overwhelming power of the atomic bomb to the Japanese government and to the rest of the world. The bombing was intended to force Japan's surrender by showcasing the destructive potential of nuclear weapons and sending a stark message about the power the United States now held.

3. Fat Man: The Second Atomic Bomb-

Development and Design-

Following the success of Little Boy, the U.S. military and the Manhattan Project turned their attention to developing a more sophisticated weapon, this time using Plutonium-239 as the fissile material. Unlike uranium-235, plutonium-239 required a more complex method of initiating a chain reaction. The bomb developed for this purpose was called Fat Man.

Fat Man used an implosion-type design, where a spherical shell of plutonium-239 was surrounded by a layer of high-explosive material. When the explosives were detonated, they compressed the plutonium core into a supercritical mass, initiating the nuclear fission chain reaction. This design was far more complicated than the gun-type design of Little Boy but ultimately proved to be more efficient in terms of the energy released and the amount of fissile material required.

The development of Fat Man was fraught with challenges. Unlike uranium-235, plutonium-239 is highly radioactive and difficult to handle, requiring advanced safety measures. Furthermore, achieving the necessary precision in the timing and synchronization of the explosive lenses was a technical challenge. However, after the success of the Trinity Test on July 16, 1945, which demonstrated the viability of plutonium-based bombs, the Fat Man design was finalized and prepared for deployment.

The Bombing of Nagasaki-

The decision to target Nagasaki was made with the same strategic and military objectives in mind as Hiroshima. However, Nagasaki was the secondary target after the primary target, Kokura, was obscured by cloud cover. The bombing mission was carried out by the B-29 bomber Bockscar, piloted by Major

Charles Sweeney.

The explosion of Fat Man occurred at 11:02 AM on August 9, 1945, and created an enormous explosion. Like Hiroshima, the bombing of Nagasaki caused widespread destruction and significant loss of life. The immediate death toll in Nagasaki is estimated at 40,000 to 75,000 people, with many more suffering from the aftereffects of radiation exposure.

The Bombing's Impact on Nagasaki-

While Hiroshima was a flat city, Nagasaki's terrain, characterized by hills and valleys, partially mitigated the bomb's impact. However, this did not prevent extensive damage. Like Hiroshima, the survivors of the Nagasaki bombing faced prolonged suffering, both from the physical effects of the bomb and from the psychological trauma. Many hibakusha from Nagasaki struggled with the stigma of being nuclear survivors, and their experiences highlighted the long-lasting, generational impact of atomic warfare.

4. Comparative Analysis of Little Boy and Fat Man-

The two bombs, while similar in their destructive power, had important technical and strategic differences. The gun-type design of Little Boy was straightforward and simple, while Fat Man's implosion design required much more advanced engineering. Despite these differences, both bombs were devastating in their effectiveness, and their deployment led to the same tragic outcome: the destruction of two cities, the death of tens of thousands of civilians, and the beginning of the nuclear age.

The impact of these bombings was felt not only in Japan but across the world. The deployment of nuclear weapons marked a new chapter in warfare, one characterized by the potential for mass destruction and the existential threat posed by nuclear weapons.

5. The Legacy of Little Boy and Fat Man-

The legacy of Little Boy and Fat Man continues to shape world history today. The bombings led directly to Japan's surrender

and the end of World War II, but they also set the stage for the Cold War, where nuclear weapons became central to military strategy. The United States, along with the Soviet Union, engaged in an arms race that would see the development of increasingly sophisticated nuclear weapons.

Furthermore, the bombings of Hiroshima and Nagasaki raised important ethical and moral questions about the use of nuclear weapons. The devastation caused by these bombs led many to question whether their use was justified, and the effects of the bombings continue to be felt by survivors and their descendants.

The nuclear arms race, the Cold War, and the subsequent rise of nuclear disarmament movements were all shaped by the events that unfolded in Hiroshima and Nagasaki. These bombings remain a powerful reminder of the devastating potential of nuclear weapons and a call for global efforts to prevent their use in the future.

The atomic bombings of Hiroshima and Nagasaki marked a pivotal moment in human history. The devastating power of Little Boy and Fat Man not only ended World War II but also signaled the dawn of the nuclear age. These events forced humanity to confront the profound ethical, moral, and existential questions posed by the use of nuclear weapons. The legacy of these bombings continues to shape our world today, reminding us of the need for vigilance, understanding, and diplomacy in managing the power of the atom.

The decision-making process behind target selection-

Introduction-

The decision to use atomic bombs against Japan during World War II was a watershed moment in military and ethical history. While the bombings of Hiroshima on August 6, 1945, and Nagasaki on August 9, 1945, are remembered for their immediate destruction, loss of life, and profound geopolitical consequences, the decision-making process that led to the selection of these two targets is equally significant. This decision was made by a small group of U.S. military and civilian leaders under intense pressure to end the war swiftly and decisively.

The process behind selecting Hiroshima and Nagasaki as targets for the atomic bomb was influenced by a combination of military objectives, geopolitical considerations, scientific experimentation, and moral calculations. This essay explores the factors that contributed to the choice of these cities, examining the role of military strategy, intelligence, and scientific expertise, as well as the ethical dilemmas faced by the leaders involved.

2. The U.S. Military Strategy in 1945-

In 1945, World War II had reached its final stages, with the Axis powers in a state of decline. Germany had surrendered in May of that year, but Japan, despite suffering heavy losses, was determined to fight to the bitter end. The Allied forces, primarily the United States, had successfully carried out a series of military campaigns in the Pacific but had yet to defeat Japan decisively. The U.S. military leadership faced a complex problem: how to end the war quickly without sacrificing more lives in a potentially bloody invasion of the Japanese homeland.

The Pacific War had been marked by fierce battles, many of them involving heavy casualties on both sides. The Americans, having captured key islands in the Pacific, were preparing for a final assault on the Japanese home islands, particularly Kyushu and Honshu. The planned invasion, codenamed Operation Downfall, was expected to cost millions of lives, including a large number of American soldiers and Japanese civilians. This potential loss of life was a key factor in the decision to use atomic bombs, as the U.S. leadership sought a means to end the war with minimal casualties.

The use of atomic bombs was seen as a way to force Japan's surrender without the need for an invasion. The idea of demonstrating overwhelming destructive power was thought to be a means of breaking Japan's resolve. At the time, the U.S. military leadership, including General Douglas MacArthur and

Admiral Chester W. Nimitz, was focused on defeating Japan by any means necessary, and the bomb provided a new tool in this effort.

3. The Development of the Atomic Bomb-

The Manhattan Project, the top-secret U.S. government initiative that developed the atomic bomb, had been underway since 1939. The project brought together some of the world's leading scientists, including J. Robert Oppenheimer, Enrico Fermi, and Niels Bohr, to create a weapon of unprecedented destructive power. By 1945, after years of research, experimentation, and successful tests, the United States had two functional atomic bombs ready for use: Little Boy, which was uranium-based, and Fat Man, which was plutonium-based.

The bombs had been developed as part of the broader goal of winning the war, and there was significant pressure to deploy them as soon as they were ready. The Trinity Test, the first successful detonation of an atomic bomb on July 16, 1945, confirmed the bomb's destructive power and demonstrated that it could be used as a military weapon. The test led to a sense of urgency among U.S. military and civilian leadership to find an appropriate target for the bombs.

4. Target Selection Criteria-

The selection of targets for the atomic bomb was not arbitrary. The U.S. military leadership established several criteria that would guide the decision-making process. These criteria were influenced by military objectives, intelligence reports, and the desire to achieve a rapid and decisive end to the war.

Military Significance: The primary criterion for target selection was the military importance of the city. Hiroshima, Nagasaki, and other potential targets were chosen because they were significant military and industrial centers. Hiroshima, for example, was a major hub for the Japanese Army and housed an important military headquarters. It was also home to several key factories producing war materials. Nagasaki, though smaller than Hiroshima, was an industrial city with a large shipbuilding industry and a significant role in Japan's military production.

Psychological Impact: Another key factor was the psychological impact the bomb would have on both the Japanese government and the civilian population. The U.S. leadership hoped that the sheer scale of the destruction, combined with the shock of using a new and terrifying weapon, would convince Japan to surrender. Hiroshima, as a large city with both military and civilian populations, was seen as a place where the bomb's effects would be visible and unforgettable, demonstrating the full power of the weapon.

Geographic and Topographic Considerations: The geography and topography of the cities played an important role in the selection process. Hiroshima was chosen because it was a large, relatively flat city, making it an ideal target for maximizing the bomb's destructive power. The terrain in Nagasaki, with its hills and valleys, limited the full effect of the bomb to some degree. Nonetheless, the city was still heavily damaged by the explosion, and it had significant military value due to its industrial base.

Avoiding Cultural and Religious Sites: U.S. military planners were aware of the cultural significance of certain cities in Japan and wanted to avoid bombing historically important sites. Tokyo, for example, was avoided as a target, as it was home to many cultural landmarks and was considered a center of Japanese civilization. Hiroshima and Nagasaki, while important military targets, were not as culturally significant as cities like Kyoto or Nara, which were spared from the bombings.

The Impact on Japanese Leadership: The American leadership believed that the atomic bomb could force the Japanese leadership to reconsider its strategy. It was thought that the devastating effects of the bomb would prompt the Japanese Emperor Hirohito and his inner circle to abandon their plans to continue the war. There was also the belief that the bomb could serve as a powerful tool in negotiating a surrender with the Japanese government, without the need for a full-scale invasion.

5. The Influence of Intelligence and Military Leaders-

Intelligence reports played a key role in the selection of Hiroshima and Nagasaki. The Allied intelligence community had gathered extensive information about Japan's industrial centers, military installations, and transportation networks. This information helped to identify cities that were crucial to Japan's war effort. Hiroshima and Nagasaki were among the cities that stood out in terms of their strategic importance.

In addition, military leaders such as General Leslie Groves and Admiral William D. Leahy were heavily involved in the decision-making process. Groves, the head of the Manhattan Project, was deeply invested in the successful deployment of the atomic bomb. He argued for using the bombs to force Japan's surrender, emphasizing the importance of maximizing their impact. Leahy, as President Truman's chief military advisor, supported the idea of using the bomb as a means to end the war quickly and without the need for a costly invasion.

Truman's decision-making was also shaped by the political context of the time. The United States was in the final stages of the war, and there was a growing sense of urgency to bring it to an end before the Soviet Union could exert its influence over post-war Japan. This context influenced Truman's decision to authorize the use of the atomic bomb on cities like Hiroshima and Nagasaki.

6. The Decision to Target Hiroshima and Nagasaki-

On July 25, 1945, President Harry S. Truman authorized the use of atomic bombs against Japan. At this point, the U.S. had already identified several potential targets, and Hiroshima, as well as Kokura, Niigata, and Nagasaki, were considered for bombing. Truman and his advisors were faced with the challenge of selecting the most appropriate targets in a situation where military necessity, political considerations, and ethical dilemmas all intersected.

The decision to bomb Hiroshima was made based on its military significance, its ability to showcase the bomb's power, and its relative lack of historical or cultural importance. Hiroshima was selected as the first target, and the bomb was dropped on August 6, 1945.

Nagasaki, which had been selected as a secondary target, was chosen after the primary target, Kokura, was obscured by clouds. The bomb was dropped on Nagasaki on August 9, 1945, resulting in a devastating explosion that killed tens of thousands of people and severely damaged the city.

The decision to use atomic bombs on Hiroshima and Nagasaki was influenced by a variety of factors, ranging from military strategy and intelligence to political and psychological considerations. The selection of these cities as targets was based on their military significance, the desire to demonstrate the power of the atomic bomb, and the belief that the bomb could force Japan to surrender and bring an end to the war. The decision-making process involved a delicate balance between achieving military objectives and considering the ethical implications of targeting civilian populations.

While the bombings of Hiroshima and Nagasaki effectively ended World War II, they also sparked profound ethical debates and set the stage for the post-war nuclear arms race. The decision to use atomic bombs on these cities remains one of the most contentious in military history, raising questions about the morality of using such devastating weapons and the long-term consequences of nuclear warfare.

Accounts from Hiroshima and Nagasaki survivors-

The survivors of the atomic bombings of Hiroshima and Nagasaki bear witness to one of the most tragic and devastating events in human history. These survivors, known as Hibakusha, endured not only the immediate physical effects of the bombs but also the long-lasting psychological and social scars. Their stories of survival, loss, and resilience offer profound insights into the horror of nuclear warfare and its impact on the human spirit.

This extended essay delves into the firsthand accounts of Hiroshima and Nagasaki survivors, exploring the physical, emotional, and societal consequences of the bombings, as well as the ongoing legacy of these survivors' advocacy for peace.

1. Introduction: The Atomic Bombings and Their Consequences-

On August 6, 1945, the United States dropped the first atomic bomb, Little Boy, on the Japanese city of Hiroshima. Just three days later, on August 9, 1945, a second atomic bomb, Fat Man, was dropped on Nagasaki. These bombings marked the first and only use of nuclear weapons in warfare and resulted in the immediate deaths of tens of thousands of people. By the end of 1945, the total death toll in Hiroshima and Nagasaki was estimated to be between 140,000 and 200,000. Many of these deaths occurred immediately, while others were the result of burns, radiation sickness, and long-term diseases such as cancer and leukemia.

The victims of these bombings, the Hibakusha, were left to deal with the profound consequences of their exposure to the atomic bombs. Their experiences serve as a reminder of the human cost of nuclear warfare, and many Hibakusha have spent their lives advocating for peace and the abolition of nuclear weapons. Through their testimonies, we gain a clearer understanding of the destructive power of nuclear weapons, both in terms of their immediate impact and the long-term toll they take on human health and society.

2. The Immediate Impact of the Bombings-

Hiroshima: The Morning of August 6, 1945-

Hiroshima, a city of over 350,000 people, was home to a military base, numerous industrial facilities, and civilian populations. At 8:15 AM on August 6, 1945, the Enola Gay, a B-29 bomber, released the first atomic bomb, Little Boy, over the city. The bomb exploded about 600 meters above the city, releasing an intense burst of heat and light, followed by a shockwave that flattened everything in its path. The explosion destroyed most of the city within a one-mile radius, leaving nothing but rubble and charred remains.

The survivors' accounts of the bombing are filled with terror and disbelief. Many Hibakusha describe a sudden flash of light that was brighter than the sun, followed by a violent explosion that knocked them to the ground. The intense heat from the bomb caused immediate, severe burns, and the shockwave sent debris flying, causing injuries to anyone within a large radius. Tadatoshi Akiba, a survivor of Hiroshima and later the mayor of the city, recalled: "It was as if the sky opened up and the earth itself was being torn apart. I was thrown to the ground by the force of the explosion, and I couldn't see anything through the dust and smoke."

In the aftermath of the explosion, the survivors were faced with a city in flames. Many of the buildings that had survived the initial blast were soon consumed by fires, and the intense heat made it nearly impossible to escape the inferno. As people tried to flee, they were confronted by the sight of the injured and dying, some of whom were burned beyond recognition. Shizuko Takada, another Hiroshima survivor, described her immediate experience after the blast: "I could hear the screams of people, but I couldn't help them. I couldn't even move. The pain from the burns was unbearable, and I could only crawl through the smoke and rubble, trying to find safety."

Nagasaki: The Morning of August 9, 1945-

Just three days later, on August 9, 1945, the second atomic bomb, Fat Man, was dropped on the city of Nagasaki. Unlike Hiroshima, which was relatively flat, Nagasaki was a hilly city with steep slopes and valleys, which had a significant effect on the bomb's impact. While the geography of Nagasaki may have helped to limit the blast radius in some areas, the devastation caused by the bomb was still immense.

At 11:02 AM, the B-29 bomber Bockscar released the bomb over the city. The explosion devastated Nagasaki, killing around 40,000 people instantly and wounding tens of thousands more.

Despite the hilly terrain, the bomb caused widespread destruction, and the fires that followed the blast led to further loss of life. Many survivors were left trapped under collapsed buildings or caught in the firestorms.

Toshiaki Murata, a Nagasaki survivor, vividly recalled the moment of the bombing: "I had just finished my morning work at a factory when I saw a flash of light. Before I could react, I was thrown to the ground by the force of the explosion. I could smell the burning flesh of my co-workers as the flames spread, and I knew I had to escape or die."

3. The Aftermath: Radiation Sickness, Burns, and Long-Term Health Effects-

Radiation Burns and Initial Suffering-

The immediate effects of the atomic bomb were devastating, but the longer-term consequences were just as horrific. The survivors of the bombings suffered from a variety of injuries, many of which were the result of radiation exposure. The intense heat generated by the explosion caused severe burns to anyone within the vicinity of the blast. Survivors who were close to the epicenter of the explosions were left with first- and second-degree burns, while those who were further away suffered from third-degree burns. The burns were often so severe that the skin would peel off, leaving raw, exposed flesh.

Takahiro Nakasone, a Hiroshima survivor, described his burns as follows: "The pain was unimaginable. My skin was burned away, and I felt like I was being consumed by fire. I couldn't understand why it was happening to me, and I couldn't do anything to stop it."

Radiation Sickness and Internal Injuries-

In addition to burns, many survivors also suffered from radiation sickness, which was caused by exposure to the intense radiation emitted by the bombs. The symptoms of radiation sickness included nausea, vomiting, diarrhea, and fever. These symptoms would often appear within hours of exposure, and in some cases, survivors would appear to recover only to experience more severe symptoms weeks later, such as internal bleeding and organ failure. Yoshiko Kato, a Nagasaki survivor, recalled: "I felt a wave of nausea wash over me, and I collapsed on the ground. I didn't understand what was happening at first, but as the days passed, I began to feel weaker and weaker."

The radiation also caused a variety of long-term health effects, such as cancer, particularly leukemia, and other forms of cancer. Many Hibakusha would later develop cancers of the thyroid, lungs, stomach, and other organs. The incidence of leukemia, particularly in the first few years after the bombings, was high among those who were exposed to the highest doses of radiation.

Kiyoshi Tanimoto, a survivor of Hiroshima, lost several friends to leukemia and spent much of his life advocating for the abolition of nuclear weapons. He described the horror of witnessing his loved ones die from radiation-related illnesses: "I saw people who had survived the blast only to succumb to a slow, painful death from leukemia. It was unbearable to watch, and I couldn't do anything to help them."

Long-Term Psychological Trauma: PTSD and Social Stigma-

Beyond the physical injuries, the survivors also had to cope with the psychological trauma caused by the bombings. Post-traumatic stress disorder (PTSD), depression, and anxiety were common among Hibakusha, many of whom experienced vivid flashbacks, nightmares, and an overwhelming sense of guilt and despair. The psychological toll was compounded by the fact that many Hibakusha faced social stigma due to their status as survivors of the atomic bomb. In the years following the bombings, survivors were often ostracized by their communities, with some people fearing that they might be contaminated by radiation.

Tadatoshi Akiba, who later became the mayor of Hiroshima, recalled the social alienation he faced: "We were treated like we were cursed. People were afraid of us because they believed we carried some kind of disease. It was as though the world had forgotten us."

Many Hibakusha also struggled with feelings of guilt. Some wondered why they had survived when so many others had perished. The psychological scars of the bombings were often just as painful as the physical injuries, and survivors carried these scars for the rest of their lives.

4. Advocacy for Peace: The Hibakusha's Role in Shaping Global Opinion-

Despite the immense suffering they endured, many Hibakusha became powerful advocates for peace and the abolition of nuclear weapons. They were determined to share their stories with the world in order to prevent future generations from experiencing the horrors of nuclear warfare. As they aged, many Hibakusha found themselves at the forefront of the global anti-nuclear movement, traveling the world to speak about their experiences and to advocate for a world free of nuclear weapons.

Kiyoshi Tanimoto, a prominent Hibakusha activist, became known for his efforts to raise awareness about the consequences of nuclear war. After the bombing of Hiroshima, Tanimoto became a Christian minister and spent much of his life traveling to various countries, speaking out against nuclear weapons. "I have seen the destruction nuclear weapons cause. I have felt it firsthand. I will never stop advocating for a world without these weapons," Tanimoto said in a public address.

The Hibakusha's testimonies played a crucial role in influencing public opinion and shaping international policies on nuclear disarmament. Many governments and organizations were moved by the survivors' accounts and recognized the urgent need to prevent the use of nuclear weapons in the future.

The Lasting Legacy of Hiroshima and Nagasaki Survivors-

The accounts of Hiroshima and Nagasaki survivors are powerful reminders of the unimaginable suffering caused by nuclear warfare. The survivors, many of whom continue to speak out about their experiences, offer invaluable lessons about the horrors of war, the resilience of the human spirit, and the importance of working toward a world free of nuclear weapons. Their stories are a testament to the human capacity for survival, healing, and hope, even in the face of unimaginable tragedy. It is through their voices that we can learn to cherish peace and work toward a more just and compassionate world.

The Hibakusha have ensured that the tragedies of Hiroshima and Nagasaki will never be forgotten. Their advocacy for peace, nuclear disarmament, and the abolition of nuclear weapons continues to inspire generations around the world. By listening to their stories and reflecting on the lessons they offer, we can honor their suffering and work toward a future where the horrors of nuclear warfare are never repeated.

Immediate aftermath and Japan's surrender-

The atomic bombings of Hiroshima and Nagasaki, in August 1945, marked a crucial and horrific turning point in the course of history. These bombings not only contributed to the end of World War II but also initiated a new era in military strategy, international relations, and ethical debates. The immediate consequences of these events were catastrophic on both the human and material levels, and they altered the trajectory of geopolitics for decades to come. While the destruction wrought by the bombs was immense, the consequences of the bombings did not end with the surrender of Japan. Instead, they sowed the seeds for the Cold War, created a lasting nuclear arms race, and prompted significant ethical and moral considerations that continue to shape global policies today. This essay examines the immediate aftermath of the bombings, Japan's response to the devastation, the events leading up to its surrender, and the far-reaching implications for the world.

1. Immediate Impact of the Bombings on Hiroshima and Nagasaki-

The Physical Devastation of Hiroshima-

When the United States dropped the atomic bomb, Little Boy, on Hiroshima on August 6, 1945, the city was instantly transformed into a scene of unimaginable destruction. Hiroshima, a city of over 350,000 people, was the target of the first-ever use of a nuclear weapon in warfare. The bomb exploded with a force of 15 kilotons of TNT at a height of approximately 600 meters above the ground. The explosion created an intense flash of light, the heat of which was so extreme that it vaporized much of the city's infrastructure and caused immediate fires that would spread rapidly across the landscape. Within minutes, about 70,000 to 80,000 people were killed, with many more suffering from burns, injuries, and radiation sickness in the following days and weeks.

The survivors of the initial explosion, known as Hibakusha, faced indescribable suffering. Medical facilities were overwhelmed, and survivors, who had been exposed to lethal doses of radiation, showed signs of radiation sickness, including nausea, hair loss, and internal bleeding. Many of these survivors faced death in the following days, weeks, and months, as radiation continued to inflict damage on their bodies. The survivors who did not succumb to the initial effects of the bomb often faced long-term health problems, including cancer and genetic mutations that were passed down to subsequent generations.

In the aftermath of the bombing, Hiroshima was left in a state of utter devastation. The city's infrastructure was obliterated. Buildings were reduced to rubble, and those that remained standing were severely damaged. The iconic Hiroshima Castle, along with most of the city's cultural and historical landmarks, were destroyed. Communications were cut off, and much of the city's administrative machinery ceased to function, adding to the confusion and chaos.

While many of the dead were civilians, a significant portion of the city's population consisted of soldiers and workers in military factories. As a result, while the immediate death toll was high, the effects of the bomb were not limited to the civilian population but also involved Japan's military structure, which had been heavily embedded in the city.

Nagasaki's Unique Geography and its Impact-

Three days after Hiroshima, the United States dropped the second atomic bomb, Fat Man, on Nagasaki on August 9, 1945. Unlike Hiroshima, Nagasaki's geography presented a unique challenge for the bomb's destructive capacity. Nagasaki is located in a valley surrounded by mountains, and the bomb's blast was somewhat contained within the topography of the area, which meant the destruction was less widespread but still devastating. The bomb exploded with an equivalent force of 21 kilotons of TNT, and an estimated 40,000 people were killed immediately. The damage to the city's infrastructure was massive, and many survivors died of burns, radiation sickness, and injuries in the weeks that followed.

The geographical features of Nagasaki led to a different kind of devastation compared to Hiroshima. Many areas of the city that were in direct line with the bomb's explosion were completely flattened. However, some structures in the mountainous regions around the valley's edge suffered less damage, though they too were severely impacted by fires and the aftermath of radiation exposure.

Like Hiroshima, Nagasaki faced a medical and humanitarian crisis. Hospitals were overwhelmed with burn victims, many of whom later died due to the compounded effects of radiation. Survivors of the bombing experienced similar health issues to those of the Hibakusha from Hiroshima. Radiation sickness, cataracts, and cancers became widespread among the survivors, and many lived with the physical and psychological scars of the attack for the rest of their lives.

2. The Japanese Government's Response to the Bombings-

Initial Confusion and Denial-

The immediate response of the Japanese government was one of confusion and disbelief. At the time of the bombings, Japan's leadership had already been dealing with widespread devastation caused by conventional Allied bombings, as well as the Soviet Union's declarations of war. The Japanese government was still divided between those who hoped for a negotiated peace and those who believed Japan could continue fighting, despite the mounting losses.

At first, the full scale and significance of the atomic bombings were not immediately understood. The Japanese government had no prior knowledge of the atomic bomb and was unsure how to respond. After the bombing of Hiroshima, military officials attempted to downplay the significance of the attack, suggesting that it was another conventional bombing. However, as reports of the destruction mounted, and as the Soviet Union declared war on Japan and began its invasion of Manchuria, the government realized that the situation was far more dire than previously believed.

Japan's military establishment, particularly the Imperial Army and Navy, remained determined to continue the fight. The idea of surrender was seen as dishonorable, and many military leaders hoped to use the bombings as a negotiating tool. Others believed that Japan could still achieve some form of victory or favorable peace terms by continuing the fight, particularly through negotiations with the Soviet Union or by relying on an increasingly desperate defense strategy.

The Role of Emperor Hirohito in the Decision to Surrender-

One of the key turning points in the Japanese response came when Emperor Hirohito became involved in the decision-making process. The Emperor, while technically holding the highest position of power in Japan, had largely refrained from direct involvement in military strategy during the war. Nevertheless, the atomic bombings and the Soviet entry into the war placed immense pressure on the Emperor to intervene.

In the wake of the bombings, Hirohito was increasingly disillusioned with the military's leadership and the ongoing war. As Japan's cities were destroyed and its resources were exhausted, the Emperor grew concerned about the fate of his people. Hirohito, who had long been revered as a divine figure, began to understand that the continuation of the war would lead to even greater suffering and loss of life. With the Soviet invasion of Manchuria and the destruction wrought by the atomic bombings, the Emperor took the unprecedented step of advocating for Japan's surrender.

On August 15, 1945, Emperor Hirohito made a national radio address, marking the first time many Japanese citizens heard his voice. In this speech, Hirohito informed the nation of Japan's decision to accept the terms of surrender as outlined in the Potsdam Declaration, which called for Japan's unconditional surrender. The speech was brief but pointed, and it conveyed the Emperor's sense of urgency in bringing the war to a conclusion.

The speech contained the phrase "The war situation has developed not necessarily to Japan's advantage," which, although diplomatic in tone, conveyed the reality that Japan's military position had become untenable. The Emperor's words marked a profound shift in the national psyche, and the war was effectively over with Japan's acceptance of the surrender terms.

The Surrender Ceremony-

On September 2, 1945, Japan formally signed the instrument of surrender aboard the USS Missouri in Tokyo Bay. The signing ceremony was attended by Allied representatives, including General Douglas MacArthur, who oversaw the event as Supreme Commander for the Allied Powers. The signing of the surrender documents marked the end of World War II and the beginning of a new chapter in world history.

The event was both somber and triumphant. For the Allied powers, the surrender represented a hard-fought victory. For Japan, it marked the conclusion of an incredibly destructive war and the beginning of a long road to recovery. The signing of the surrender was also symbolic of the devastation that Japan had endured, as the consequences of the atomic bombings and conventional warfare had left the nation in ruins.

3. Long-Term Consequences of the Bombings-
Global Repercussions-

The bombings of Hiroshima and Nagasaki had a profound impact not just on Japan, but also on the global stage. In the immediate aftermath, the bombings raised fundamental questions about the morality and ethics of nuclear weapons. The sheer devastation caused by the atomic bombs prompted global concern about the possibility of nuclear warfare. The horrors witnessed by the survivors of the bombings, who would later become active advocates for peace and disarmament, led to widespread calls for the abolition of nuclear weapons.

These calls were not without merit, as the experience of Hiroshima and Nagasaki underscored the terrifying potential of nuclear weapons. The United States and the Soviet Union, both of whom had developed nuclear arsenals, engaged in an intense nuclear arms race throughout the Cold War. The proliferation of nuclear weapons, and the doctrine of Mutually Assured Destruction (MAD), became central to global military strategy, as both superpowers faced the terrifying prospect of total annihilation in the event of a nuclear war.

The Birth of the Nuclear Age-

The bombings of Hiroshima and Nagasaki also marked the beginning of the nuclear age, which would define much of the 20th century and beyond. In the years following the war, nuclear technology played a significant role in energy production, medical advancements, and scientific research. However, it also became a symbol of the destructive potential of human ingenuity and a constant reminder of the dangers of unchecked technological progress.

The bombings led to a global discourse on the control and regulation of nuclear weapons. In the years following World War II, several arms control treaties were established, including the Non-Proliferation Treaty (NPT), which aimed to prevent the spread of nuclear weapons and promote disarmament. However, the continued development and testing of nuclear weapons by various nations highlighted the difficulties in achieving global disarmament.

The Ongoing Struggle for Nuclear Disarmament-

Despite the moral lessons learned from Hiroshima and Nagasaki, the specter of nuclear war continues to loom over humanity. The bombings of Japan served as a stark reminder of the immense destructive power that nuclear weapons hold. In the years since the bombings, various groups and organizations have advocated for nuclear disarmament, arguing that the only way to ensure a safer world is to rid the planet of these weapons altogether.

Lessons from the Bombings of Hiroshima and Nagasaki-

The bombings of Hiroshima and Nagasaki marked the end of World War II but began a new era marked by the threat of nuclear warfare. These bombings resulted in immense human suffering, and the global response to the devastation underscored the importance of striving for peace and disarmament. The bombings forced the world to confront the question of the morality of nuclear weapons and their potential to cause irreversible damage to both humanity and the environment.

The decision to use atomic bombs on Japan has been debated for decades. Still, there is little debate about the profound consequences of these attacks, which reshaped the world order, forced the surrender of Japan, and fundamentally changed the way that nations view conflict and diplomacy.

The legacy of Hiroshima and Nagasaki is one of deep sorrow, and it serves as an enduring reminder of the potential for destruction inherent in modern warfare. The Hibakusha, the survivors of the bombings, continue to advocate for peace, and their voices serve as a powerful reminder that nuclear weapons, regardless of their perceived military utility, should never again be used.

As we reflect on these events, the world must continue to grapple with the moral, ethical, and political challenges posed by nuclear weapons. The lessons of Hiroshima and Nagasaki must be passed on to future generations, ensuring that the horrors of nuclear warfare are never repeated.

CHAPTER NINE

THE LEGACY OF MANHATTAN – THE NUCLEAR AGE

The role of the Manhattan Project in ending WWII-

The Manhattan Project, a pivotal secret research and development program during World War II, stands as one of the most significant and transformative endeavors in history. This highly classified project led to the creation of the world's first atomic bombs, ultimately playing a crucial role in the end of the Second World War. The development of atomic weapons marked a dramatic shift in warfare, diplomacy, and geopolitics, leaving a lasting legacy on international relations and technological advancements. In this essay, we will explore the role of the Manhattan Project in ending World War II, examining its origins, key figures, technological breakthroughs, and the moral and political implications of using atomic weapons to force Japan's surrender.

1. The Origins of the Manhattan Project-

The roots of the Manhattan Project can be traced back to the late 1930s, when scientists in Europe began to explore the possibilities of nuclear fission, the process by which atomic nuclei are split to release enormous amounts of energy. The discovery of fission in uranium by German scientists Otto Hahn and Fritz Strassmann in 1938, followed by the realization by Lise Meitner and Otto Frisch that this process could potentially create a self-sustaining chain reaction, set the stage for the development of atomic weapons.

In the early years of World War II, the fear that Nazi Germany might develop atomic weapons prompted significant concern among the Allied powers. In 1939, physicists such as Albert Einstein and Leo Szilard, recognizing the potential dangers of nuclear weapons, sent a famous letter to President Franklin D. Roosevelt urging the United States to initiate its own nuclear research program. This letter, known as the Einstein-Szilard letter, warned that Germany was likely pursuing similar research and that the U.S. should begin work on developing atomic bombs.

This letter, along with growing concerns about Germany's military advances, led to the formation of the Uranium Committee in 1941, which eventually evolved into the Manhattan Project. The U.S. government, recognizing the importance of securing nuclear weapons in the war effort, provided significant funding and resources to the project. As the U.S. joined the war in 1941 following the attack on Pearl Harbor, the urgency of developing an atomic weapon intensified.

2. The Establishment and Leadership of the Manhattan Project-

The Manhattan Project officially began in 1942 under the direction of General Leslie R. Groves of the U.S. Army Corps of Engineers. Groves was tasked with overseeing the entire project, and his organizational skills were pivotal in bringing together the scientific and industrial resources necessary to create an atomic bomb. One of Groves's early decisions was to appoint J. Robert Oppenheimer, a brilliant theoretical physicist, as the scientific director of the project. Oppenheimer's leadership and scientific vision were essential in guiding the project to its successful conclusion.

The project was spread across multiple locations in the United States, with the primary research and development facility being located at Los Alamos, New Mexico, which was isolated to ensure secrecy. Other key sites included Oak Ridge, Tennessee, where uranium was enriched, and Hanford, Washington, where plutonium was produced. These sites, along with a host of industrial partners and universities, collaborated to turn the concept of nuclear weapons into reality.

The project attracted some of the world's most brilliant scientific minds, including physicists such as Enrico Fermi, Niels Bohr, and Richard Feynman. The diverse team of scientists worked tirelessly, often under strict secrecy, to design and construct the two types of atomic bombs that would eventually be used in the war: a uranium-based bomb (Little Boy) and a plutonium-based bomb (Fat Man).

3. The Technological Breakthroughs and the Development of Atomic Weapons-

The Manhattan Project represented a massive scientific and technological challenge. The development of an atomic bomb required breakthroughs in several fields, including nuclear physics, materials science, and engineering. The project's primary goal was to harness the energy released by nuclear fission and to create a weapon that could unleash that power in an instant.

Uranium Enrichment-

One of the key technical challenges faced by the Manhattan Project was obtaining sufficient quantities of enriched uranium—a form of uranium in which the isotope U-235 is concentrated. Naturally occurring uranium consists mostly of the isotope U-238, which is not readily fissionable. To create an atomic bomb, the U.S. needed uranium enriched with the fissionable isotope U-235.

The enrichment process was a massive industrial effort that involved the construction of the Oak Ridge facility in Tennessee.

The Oak Ridge site used a variety of methods to enrich uranium, including gaseous diffusion, centrifugation, and electromagnetic separation. These methods allowed scientists to isolate the small amount of U-235 from natural uranium, which could then be used in the construction of the bomb.

Plutonium Production-

In addition to uranium, the project needed to obtain sufficient quantities of plutonium, another fissionable material. Plutonium-239 is produced by bombarding uranium-238 with neutrons in a nuclear reactor. The production of plutonium was one of the most challenging aspects of the Manhattan Project, requiring the construction of the Hanford Site in Washington state, which housed a number of nuclear reactors for plutonium production.

Once plutonium was produced, it had to be separated from the other elements in the reactor's spent fuel. This process was incredibly difficult and involved a series of chemical and mechanical steps. The successful production and purification of plutonium were key to the development of the Fat Man bomb, which used plutonium as its core material.

Weapon Design and Testing-

With uranium and plutonium available, the project's scientists faced the daunting task of designing a functional bomb. Two distinct designs were pursued for the atomic bomb: the "Little Boy" uranium bomb and the "Fat Man" plutonium bomb.

The Little Boy bomb, which used enriched uranium-235, was based on a relatively simple design known as the "gun-type" design. In this design, two subcritical masses of uranium-235 were brought together by a conventional explosive, initiating a chain reaction that would release a tremendous amount of energy. However, the Little Boy bomb was large and inefficient, and it required a large amount of enriched uranium to achieve a viable explosion.

The Fat Man bomb, which used plutonium-239, was based on a much more complex implosion-type design. This design required the use of a shell of high explosives surrounding a subcritical core of plutonium, compressing it to a supercritical state and initiating a chain reaction. The implosion-type design was more efficient than the gun-type design and required less fissile material.

The success of these designs depended not only on the ability to produce the necessary materials but also on the precision and coordination of the engineering and physics involved. A critical part of this was the construction and testing of the first atomic bomb at the Trinity test site in New Mexico, on July 16, 1945.

4. The Trinity Test and Its Consequences-

On the morning of July 16, 1945, the Manhattan Project conducted the first-ever test of an atomic bomb at the Trinity test site in the New Mexico desert. The test was code-named "Trinity," and it involved the detonation of a plutonium-based implosion-type device. The explosion created a blinding flash of light, followed by a mushroom cloud that rose more than 7.5 miles into the sky. The blast was so powerful that it was felt hundreds of miles away.

The Trinity test demonstrated that atomic bombs were not only feasible but also incredibly destructive. The successful detonation of the bomb marked the culmination of years of research and development by the Manhattan Project. For the scientists and military personnel involved, the test was both a triumph of scientific achievement and a stark reminder of the destructive power they had unleashed.

In the aftermath of the Trinity test, Oppenheimer famously quoted the Hindu scripture, the Bhagavad Gita, saying, "Now I am become Death, the destroyer of worlds." This statement captured the deep moral and ethical dilemmas that many of the scientists and military leaders faced in the wake of the successful test. The bomb had proven that it could be built, but it was now a question of how, and if, it should be used.

5. The Use of Atomic Bombs on Hiroshima and Nagasaki-

The decision to use atomic bombs on Japan remains one of the most contentious and debated actions in military history. After the successful Trinity test, the U.S. government faced a difficult decision: whether to use the bombs in an effort to end the war quickly, or to wait for Japan to surrender through other means. President Harry S. Truman, who had succeeded Franklin D. Roosevelt in April 1945, was under immense pressure to bring the war to a swift conclusion and to avoid a costly invasion of Japan's home islands.

After a series of failed diplomatic efforts and warnings to Japan, the U.S. dropped Little Boy on Hiroshima on August 6, 1945, followed by Fat Man on Nagasaki three days later, on August 9. These bombings killed an estimated 100,000 people instantly and caused many more deaths in the weeks and months following the attacks due to radiation exposure and injuries.

The bombings of Hiroshima and Nagasaki played a critical role in bringing about Japan's surrender. Japan, devastated by the destruction of its cities and faced with the threat of further atomic bombings, officially announced its surrender on August 15, 1945. The formal signing of Japan's surrender took place on September 2, 1945, aboard the USS Missouri, marking the official end of World War II.

6. The Aftermath and Legacy of the Manhattan Project-

The successful conclusion of the Manhattan Project had profound implications not only for the end of World War II but also for the postwar world order. The bombings of Hiroshima and Nagasaki brought about Japan's surrender, but they also introduced a new era of nuclear weaponry, with the potential to annihilate entire civilizations.

The legacy of the Manhattan Project is complex and multifaceted. On the one hand, it contributed significantly to the end of World War II by hastening Japan's surrender and sparing countless lives that might have been lost in a prolonged war or invasion. On the other hand, the bombings of Hiroshima and Nagasaki raised profound moral and ethical questions about the use of nuclear weapons and their impact on humanity.

The creation of the atomic bomb also had long-lasting geopolitical ramifications, as the United States emerged as the world's dominant nuclear power and the only nation to have used atomic bombs in combat. The fear of nuclear warfare shaped much of the Cold War that followed, as the Soviet Union quickly developed its own nuclear weapons in response.

In the years since the end of World War II, the legacy of the Manhattan Project has been debated by historians, politicians, and the general public. Many view the bombings of Hiroshima and Nagasaki as necessary to bring a swift end to the war, while others argue that they were unjustified and immoral. Regardless of the perspectives on the bombings, the Manhattan Project stands as a pivotal moment in world history, one that reshaped the global balance of power and established nuclear weapons as a permanent part of international relations.

The Manhattan Project's influence is still felt today in ongoing debates about nuclear disarmament, the ethics of warfare, and the responsibility of scientists and governments in the development of powerful technologies. The project serves as both a triumph of human ingenuity and a cautionary tale of the dangers of unchecked scientific and technological advancement.

The arms race and the beginning of the Cold War-

The arms race and the beginning of the Cold War are integral chapters in the history of the 20th century. The period from the end of World War II in 1945 to the collapse of the Soviet Union in 1991 was marked by political, military, and ideological confrontations between two superpowers: the United States and the Soviet Union. The Cold War was a time of profound tension and conflict, but also of remarkable scientific and technological progress. At the heart of this conflict was the arms race, a race to develop, stockpile, and refine nuclear weapons, which became a central factor in international relations, military strategy, and geopolitics. The Cold War and the arms race were intertwined, with the two superpowers, backed by competing ideologies and visions for the future, vying for global dominance. This period, characterized by the struggle for military supremacy, economic influence, and political power, left an indelible mark on the world, shaping the modern geopolitical landscape.

1. The End of World War II and the Emergence of Superpowers-

The end of World War II marked the conclusion of an era of global conflict, but it simultaneously set the stage for a new kind of confrontation—one based not on traditional warfare, but on political, economic, and technological rivalry. In 1945, the United States and the Soviet Union emerged as the two most powerful nations in the world. Although both countries had been allies during the war, their cooperation quickly began to break down in the aftermath of the conflict. World War II had left Europe devastated, and a power vacuum emerged as the Axis powers were defeated. The world was divided into spheres of influence, with the U.S. and the Soviet Union each vying for control of the postwar order.

The United States, with its capitalist economy and democratic ideals, sought to establish a new world order based on free markets, political democracy, and the spread of Western values. The U.S. was determined to prevent the spread of communism and sought to rebuild war-torn Europe through the Marshall Plan, a comprehensive economic aid program designed to promote stability and prosperity in the Western European nations.

On the other hand, the Soviet Union, under the leadership of Joseph Stalin, sought to expand the influence of communism. The USSR aimed to spread socialist revolutions across the world, particularly in Eastern Europe, where it had installed communist governments following the defeat of Nazi Germany. The Soviet Union sought to create a buffer zone between itself and the Western democracies, with the ultimate goal of spreading the ideology of Marxism-Leninism globally.

The breakdown of cooperation between the U.S. and the Soviet Union led to the emergence of the Cold War. The competition between the two superpowers was not limited to politics, but extended to military and technological superiority. The advent of nuclear weapons, which had been developed during the final stages of World War II, became a key factor in this rivalry.

2. The Emergence of Nuclear Weapons: The Beginning of the Arms Race-

The development and use of atomic bombs by the United States during World War II marked a turning point in military history. The dropping of the atomic bombs on Hiroshima and Nagasaki in 1945 not only contributed to the end of the war but also triggered a new era of warfare in which nuclear weapons played a central role. The United States, having successfully developed and used atomic bombs, became the first nation to possess nuclear weapons. However, this monopoly was short-lived.

In 1949, the Soviet Union successfully tested its own atomic bomb, "First Lightning", also known as the Joe-1 bomb. This marked the beginning of the nuclear arms race between the U.S. and the USSR. The Soviet Union's successful detonation of an atomic bomb shocked the United States, which had believed that it would maintain a monopoly on nuclear weapons for several more years. The Soviets' ability to develop their own nuclear bomb signaled the start of a new phase in the Cold War, as both superpowers now possessed the ability to destroy each other with nuclear weapons.

The development of nuclear weapons by both the U.S. and the Soviet Union set the stage for a technological and military rivalry that would last for nearly five decades. The early years of the arms race were marked by a series of tests and developments aimed at achieving superiority in nuclear weaponry.

3. The Hydrogen Bomb and the Escalation of the Arms Race

In the early 1950s, the arms race took on a new dimension with the development of the hydrogen bomb (H-bomb), a weapon that was far more powerful than the atomic bomb. The hydrogen bomb, or thermonuclear bomb, relied on nuclear fusion, the process by which lighter elements, such as hydrogen, are fused together under extreme conditions to release enormous amounts of energy. This fusion reaction was far more potent than the fission reaction used in atomic bombs.

The United States was the first country to successfully develop the hydrogen bomb. In 1952, the U.S. conducted its first successful test of the H-bomb, code-named Ivy Mike, on the Bikini Atoll in the Pacific Ocean. The explosion was a significant leap forward in nuclear weaponry, producing an explosion of immense destructive power. The United States' success in developing the hydrogen bomb was seen as a critical milestone in the arms race and intensified the sense of urgency within the Soviet Union to match this development.

In 1953, the Soviet Union followed suit, testing its own hydrogen bomb, which was a direct response to the U.S. test. The detonation of the Soviet H-bomb further escalated the arms race and signaled that both superpowers now possessed weapons of unprecedented destructive capability. This marked the beginning of a new phase in the Cold War, in which the development of increasingly powerful nuclear weapons would dominate the strategic calculations of both nations.

4. The Policy of Deterrence and Mutually Assured Destruction (MAD)-

By the late 1950s and early 1960s, the arms race had reached a new level of intensity. Both the United States and the Soviet Union had developed large arsenals of nuclear weapons, and the potential for global destruction became more apparent than ever before. This period marked the rise of nuclear deterrence, a military strategy based on the premise that neither side would launch a nuclear attack on the other due to the certainty of devastating retaliation.

This strategy was encapsulated in the doctrine of Mutually Assured Destruction (MAD), which held that if either the United States or the Soviet Union were to launch a nuclear strike, the other would respond with an equally destructive retaliatory strike, leading to the total annihilation of both sides. MAD became the central principle guiding the nuclear policies of both superpowers during the Cold War.

The fear of nuclear annihilation created a paradox in which both nations were compelled to build and stockpile more nuclear weapons to maintain the balance of power, yet they also sought to avoid direct conflict that could trigger a nuclear war. This delicate balance led to a standoff that lasted for decades, with both sides engaged in a constant struggle to maintain their nuclear superiority.

5. The Arms Race and the Space Race-

The arms race was not confined to the development of nuclear weapons alone. It also extended into the realm of space exploration. Both the United States and the Soviet Union understood the strategic importance of space technology, not only for military applications but also for technological and political prestige. The launch of Sputnik, the first artificial satellite, by the Soviet Union in 1957 marked the beginning of the Space Race, a competition between the two superpowers to achieve technological superiority in space exploration.

The Space Race was deeply intertwined with the arms race, as the technologies developed for space exploration were often dual-use technologies that could also be used for military purposes, such as the development of intercontinental ballistic missiles (ICBMs). ICBMs, which were capable of carrying nuclear warheads over long distances, became a critical part of the nuclear arsenals of both nations. The Space Race thus became a reflection of the larger Cold War rivalry, with each side seeking to outdo the other in terms of technological achievement and military capability.

6. The Cuban Missile Crisis: A Critical Turning Point-

The arms race and the Cold War reached their most dangerous point during the Cuban Missile Crisis of October 1962. This 13-day standoff between the United States and the Soviet Union brought the world to the brink of nuclear war. The crisis was triggered by the discovery that the Soviet Union had placed nuclear missiles in Cuba, just 90 miles off the coast of the United States. The presence of these missiles dramatically shifted the balance of power in the Western Hemisphere, and President John F. Kennedy responded by ordering a naval blockade of Cuba and demanding the removal of the missiles.

The Cuban Missile Crisis was the closest the world came to full-scale nuclear war. Both superpowers faced the prospect of annihilation, and the tensions of the arms race reached their peak. However, after intense negotiations, the crisis was defused. The Soviet Union agreed to remove the missiles from Cuba in exchange for a U.S. promise not to invade the island and the secret removal of U.S. missiles from Turkey. This event highlighted the dangers of the arms race and underscored the necessity of careful diplomacy to avoid catastrophic consequences.

7. The Arms Control Movements: Efforts to Limit the Arms Race-

Despite the dangers of the arms race, there were significant efforts to limit the proliferation of nuclear weapons and reduce the likelihood of nuclear war. Throughout the Cold War, arms control became an important aspect of the diplomatic efforts between the United States and the Soviet Union.

In 1963, the Partial Test Ban Treaty was signed, prohibiting nuclear tests in the atmosphere, outer space, and underwater. This treaty was followed by a series of other arms control agreements, such as the Strategic Arms Limitation Talks (SALT) in the 1970s and the Intermediate-Range Nuclear Forces (INF) Treaty in 1987. These agreements sought to slow the growth of nuclear arsenals and reduce the risk of nuclear war.

8.The End of the Arms Race and the Cold War-

The arms race, which had defined much of the Cold War, began to wind down in the late 1980s. The Soviet Union, under the leadership of Mikhail Gorbachev, pursued policies of glasnost (openness) and perestroika (restructuring), leading to a thaw in relations between the U.S. and the USSR. The signing of the INF Treaty in 1987, which eliminated an entire class of nuclear weapons, marked a significant milestone in arms control.

The collapse of the Soviet Union in 1991 marked the end of the Cold War and the arms race. The United States emerged as the sole superpower, but the legacy of the arms race continues to shape global security concerns today. The arms race of the Cold War era may have ended, but the existence of nuclear weapons remains a central issue in international relations and geopolitics.

The Cold War arms race left an indelible mark on the world, shaping the political landscape, technological advancements, and global security concerns. The development and proliferation of nuclear weapons during this period created a new paradigm for international relations, one in which the threat of nuclear war continues to loom large over the world. The lessons of the arms race and the Cold War remain relevant as we navigate the complexities of modern geopolitics and the ongoing challenges of nuclear disarmament.

Establishment of international nuclear treaties and controls-

The establishment of international nuclear treaties and controls, such as the Nuclear Non-Proliferation Treaty (NPT) and the International Atomic Energy Agency (IAEA), represents a crucial aspect of global efforts to manage the development and use of nuclear technology for peaceful purposes while preventing its spread for military purposes. These treaties and organizations emerged out of the geopolitical tensions of the Cold War and the post-war desire to prevent the catastrophic consequences of nuclear conflict. Over time, these international mechanisms have aimed to strike a balance between promoting the peaceful use of nuclear energy and ensuring that nuclear weapons are not proliferated, thereby maintaining global peace and security.

In this context, the NPT and IAEA are two of the most prominent examples of international agreements that have shaped the landscape of nuclear control. These treaties have been central to the promotion of nuclear non-proliferation, peaceful nuclear cooperation, and the advancement of nuclear disarmament. Their formation, evolution, and impact have played a central role in reducing the risk of nuclear warfare and limiting the spread of nuclear weapons.

1. The Rise of Nuclear Weapons and the Need for International Control-

The creation and use of nuclear weapons during World War II changed the nature of international relations and posed new challenges for global governance. The United States' use of atomic bombs on Hiroshima and Nagasaki in 1945 demonstrated the devastating potential of nuclear weapons, while the subsequent testing of nuclear bombs by the Soviet Union in 1949 marked the beginning of the nuclear arms race between the two superpowers. The development of nuclear weapons was seen not only as a military and strategic necessity by the United States and the Soviet Union, but also as a new form of political power in the international system. This new reality raised concerns among other countries that the uncontrolled spread of nuclear weapons could lead to global catastrophe.

The devastating power of nuclear weapons and the increasing number of nations with nuclear capabilities led to the recognition that some form of international regulation and control was necessary to prevent nuclear war and the further spread of nuclear weapons. In this context, two key mechanisms for international control—the Nuclear Non-Proliferation Treaty (NPT) and the International Atomic Energy Agency (IAEA)—were established as critical steps in ensuring nuclear stability and security.

2. The Nuclear Non-Proliferation Treaty (NPT)-

The Nuclear Non-Proliferation Treaty (NPT), which was first opened for signature in 1968 and entered into force in 1970, is the cornerstone of global efforts to prevent the spread of nuclear weapons. The NPT is a multilateral treaty that aims to prevent the proliferation of nuclear weapons and promote the peaceful use of nuclear energy, while working toward nuclear disarmament. The treaty is based on three main objectives: non-proliferation, disarmament, and the peaceful use of nuclear energy.

The Three Pillars of the NPT-

Non-Proliferation: The primary goal of the NPT is to prevent the spread of nuclear weapons to countries that do not already possess them. The treaty creates a framework in which nuclear-weapon states agree not to transfer nuclear weapons or nuclear weapon technology to non-nuclear-weapon states. Similarly, non-nuclear-weapon states commit to not developing or acquiring nuclear weapons.

Disarmament: The NPT calls for the eventual elimination of nuclear weapons. Although this goal has not yet been fully realized, the treaty has created a framework for nuclear disarmament negotiations and has contributed to arms reduction efforts. The treaty obligates the nuclear-armed states to pursue negotiations on disarmament, although progress has been slow and uneven.

Peaceful Use of Nuclear Energy: The NPT recognizes the right of all countries to pursue the peaceful use of nuclear energy for purposes such as energy generation, medicine, and agriculture. The treaty encourages the sharing of nuclear technology for peaceful purposes while ensuring that it does not contribute to nuclear weapons development. It is through the International Atomic Energy Agency (IAEA) that these peaceful uses are monitored and regulated.

Key Provisions of the NPT-

Article I: Nuclear-weapon states (the U.S., Russia, China, France, and the United Kingdom) commit not to transfer nuclear weapons or assist other states in acquiring them.

Article II: Non-nuclear-weapon states agree not to develop or acquire nuclear weapons and to accept safeguards to verify their compliance with this commitment.

Article III: Non-nuclear-weapon states must place their nuclear facilities under IAEA safeguards to ensure that they are used only for peaceful purposes.

Article VI: Nuclear-weapon states agree to pursue nuclear disarmament and negotiate toward a treaty on general and complete disarmament.

Article IV: All parties to the treaty have the right to access nuclear technology for peaceful purposes, subject to safeguards and international monitoring.

Significance of the NPT-

The NPT has had a profound impact on global nuclear governance. As of 2021, 191 countries are parties to the NPT, making it one of the most widely accepted arms control treaties in history. The treaty has succeeded in preventing the proliferation of nuclear weapons to many countries that might have pursued nuclear weapons programs otherwise. The NPT has also played a key role in promoting the peaceful use of nuclear energy, facilitating the development of nuclear power for energy generation while minimizing the risk of diversion to military applications.

However, the NPT is not without its criticisms. Some countries have argued that the treaty has failed to deliver on its disarmament goals, as nuclear-armed states have not made significant progress toward the elimination of their nuclear arsenals. Others, such as India, Israel, and Pakistan, have criticized the treaty for permitting the nuclear weapons of certain countries while denying others the right to develop their own nuclear capabilities. Despite these criticisms, the NPT remains a cornerstone of international efforts to prevent nuclear proliferation and promote peaceful nuclear cooperation.

3. The Role of the International Atomic Energy Agency (IAEA)-

The International Atomic Energy Agency (IAEA), established in 1957, is an independent international organization that plays a central role in monitoring and verifying nuclear activities to ensure that nuclear energy is used for peaceful purposes. The IAEA's role is vital in implementing the NPT's provisions, particularly those related to the peaceful use of nuclear energy and the prevention of nuclear proliferation.

Key Functions of the IAEA-

Safeguards and Inspections: The IAEA is responsible for implementing safeguards to ensure that nuclear materials and technology are not diverted from peaceful uses to nuclear weapons development. The IAEA conducts inspections of nuclear facilities and materials in member states to verify compliance with the NPT and other non-proliferation agreements.

Technical Assistance and Cooperation: The IAEA provides technical assistance to countries seeking to develop nuclear technology for peaceful purposes. This assistance includes the provision of expertise, training, and equipment to support nuclear energy programs, medical applications, and other uses of nuclear technology.

Promoting Nuclear Safety and Security: The IAEA works to establish and promote international standards for the safe and secure use of nuclear energy. This includes ensuring that nuclear facilities are designed, operated, and maintained to prevent accidents and minimize the risk of nuclear proliferation.

Facilitating Research and Development: The IAEA supports research in nuclear science and technology, fostering international collaboration and helping countries improve their nuclear capabilities for peaceful purposes.

IAEA Safeguards and Nuclear Inspections-

One of the IAEA's most important functions is the implementation of safeguards, which are designed to detect and prevent the diversion of nuclear materials from peaceful uses to the production of nuclear weapons. These safeguards involve a comprehensive system of inspections, monitoring, and reporting that ensures nuclear materials are used in accordance with international agreements.

IAEA safeguards include the following elements:-

Comprehensive Safeguards Agreements (CSA): These agreements require countries to declare and allow inspection of all nuclear material and facilities. Under the NPT, non-nuclear-weapon states are required to place all nuclear activities under IAEA safeguards.

Additional Protocol: This supplementary agreement allows the IAEA to conduct more comprehensive inspections, including access to undeclared facilities, to verify that nuclear materials are not being diverted for military purposes.

Monitoring of Nuclear Materials: The IAEA tracks the movement and usage of nuclear materials, such as uranium and plutonium, to ensure that they are not diverted to weapons programs.

IAEA Challenges and Controversies-

While the IAEA has been effective in promoting the peaceful use of nuclear energy, it has faced significant challenges in ensuring full compliance with the NPT and preventing the spread of nuclear weapons. The agency has been involved in a number of high-profile cases, such as its inspections in Iraq and Iran, where allegations of illicit nuclear activities were raised. The IAEA's ability to enforce compliance is often limited by political considerations and the unwillingness of certain countries to cooperate fully with inspections.

Despite these challenges, the IAEA continues to play a critical role in the global non-proliferation regime. Its efforts to strengthen nuclear safeguards, promote disarmament, and ensure the peaceful use of nuclear energy are essential to reducing the risk of nuclear conflict and ensuring that nuclear technology is used for the benefit of all humanity.

4. Key Nuclear Treaties and Agreements Beyond the NPT-

In addition to the NPT, there are several other important nuclear treaties and agreements that have been developed to support non-proliferation, disarmament, and the peaceful use of nuclear energy. These include:

The Comprehensive Nuclear-Test-Ban Treaty (CTBT): This treaty, adopted by the UN General Assembly in 1996, bans all nuclear explosions for both military and civilian purposes. While the treaty has not yet entered into force due to the non-ratification of key states, it represents a significant step toward limiting the development of new nuclear weapons and reducing nuclear testing.

The Treaty on the Prohibition of Nuclear Weapons (TPNW): Adopted in 2017, the TPNW is the first international treaty to comprehensively ban nuclear weapons. While not yet widely ratified by nuclear-armed states, the treaty is seen as a major step in the global movement toward nuclear disarmament.

The Strategic Arms Reduction Treaty (START): This series of treaties between the United States and Russia aims to reduce the number of strategic nuclear weapons held by each country. The treaties have played a critical role in arms control and reducing the risk of nuclear conflict between the two superpowers.

5. The Ongoing Challenge of Nuclear Control-

The establishment of the NPT and the IAEA represents one of the most significant achievements in international diplomacy, providing a framework for the non-proliferation of nuclear weapons, the promotion of peaceful nuclear energy, and the pursuit of nuclear disarmament. While challenges remain, including the reluctance of some countries to fully comply with non-proliferation norms, the NPT and the IAEA have played a central role in limiting the spread of nuclear weapons and promoting nuclear safety and security.

The ongoing challenge of nuclear control remains as relevant today as ever, with nuclear weapons continuing to pose a significant threat to global security. Efforts to strengthen international nuclear treaties and organizations, promote disarmament, and ensure that nuclear technology is used responsibly will be crucial in shaping the future of nuclear governance and ensuring a stable and secure world for future generations.

The shadow of nuclear weapons on global politics and warfare-

The application of nuclear technology in medicine, energy, and industry represents a significant facet of modern technological development. While the destructive power of nuclear weapons often overshadows these peaceful uses, they play a vital role in shaping industries, enhancing the quality of life, and providing solutions to some of the world's most pressing challenges. This essay explores the positive uses of nuclear technology, as well as the ongoing geopolitical and strategic concerns surrounding nuclear weapons. The dual-use nature of nuclear technology, where advancements meant for peaceful purposes can also be used for military gain, has left a lasting shadow on global politics, fueling tensions and shaping international relations. This complex relationship between the peaceful and military uses of nuclear technology has evolved throughout the 20th and 21st centuries, and continues to be one of the most significant issues in global diplomacy.

1. Nuclear Technology in Medicine-

Nuclear technology has profoundly impacted medicine, offering innovative tools for diagnosis, treatment, and research. Its application ranges from cancer treatment to medical imaging, enabling doctors and scientists to explore the inner workings of the human body and develop effective therapies for a variety of diseases.

Nuclear Imaging and Diagnostics-

Nuclear medicine involves the use of radioactive isotopes to diagnose and treat diseases. One of the most important techniques in nuclear medicine is positron emission tomography (PET), which allows doctors to observe the metabolic processes within the body. PET scans use radioactive tracers to detect diseases at an early stage, such as cancer, heart disease, and neurological disorders. By tracking the movement of these tracers, which emit positrons, physicians can gain insight into abnormal tissue activity, aiding in accurate diagnoses.

Another key imaging technology is single-photon emission computed tomography (SPECT), which also uses radioactive tracers to create detailed 3D images of organs. SPECT is particularly effective for assessing the heart, brain, and bones. These non-invasive imaging techniques provide crucial information for medical professionals, often leading to early diagnosis and improved outcomes for patients.

In addition to PET and SPECT, nuclear technology is employed in radiology through the use of X-rays and CT scans. These techniques use ionizing radiation to produce detailed images of internal body structures, which are indispensable for diagnosing a wide array of conditions.

Cancer Treatment-

Nuclear technology is perhaps best known for its role in the treatment of cancer, particularly through radiotherapy. Radiotherapy uses high-energy radiation to target and kill cancerous cells. This treatment is effective for a range of cancers, including lung, breast, prostate, and head and neck cancers. External beam radiation is commonly used, where radiation is directed at the tumor from outside the body. In some cases, internal radiation, also known as brachytherapy, is used, where radioactive sources are placed inside or very close to the tumor.

One of the most significant advancements in cancer treatment using nuclear technology is the development of radioisotopes. These isotopes emit radiation that can be used to destroy cancer cells. For example, iodine-131 is widely used to treat thyroid cancer, while cobalt-60 is used in external radiation therapy. These isotopes can be precisely delivered to the cancerous tissue, minimizing damage to surrounding healthy tissues.

Sterilization and Disease Prevention-

Nuclear technology also plays a key role in sterilizing medical equipment. Gamma radiation, produced by isotopes such as cobalt-60, is used to sterilize surgical instruments, implants, and other medical devices. This method ensures that the instruments are free of harmful bacteria, viruses, and fungi, reducing the risk of infections during medical procedures.

Moreover, nuclear techniques are employed in the prevention and treatment of infectious diseases. For instance, the radiation-induced mutation of viruses is an approach to developing new vaccines and therapies. Radiation can alter the genetic material of viruses, rendering them incapable of infecting human cells. This approach has been used to produce vaccines for diseases like polio, and ongoing research aims to extend these techniques to other infectious agents.

2. Nuclear Technology in Energy-

The peaceful use of nuclear technology in energy production is one of the most significant advancements of the 20th century. Nuclear power plants harness the energy released from nuclear reactions to generate electricity, providing a significant portion of the world's energy needs. This form of energy is seen as an alternative to fossil fuels, offering a low-carbon source of electricity and reducing reliance on coal, oil, and natural gas.

Nuclear Fission and Power Generation-

The basic process behind nuclear power generation is nuclear fission, the splitting of atomic nuclei. When a heavy isotope such as uranium-235 or plutonium-239 is bombarded with neutrons, it splits into smaller nuclei, releasing a large amount of energy in the form of heat. This heat is used to produce steam, which drives turbines connected to generators, creating electricity.

Nuclear power plants operate on the same principle as conventional thermal power plants, with the key difference being the source of heat. Unlike fossil fuel plants, which burn coal or gas to produce heat, nuclear plants rely on fission reactions to generate the required energy. The advantage of nuclear power is that it produces large amounts of energy with relatively low fuel consumption and minimal greenhouse gas emissions. As concerns over climate change continue to grow, nuclear energy is seen by some as a key component in the transition to a sustainable, low-carbon energy future.

Challenges and Safety Concerns-

Despite the benefits of nuclear energy, there are significant challenges and concerns associated with its use. The most pressing of these concerns is the issue of nuclear safety. The potential for catastrophic accidents, such as the disasters at Chernobyl (1986) and Fukushima (2011), has led to widespread fear about the safety of nuclear power plants. These accidents, caused by reactor failures, resulted in radioactive contamination and long-term health and environmental consequences.

Furthermore, the disposal of nuclear waste is a persistent challenge for the nuclear energy industry. Spent nuclear fuel remains radioactive for thousands of years, requiring safe and secure storage solutions. The development of permanent storage facilities, such as geological repositories, is essential to ensure that nuclear waste does not pose a threat to human health and the environment.

Despite these challenges, many countries continue to invest in nuclear energy as part of their energy mix. Advances in reactor technology, including small modular reactors (SMRs) and thorium reactors, promise to improve the safety and sustainability of nuclear power in the coming decades.

Nuclear Fusion: The Holy Grail of Energy Production-

In addition to nuclear fission, there is ongoing research into nuclear fusion, the process by which atomic nuclei combine to release energy. Fusion is the process that powers the sun, and its potential for clean, virtually limitless energy has made it the "holy grail" of energy research. Unlike fission, fusion does not produce long-lived radioactive waste and carries no risk of catastrophic meltdown. However, achieving controlled nuclear fusion on Earth has proven to be extremely challenging, as it requires extremely high temperatures and pressures to overcome the repulsive forces between atomic nuclei.

Recent progress in fusion research, particularly with projects like the International Thermonuclear Experimental Reactor (ITER), offers hope that nuclear fusion could one day become a viable source of clean energy. If successful, fusion could revolutionize global energy production, providing an abundant, safe, and environmentally friendly alternative to both fossil fuels and nuclear fission.

3. Nuclear Technology in Industry-

Nuclear technology is also widely used in various industrial applications, from materials testing and quality control to environmental monitoring. These applications make use of the unique properties of radioactive isotopes and radiation to achieve precise measurements, improve manufacturing processes, and ensure safety.

Industrial Radiography-

One of the most common industrial applications of nuclear technology is radiographic testing, which uses gamma rays or X-rays to inspect the integrity of materials and structures. In this process, a radiation source is placed on one side of a material, while a detector is placed on the other side. The amount of radiation that passes through the material reveals any internal defects, such as cracks, voids, or corrosion. Radiographic testing is widely used in industries such as aerospace, oil and gas, and construction to ensure the quality and safety of products and infrastructure.

Tracer Studies-

Nuclear tracers are used to study and optimize various industrial processes. A small amount of a radioactive isotope is introduced into a system, and its movement is tracked to gather information about the system's behavior. This technique is commonly used in the oil and gas industry to optimize the extraction of resources and in environmental studies to track the movement of pollutants.

Irradiation in Food Preservation-

Another important industrial use of nuclear technology is irradiation, a process that uses ionizing radiation to kill bacteria, parasites, and other pathogens in food. This technique extends the shelf life of food products and helps to ensure food safety, particularly in the case of meat, poultry, and produce. Irradiation also helps to preserve nutrients in food by preventing spoilage, reducing waste, and ensuring that food remains safe for consumption.

4. The Shadow of Nuclear Weapons on Global Politics and Warfare-

While the peaceful applications of nuclear technology are significant, the existence of nuclear weapons casts a long shadow over global politics, shaping international relations and military strategy. The development of nuclear weapons during World War II marked a turning point in the history of warfare, with nuclear weapons offering the potential for unparalleled destruction. The existence of these weapons has influenced global power dynamics and created a permanent fear of nuclear conflict.

The Nuclear Arms Race and Cold War Politics

The advent of nuclear weapons led to the nuclear arms race between the United States and the Soviet Union during the Cold War. Both superpowers sought to build increasingly powerful nuclear arsenals, each hoping to deter the other from using nuclear weapons through the doctrine of mutually assured destruction (MAD). This concept relied on the belief that no side would launch a nuclear attack because it would result in the complete annihilation of both parties.

The development of nuclear weapons shifted the focus of international relations from traditional military power to the threat of nuclear escalation. Nations began to build and stockpile nuclear weapons not just as a means of deterrence, but as a way to project power and influence. The presence of nuclear weapons created new power structures and alliances, fundamentally altering the balance of global politics.

The Legacy of Nuclear Weapons on Warfare-

The destructive potential of nuclear weapons has led to a fundamental change in the nature of warfare. The fear of total annihilation from nuclear conflict has led to an unprecedented level of diplomacy and negotiation between nuclear powers. It also resulted in various arms control agreements, such as the Nuclear Non-Proliferation Treaty (NPT) and the Strategic Arms Reduction Treaties (START), which aimed to limit the spread and proliferation of nuclear weapons.

Despite these efforts, the threat of nuclear warfare continues to shape global security concerns. The nuclear triad—comprising land-based intercontinental ballistic missiles (ICBMs), submarine-launched ballistic missiles (SLBMs), and strategic bombers—remains a key component of the military strategy of nuclear-armed states.

The Ethical Dilemma: Peaceful vs. Military Use of Nuclear Technology-

The dual-use nature of nuclear technology—where advancements in energy and medicine can be repurposed for military use—presents an ongoing ethical dilemma. While nuclear technology offers significant benefits in fields such as health and energy, the potential for misuse in military applications raises profound ethical questions. The horrific consequences of nuclear warfare, exemplified by the bombings of Hiroshima and Nagasaki, continue to fuel debates about the morality of nuclear weapons and the responsibility of nations to control their development.

The prospect of further nuclear proliferation, with new nations seeking to acquire nuclear capabilities, adds another layer of complexity to the issue. As more countries develop nuclear weapons, the risk of nuclear conflict or accidents increases, with potentially catastrophic consequences for humanity.

5.The Dual Legacy of Nuclear Technology-

Nuclear technology represents a paradox. On the one hand, it has brought immense benefits in medicine, energy, and industry, improving human health, providing sustainable energy sources, and enabling advanced industrial processes. On the other hand, its potential for destruction through nuclear weapons has left a dark shadow over global politics and warfare. The tension between these peaceful uses and the military applications of nuclear technology will continue to shape international relations for the foreseeable future.

As the world moves forward, it is crucial to continue efforts to promote peaceful uses of nuclear technology while preventing the spread of nuclear weapons. The global community must work together to find solutions to the challenges posed by nuclear proliferation and ensure that nuclear technology is used responsibly, with the well-being of humanity in mind.

CHAPTER TEN

HE UNSUNG HEROES – WORKERS BEHIND THE SCENES

The thousands of workers who made the project possible-

The Manhattan Project, which was responsible for developing the first atomic bombs during World War II, was not only a monumental scientific and technological achievement but also a massive collective effort that involved thousands of individuals from diverse fields. These workers, who came from various backgrounds and expertise, contributed their talents to the project's success, despite often being unaware of the full scope and ultimate purpose of their work. The project was not merely a scientific breakthrough; it was the result of a massive mobilization of human resources, knowledge, and effort.

1. The Scale and Scope of the Manhattan Project-

The Manhattan Project was launched in 1942, and by the time it ended in 1945, it had evolved into one of the largest and most secretive scientific endeavors in history. It involved over 130,000 people across a network of laboratories, research facilities, military bases, and industrial plants in the United States and abroad. The project required the collaboration of physicists, engineers, chemists, mathematicians, and many other specialists. Additionally, it demanded the work of thousands of laborers, clerks, technicians, and secretaries who carried out essential but often invisible tasks.

The workers who contributed to the Manhattan Project were spread across the United States, working at various sites that included the Los Alamos Laboratory, the Oak Ridge National Laboratory, the Hanford Engineer Works, and the University of Chicago's Metallurgical Laboratory. Each site had its own specialized focus, but they all contributed to the overall goal of developing the atomic bomb.

2. The Role of Scientists and Engineers-

The most well-known figures of the Manhattan Project are the scientists and engineers who led the research and development of the atomic bomb. These individuals were responsible for the breakthroughs in nuclear physics and engineering that made the project a reality. Key figures like J. Robert Oppenheimer, the scientific director at Los Alamos, Enrico Fermi, the physicist behind the first controlled nuclear chain reaction, and Leo Szilard, who first conceived the idea of nuclear chain reactions, were instrumental in the project's success.

However, behind these well-known figures were many others whose contributions were crucial but less publicly recognized. Thousands of scientists and engineers worked under intense pressure, often long hours, and at great personal sacrifice. Many were assigned to specific aspects of the project, such as the development of the uranium enrichment process or the creation of the plutonium production reactors. Their work required a blend of specialized knowledge and practical ingenuity, as well as the ability to solve unprecedented scientific and engineering problems.

For example, Nobel laureate Glenn T. Seaborg played a critical role in the discovery of plutonium and its role in the bomb's design. His work, alongside colleagues, enabled the creation of the plutonium isotope needed for the bomb's core. Meanwhile, Richard Feynman, later famous for his contributions to quantum mechanics and for his role in investigating the Challenger disaster, contributed to the development of the bomb's detonators.

Many engineers were tasked with turning the theoretical concepts into tangible machinery. The implosion method used to trigger the explosion of the plutonium bomb, famously tested at the Trinity Test in July 1945, was a groundbreaking technical achievement that required the work of many individuals in areas such as explosive physics and high-precision mechanical engineering.

3. The Role of Technicians and Laborers-

While the scientists and engineers are often the most celebrated figures of the Manhattan Project, the technicians, laborers, and support staff were just as essential. Many of the workers at the various facilities had no idea what they were working on; they were given only the specific task they needed to perform without knowledge of the greater project.

At Oak Ridge, where uranium was enriched for use in the atomic bomb, thousands of workers were involved in building and operating massive uranium enrichment plants. Many of these workers were young women, some of whom were from rural backgrounds and had no scientific education but were trained to operate the complex machinery required for the separation of uranium isotopes. One of the key techniques used at Oak Ridge was the gaseous diffusion method, which separated uranium-235 from uranium-238. This process required an enormous amount of manpower, with workers laboring in the plant's complex, and often dangerous, conditions. The plant's operation was classified, and workers were given limited knowledge about what they were producing.

In addition to uranium enrichment, workers at Hanford Engineer Works in Washington were tasked with producing plutonium through nuclear reactors. The facility employed thousands of laborers, many of whom were involved in construction and maintenance. The reactors at Hanford were crucial in producing the plutonium required for the atomic bomb, but workers had little knowledge of the importance of the project they were involved in. Many were simply told they were helping with "war efforts," with no further details provided.

The safety conditions at these sites were often poor, and workers were exposed to dangerous levels of radiation without fully understanding the risks. Despite this, many workers played an essential role in ensuring the completion of the project. Many individuals who worked in the uranium enrichment and plutonium production plants were unaware that they were working directly on the atomic bomb, as the project was highly compartmentalized. In fact, workers were typically only aware of their specific task and were instructed not to inquire further.

In addition to the manual laborers and technicians, the project employed clerks, secretaries, and administrative personnel to help with logistics, communication, and coordination. These workers ensured that supplies were delivered on time, paperwork was processed efficiently, and the various sites operated smoothly. Their work, although less glamorous, was vital to the operation of the project.

4. The Women Who Contributed-

One of the most underreported aspects of the Manhattan Project was the role played by women, especially in areas like laboratory work and clerical duties. Many women took on vital roles in the workforce during World War II, and the Manhattan Project was no exception. Women worked as lab assistants, clerks, and secretaries at various sites, often managing the vast amount of data generated by the project or working alongside scientists and engineers in research tasks.

For example, Lise Meitner, a physicist who had previously fled Nazi-occupied Europe, played a crucial role in understanding nuclear fission. While she was not directly involved in the

Manhattan Project due to her absence from the United States, her work laid the foundation for the development of the bomb. Many women also worked as "computers," performing the tedious calculations necessary for the bomb's design before the advent of electronic computers.

In Los Alamos, Dorothy McKibbin was known as the "First Lady of Los Alamos," managing the personnel and administrative functions at the laboratory. She was one of the few women involved in high-level operations and was central to coordinating the arrival of staff at Los Alamos and ensuring the smooth running of the facility.

Women also worked in Oak Ridge and Hanford in various roles, many of them contributing to the uranium enrichment process and plutonium production. Thousands of women were employed in these areas, performing essential tasks that were critical to the success of the project. These women were integral to the war effort, even though their contributions were often not publicly acknowledged.

5. The Secrecy and Security of the Project-

The success of the Manhattan Project was made possible not only by the brilliant minds of scientists and engineers but also by the extreme secrecy and security measures implemented to keep the project hidden from the enemy. The project operated under the highest levels of secrecy, with workers assigned to tasks without knowing the larger context of their work. They were instructed not to discuss their work with anyone, including family members, and those who were privy to any information about the project had to undergo security clearance procedures.

At Los Alamos, scientists were housed in a remote location in the New Mexico desert to ensure the project remained undisclosed. The workers, including those in security and administration, were all involved in maintaining the secrecy of the project. There were even "spies" employed within the ranks, tasked with ensuring that no one discussed sensitive information or revealed anything that could compromise the project.

The extreme secrecy of the project is a testament to the level of trust placed in the thousands of workers involved. While many workers had only a vague sense of the project's purpose, they were often told that their work was of national importance, contributing directly to the war effort. Many employees found themselves caught in a morally complex situation, unsure of whether their work would lead to a weapon of mass destruction or a tool for peace.

6. The Legacy of the Workers-

The workers who contributed to the Manhattan Project played an essential role in the development of the atomic bomb and, by extension, in the history of World War II. While many workers remained unaware of the implications of their work, the significance of their contributions cannot be overstated. These men and women, from scientists and engineers to laborers and technicians, were the backbone of the Manhattan Project.

The legacy of these workers is a complex one. On the one hand, their efforts helped bring an end to the Second World War, with the bombings of Hiroshima and Nagasaki accelerating Japan's surrender. On the other hand, the destructive power of nuclear weapons has left a legacy of global fear, tension, and the need for ongoing control and diplomacy regarding nuclear proliferation.

Despite the ethical dilemmas surrounding the use of atomic weapons, the workers who contributed to the Manhattan Project made an undeniable mark on history. Many of them, in the years following the war, reflected on their involvement with a sense of ambivalence, grappling with the consequences of their work. However, it is clear that their efforts were essential to a critical moment in world history, marking the dawn of the atomic age and forever changing the course of global politics.

As we look back on the Manhattan Project, it is important to remember the thousands of people—many of whom worked in secret, with little recognition—whose combined efforts made the project possible. The lessons learned from this project continue to shape global security, ethics, and scientific responsibility today.

Contributions from women and minorities in science and industry-

The contributions of women and minorities in science and industry, particularly in pivotal historical moments like the Manhattan Project, have often been underrepresented or overlooked. However, their roles have been essential not only in the technological and scientific advancements of the 20th century but also in shaping the future of various fields, including physics, chemistry, engineering, and industry. In examining their contributions, it becomes clear that without the participation and dedication of women and minorities, many of the most significant scientific and industrial achievements would not have been possible.

1. The Historical Context: Barriers to Inclusion-

Before delving into the specifics of how women and minorities contributed to science and industry, it's crucial to understand the societal and institutional barriers that have historically excluded or marginalized these groups. The scientific and industrial fields in the early 20th century were largely dominated by white men, and most of the educational opportunities and research funding were directed toward them. Women and minorities, especially Black, Latinx, Indigenous, and Asian individuals, faced immense challenges in gaining access to higher education, scientific training, and career opportunities in these fields.

Women, in particular, were often excluded from formal scientific education or research positions and were relegated to more "appropriate" roles, such as teaching, secretarial work, or clerical tasks. Similarly, people of color faced racial discrimination, not only in the classroom but also in professional and industrial settings. Despite these barriers, women and minorities persisted, making significant strides in breaking down these obstacles and leaving their marks on the scientific and industrial fields.

2. Women's Contributions to Science-

The early 20th century saw many women, despite facing institutionalized discrimination, breaking into the scientific community and making significant contributions to their respective fields. Some of these women are now widely recognized, but many others remained in the shadows of history, their names barely mentioned in scientific textbooks and research papers. Yet, their discoveries and work were pivotal in advancing both theoretical and applied science.

Marie Curie

One of the most iconic figures in science and an example of a woman overcoming immense barriers was Marie Curie, a Polish-born physicist and chemist. Curie was the first woman to win a Nobel Prize and remains the only person to have won Nobel Prizes in two different scientific fields—Physics in 1903 (shared with her husband, Pierre Curie, and Henri Becquerel) and Chemistry in 1911 for her work in discovering the elements radium and polonium. Her work on radioactivity laid the foundation for the development of nuclear physics and had far-reaching consequences for medicine, particularly in the development of cancer treatments using radiation.

Her accomplishments were groundbreaking, but the challenges she faced as a woman in a male-dominated field were profound. She was often denied access to the resources that her male colleagues enjoyed, yet she persevered, managing to establish research institutes in Paris that remain influential to this day.

Rosalind Franklin

Another key figure in molecular biology is Rosalind Franklin, whose X-ray diffraction images of DNA were critical to the discovery of the double helix structure of DNA. Her famous "Photograph 51" provided the evidence that led James Watson and Francis Crick to their discovery. Unfortunately, Franklin's contributions were overshadowed, as much of the recognition for the discovery of the DNA structure went to Watson, Crick, and Maurice Wilkins, who had access to her work without her full acknowledgment. Nevertheless, Franklin's work was crucial to the understanding of genetics and laid the groundwork for modern molecular biology.

Lise Meitner-

Lise Meitner, an Austrian-Swedish physicist, was instrumental in the discovery of nuclear fission, a finding that later contributed to the development of nuclear energy and weapons. Despite being a key player in the work done at the Kaiser Wilhelm Institute, she was not awarded the Nobel Prize in Chemistry for the discovery of fission (which was instead given to Otto Hahn, her colleague and collaborator). Meitner's exclusion from the prize is often attributed to the sexism of the time, but her scientific achievements were groundbreaking, and she is now recognized as one of the most important figures in nuclear physics.

Katherine Johnson-

In the United States, Katherine Johnson, an African American mathematician, worked at NASA, where she calculated the trajectories for early space flights. Her work was pivotal in the success of the Apollo missions, including John Glenn's orbital flight in 1962. Johnson's role, along with those of her colleagues at NASA, was a crucial factor in the United States' victory in the space race against the Soviet Union. Her contributions to space exploration were significant, but it was not until much later in her life that her work gained the widespread recognition it deserved, particularly following the publication of the book and movie Hidden Figures, which highlighted the vital role that women like Johnson played at NASA.

3. Contributions of Minorities in Science and Industry-

The contributions of racial and ethnic minorities in science and industry have similarly been undervalued or overlooked. People of color, particularly Black, Latinx, Indigenous, and Asian individuals, faced systemic racism, segregation, and discrimination, which hindered their ability to gain access to higher education, professional careers, and scientific recognition. However, despite these significant challenges, many individuals overcame these barriers to make crucial contributions in various fields.

George Washington Carver-

One of the most prominent African American scientists in the early 20th century was George Washington Carver, an agricultural scientist and inventor who is best known for his work with peanuts and crop rotation. Carver's research revolutionized the agricultural industry by developing alternative crops to cotton, which were critical for improving soil quality in the Southern United States. His work not only helped farmers economically but also led to the development of numerous products from peanuts, including food, cosmetics, and industrial products. Despite facing racial discrimination and limited resources, Carver's legacy endures in modern agriculture.

Marie Maynard Daly-

Another significant African American scientist was Marie Maynard Daly, the first African American woman to earn a PhD in chemistry in the United States. Daly's work focused on the physiological effects of hypertension, particularly the relationship between high blood pressure and heart disease. Her research was groundbreaking in its exploration of the mechanisms by which diet, particularly the intake of salt, affects cardiovascular health. Though she faced significant challenges in her academic and professional career due to her race and gender, Daly's contributions helped lay the foundation for modern cardiovascular medicine.

Ben Barris and the Development of Nuclear Physics-

instrumental in the development of nuclear physics and the advancement of atomic research in the post-war period. Barris's work as a physicist has often been overlooked, but his contributions in quantum mechanics and atomic structure have had lasting impacts on the understanding of nuclear reactions. Barris, much like other Indigenous scholars, often had to overcome cultural and societal barriers to establish himself in the scientific community, but his work has influenced generations of nuclear scientists.

Santiago Ramón y Cajal-

Santiago Ramón y Cajal, a Spanish neuroscientist, was one of the key figures in the development of modern neuroscience. While he was not a minority in the traditional sense, his work, which focused on the structure of the nervous system, broke new ground in a field dominated by European and American scientists. His meticulous studies on the structure of neurons and their function provided the foundation for much of modern neuroscience. Cajal's work has been widely acknowledged, particularly after his Nobel Prize in Physiology or Medicine in 1906, shared with Camillo Golgi. His contributions to the understanding of the human brain were crucial and have influenced various fields of medicine, including the study of neurological disorders.

4. Women and Minorities in the Manhattan Project-

The contributions of women and minorities were critical to the success of the Manhattan Project, even though these groups were often relegated to lower-profile roles. At Los Alamos, Oak Ridge, and Hanford, women and minorities made significant contributions in fields ranging from nuclear physics to the operation of complex machinery.

Women working in the laboratories of Los Alamos, such as Dorothy McKibbin, who handled administrative tasks, were essential to the organization and communication between scientists. Others worked as laboratory assistants, performing the grunt work of sorting and categorizing data, and doing calculations. However, many of the women and minorities working at Los Alamos and other sites during the Manhattan Project were never fully recognized for their work in the development of the atomic bomb.

Women also worked in Oak Ridge, where the uranium enrichment process took place. Thousands of women were involved in operating the equipment necessary to separate uranium-235 from uranium-238, even though they were given little understanding of the importance of their work. Many of these women were brought in from rural areas with little prior scientific education, but they were quickly trained and made invaluable contributions to the project.

At the Hanford Engineer Works, the production of plutonium required the efforts of countless technicians, engineers, and manual laborers, many of whom were women and minorities. These workers helped construct and operate the nuclear reactors that produced plutonium for the bomb. Again, these individuals worked in harsh conditions, often without fully understanding the significance of their tasks.

The legacy of these women and minority workers, particularly their unsung roles in the development of the atomic bomb, remains an important part of the history of the Manhattan Project. Without their labor, the project could not have succeeded, and the world would not have experienced the technological advancements that followed.

5. Moving Forward: The Importance of Diversity in Science-

The contributions of women and minorities to science and industry, particularly in the context of critical moments like the Manhattan Project, remind us of the importance of diversity in scientific endeavors. Diversity in thought, background, and perspective leads to more creative solutions to problems, the exploration of different research avenues, and the development of a broader array of innovations.

As we look to the future, it is crucial that we continue to remove the barriers to entry that have historically kept women and minorities out of science and industry. Education and mentorship programs that encourage young girls and students from underrepresented communities to pursue careers in science, technology, engineering, and mathematics (STEM) are essential for ensuring that future scientific achievements are made by the most talented and diverse group of people possible.

The contributions of women and minorities to science and industry, though often overlooked or underappreciated, have been invaluable to the scientific advancements of the 20th century and beyond. From groundbreaking work in physics and biology to essential contributions during the Manhattan Project, these individuals shaped the course of history. As we continue to celebrate the achievements of these often-forgotten pioneers, it is important to recognize the vital roles they played and ensure that their contributions are not lost to history. The work of women and minorities in science should be celebrated and remembered, not only for its historical significance but for the continued inspiration it provides to future generations of scientists.

Stories of espionage and security breaches-

The topic of espionage and security breaches during the era of the Manhattan Project, and the subsequent effects on the development of nuclear weapons, is of great historical and geopolitical significance. The breach of scientific and military secrecy had repercussions that reshaped not only the Cold War but also the trajectory of nuclear diplomacy, national security policies, and the global balance of power. Espionage during this period is closely tied to the fear and uncertainty of the early Cold War years, where secrecy, suspicion, and ideology played pivotal roles in the race for nuclear superiority between the United States and the Soviet Union.

1. Introduction: The Atmosphere of Secrecy and the Emergence of Espionage-

The Manhattan Project, the U.S. effort to develop the atomic bomb during World War II, was a secretive and massive endeavor. Hundreds of thousands of workers contributed to the project across several sites in the United States, and it was deemed essential for the success of the war effort. The need for security and secrecy was paramount, as the United States was racing against Nazi Germany to develop nuclear weapons. The project's importance made it a target for espionage. The consequences of any leakage of information about atomic bomb technology were dire; not only would it jeopardize the war effort but it could shift the balance of power in the post-war world. As tensions between the Soviet Union and the United States began to escalate, the stakes of the arms race heightened, and espionage became a significant tool of Cold War strategy.

The fear of infiltration and the loss of vital information led to an increased emphasis on securing scientific data related to nuclear research. The war efforts, especially in the context of atomic weapons development, were incredibly secretive. Still, espionage infiltrated the ranks of those working on the project. Some spies were ideologically driven, others were motivated by greed or coercion, and some were even recruited by foreign powers due to their technical expertise. Regardless of their motivations, these individuals had a profound impact on the course of history. Their actions fueled an arms race, a nuclear arms race that would define much of the second half of the 20th century.

2. Klaus Fuchs: The Scientist Who Spied for the Soviet Union-

One of the most well-known cases of espionage in the history of the Manhattan Project was Klaus Fuchs, a German-born physicist who worked on the British nuclear weapons project, later transferring to the Manhattan Project in the United States. Fuchs was a prominent scientist in the field of nuclear physics, and his expertise was invaluable to the Allied effort to develop the atomic bomb. However, Fuchs had a secret: he was also spying for the Soviet Union. His motivations for espionage were complex, but they can largely be traced back to his strong communist beliefs and his ideological opposition to fascism.

Born in Germany in 1911, Fuchs was a committed socialist and, after fleeing Nazi persecution, moved to the United Kingdom in the 1930s. There, he began working on nuclear research and quickly became involved in the British atomic bomb project, known as Tube Alloys. During the war, Fuchs was sent to the United States to contribute his expertise to the Manhattan Project. By 1943, he was stationed at the Los Alamos Laboratory in New Mexico, working under the direction of J. Robert Oppenheimer, one of the leading figures of the project. Fuchs had access to highly classified information about the atomic bomb, including its design, the development of plutonium, and the processes of uranium enrichment.

Fuchs's espionage activities began almost immediately upon his arrival in the U.S. His relationship with the Soviet Union began in 1941, when he was recruited by Soviet intelligence operatives. Fuchs provided the Soviet Union with critical information about the Manhattan Project, including detailed descriptions of the bomb's design, the technical workings of the bomb's trigger mechanism, and the necessary components for producing fissile material like plutonium and uranium. This information proved invaluable to the Soviets, who were conducting their own atomic bomb research and development. With the intelligence provided by Fuchs, the Soviet Union was able to accelerate its efforts and develop its own atomic bomb by 1949, only four years after the U.S. had successfully tested its first bomb. Fuchs's espionage dramatically shortened the Soviet Union's path to nuclear weapons, creating a strategic shift in the Cold War power dynamic.

Fuchs was arrested in 1950, after a tip from an informant, and he confessed to his espionage activities. He was convicted of espionage in the United Kingdom and served a prison sentence of nine years. After his release, Fuchs moved to East Germany, where he continued to work as a scientist under the communist regime. His espionage activities remain one of the most well-documented cases of nuclear espionage, as he was directly responsible for providing the Soviet Union with the knowledge it needed to develop its nuclear weapons in such a short time.

Fuchs's motivations for spying have been the subject of much debate. Some scholars suggest that he was ideologically driven by his commitment to the Soviet Union's cause and believed that atomic weapons would ultimately lead to global peace by preventing the United States from exercising nuclear superiority. Others argue that he may have been motivated by a sense of injustice against the United States and Britain for their treatment of him as a foreign-born scientist. Despite these motivations, his espionage significantly changed the course of the Cold War, and his actions were instrumental in the Soviet Union's successful atomic bomb tests.

3. The Rosenbergs: A Family Affair-

One of the most sensational and controversial espionage cases from the Cold War era involved the Rosenbergs, Julius and Ethel, who were accused of providing the Soviet Union with vital information about the atomic bomb. The Rosenbergs' case remains one of the most debated and polarizing events of the Cold War, with some arguing that they were innocent victims of political persecution, while others contend that they were indeed spies who betrayed their country.

Julius Rosenberg, a former engineer and a member of the Communist Party, was recruited by Soviet agents to provide them with information about the atomic bomb's design. Julius's primary role in the espionage network was to pass on scientific and technical data to the Soviet Union. He allegedly provided critical information regarding the bomb's components, including the designs for the bomb's trigger mechanism and the process for creating fissile material. The Soviet Union, eager to catch up with the United States' lead in nuclear weapons, relied heavily on Julius Rosenberg for information that would allow them to develop their own atomic bomb.

Ethel Rosenberg's involvement in the espionage case is more contentious. Some historians argue that Ethel was not directly involved in espionage and was only indicted because of her association with her husband and her involvement in the Communist Party. Others suggest that Ethel may have played a more active role in the espionage operation, possibly in recruiting her brother, David Greenglass, a machinist working on the Manhattan Project, to help pass on atomic secrets. Greenglass was the one who allegedly provided the Soviets with information about the bomb's design, and his testimony was central to the Rosenbergs' conviction.

The trial of Julius and Ethel Rosenberg in 1951 was marked by political and ideological tensions. The United States, at the height of the McCarthy-era Red Scare, was deeply concerned about the threat of communism and the possibility of Soviet infiltration. Many viewed the Rosenbergs as symbols of the communist threat within American society. The trial was controversial for several reasons, including the lack of conclusive evidence against Ethel and the harsh sentences handed down to the couple. The Rosenbergs were convicted of espionage and sentenced to death. Despite appeals and protests from international communities, they were executed in 1953.

The execution of the Rosenbergs raised questions about the fairness of the trial, as well as concerns about civil liberties during a period of intense political repression. Their deaths became a symbol of the Cold War's ideological struggle, with many believing that the trial was politically motivated and an attempt to silence communism in the United States. In the years following their deaths, the release of new evidence, including declassified Soviet intelligence documents, led some to believe that Julius Rosenberg had indeed provided valuable atomic secrets to the Soviet Union, while Ethel's role in the espionage plot remained more ambiguous.

4. Espionage's Impact on the Cold War and Nuclear Proliferation-

The espionage cases of Klaus Fuchs and the Rosenbergs had far-reaching implications for the Cold War, the arms race, and the development of nuclear weapons. Their actions, along with the growing concerns over national security, contributed to the increasing tension between the United States and the Soviet Union. Following the revelation of Fuchs's espionage activities, the U.S. government became much more cautious and security-conscious regarding its nuclear research. In particular, it sparked a wave of investigations, heightened security measures, and a greater emphasis on controlling access to classified nuclear information.

For the Soviet Union, the stolen atomic secrets were invaluable. The rapid acquisition of information about the atomic bomb allowed the Soviet Union to develop its own weapons in a fraction of the time it would have otherwise taken. The Soviet Union's first successful atomic test in 1949, just four years after the U.S. had tested its first bomb, marked a turning point in the Cold War. It shifted the balance of power between the two superpowers and escalated the arms race to unprecedented levels. The development of nuclear weapons by both nations led to a fear of global destruction, and the subsequent deployment of hydrogen bombs only intensified this threat. The Cold War, marked by the specter of nuclear warfare, would dominate global politics for decades.

Espionage played a critical role in the arms race. The United States and the Soviet Union continued to engage in a series of covert operations and intelligence gathering throughout the Cold War to acquire information about each other's military capabilities. The stakes of the nuclear arms race were high, and espionage became a tool for each side to gain an upper hand. The ideological motivations of espionage agents, combined with the geopolitical rivalry between the two superpowers, created an environment where national security was always in question.

5.Espionage and the Shaping of the Modern Nuclear Age-

Espionage during the Manhattan Project and the early Cold War period significantly impacted the course of history. It not only altered the trajectory of the arms race but also shaped the geopolitics of the 20th century. The rapid development of nuclear weapons by both the United States and the Soviet Union, fueled in part by espionage, created an atmosphere of fear and tension. The actions of individuals like Klaus Fuchs and the Rosenbergs exemplify the role of intelligence and secrecy in the development of nuclear weapons. They also underscore the precariousness of security during times of intense geopolitical competition. Their actions altered the course of the Cold War and provided an early lesson on the dangers of nuclear proliferation, which continues to influence global security policy today.

The human cost: Health risks, secrecy, and sacrifices-

The human cost of the Manhattan Project and the subsequent development of nuclear weapons is an often underappreciated aspect of the story of the atomic bomb. The development of nuclear weapons, while viewed as a scientific and military achievement, came at a tremendous human cost—both in terms of the health risks faced by those working on the project and the secrecy that often concealed these risks, as well as the sacrifices made by individuals involved in the project. From the workers who labored under dangerous conditions at various research sites to the soldiers and civilians who were affected by the deployment of these weapons, the human toll of the atomic age is profound.

This narrative is a complex one, with layers of ethical, scientific, and political issues at play. The Manhattan Project, a secret U.S. government project that developed the first atomic bombs during World War II, involved tens of thousands of individuals working in highly classified conditions at research sites across the country. While the project's success ultimately led to the creation of the atomic bomb and its use in Hiroshima and Nagasaki, the human cost of this achievement was significant—both for those involved directly in the project and for the countless others affected by the consequences of nuclear weapons.

In examining the human cost of the Manhattan Project, it is important to consider not only the health risks associated with the work involved but also the sacrifices made by individuals, the secrecy surrounding the project's operations, and the long-term consequences of nuclear weapons on global politics, warfare, and human lives. This comprehensive exploration of the human cost examines the ethical dilemmas, public health risks, and human suffering associated with nuclear technology, highlighting the sacrifices made by workers, scientists, soldiers, and civilians alike.

1. The Manhattan Project: A Breeding Ground for Secrecy and Risk-

The Manhattan Project was a sprawling and ambitious effort involving the collaboration of the U.S. government, leading scientists, engineers, and military personnel. It had one central goal: to develop the atomic bomb before Nazi Germany. With the rise of the Nazi regime in Europe and the impending threat of global war, the United States, along with its Allied partners, believed that a new kind of weapon—one that harnessed the power of atomic energy—would prove decisive.

By 1942, the United States had begun to pour resources into the Manhattan Project, which became one of the largest and most secretive research and development programs in history. Headed by General Leslie Groves and the brilliant physicist J. Robert Oppenheimer, the project employed scientists and workers from across the country, most of whom had little understanding of the larger scope of their work or its potentially catastrophic consequences. In all, an estimated 130,000 people worked on the project at various sites in the U.S., including Los Alamos, Oak Ridge, and Hanford.

While these workers and scientists contributed to the development of the atomic bomb, they were often unaware of the true nature of their work, and even less so about the long-term risks involved. They were kept in the dark, not only about the potential consequences of the bomb but also about the dangers posed by the very materials they worked with. Secrecy and security were paramount, and this often came at the cost of transparency, especially in regards to the health risks posed by the project. The workers, many of whom were not well-versed in the properties of radioactive materials, were often exposed to harmful radiation, toxins, and hazardous chemicals without adequate protection or information about the risks.

2. The Health Risks: Radiation Exposure and Its Consequences-

One of the most significant and tragic aspects of the Manhattan Project was the exposure of workers to ionizing radiation, which would have long-lasting health effects for many of those involved. Workers at various research sites were exposed to dangerous levels of radiation, much of which was not understood at the time. Radiation exposure can lead to a variety of health problems, including cancers, leukemia, genetic mutations, and a variety of other long-term effects. At the time, however, the full scope of the dangers of radiation was not fully understood, and workers were not given the proper protective equipment or information about the hazards they faced.

At the Oak Ridge National Laboratory in Tennessee, one of the main facilities for uranium enrichment, workers were exposed to high levels of radiation while working with the uranium isotopes. Many of these workers were unaware of the potential risks posed by their work. Additionally, they were often exposed to dangerous chemicals, such as beryllium, which caused a variety of health issues, including lung diseases and cancer. The workers at Oak Ridge were among the most exposed to radiation and other hazardous materials, and many suffered long-term health problems as a result.

At the Hanford Site in Washington State, where plutonium was produced for the atomic bomb, workers were also exposed to radiation, often without adequate safety precautions. Hanford became one of the most significant sites for nuclear production during the Manhattan Project and continued to play a central role in the Cold War's nuclear weapons program. Unfortunately, the risks associated with radiation exposure were not fully understood at the time, and workers faced long-term health consequences. Many employees at Hanford developed cancers, respiratory diseases, and other health problems as a result of their exposure to radioactive materials.

In the early years of the project, the workers were not provided with any protective gear to shield them from the radiation or given adequate medical monitoring. It was not until after the war that the true extent of the damage caused by radiation exposure became apparent. Even then, many of the workers, particularly those in the lower ranks, did not receive compensation or recognition for the damage done to their health. Only later, after years of lobbying and legal challenges, were some workers able to receive compensation for the illnesses caused by their exposure to radiation.

The long-term health effects of exposure to radiation were not fully recognized until after the war. Many of those involved in the project did not live to see the full consequences of their exposure. Radiation-induced cancers and other health conditions would take years to manifest, and many of the survivors of the project lived out their lives with chronic health issues, some of which could be traced back to their work on the Manhattan Project.

3. The Sacrifices Made by Workers and Scientists-

The human cost of the Manhattan Project was not only a matter of health risks and radiation exposure but also included the personal sacrifices made by those who contributed to the project. For many of the workers and scientists involved in the Manhattan Project, the experience was a deeply transformative one. The work was grueling, secretive, and often dangerous, and many workers faced emotional and psychological stress as they grappled with the implications of their work.

Many scientists, including key figures such as Oppenheimer, Fermi, and Niels Bohr, wrestled with the moral implications of their work. While they understood the importance of defeating Nazi Germany, they were also aware that the development of nuclear weapons could change the nature of warfare and pose a grave threat to humanity. Some, like Leo Szilard and others, were vocal in their opposition to the use of the bomb on civilian targets, warning that the weapon's use would mark a new and frightening chapter in human history.

The secrecy surrounding the project meant that workers often did not understand the full scope of the implications of their work. For many, the end of the war brought a sense of relief, but it also raised moral and ethical questions that continued to haunt those who had been involved. For scientists like Oppenheimer, the aftermath of the project was particularly troubling. Oppenheimer himself later expressed regret over the use of the bomb, particularly in the context of Hiroshima and Nagasaki. While he initially supported the development of the atomic bomb, his views shifted in the years following the war. The psychological toll of having played a role in creating a weapon of mass destruction weighed heavily on him, leading to feelings of guilt and moral conflict.

For many of the workers, the psychological toll of their involvement was just as devastating as the physical effects. The secrecy surrounding the project meant that they were often isolated from their families and communities, and the pressure of keeping such a monumental secret created feelings of anxiety and guilt. As the years passed, many of the workers began to question the morality of their work. The bomb had ended the war, but it had also set the stage for a new era of nuclear warfare and global political instability.

The sacrifices made by these individuals, in terms of both health and personal well-being, are often overlooked in discussions of the Manhattan Project. They were ordinary people—scientists, engineers, and laborers—who had little understanding of the implications of the work they were doing. For many, the cost of their involvement in the project was high, and it continued to affect them long after the war was over.

4. The Secrecy: Ethical Implications and Lack of Accountability-

Secrecy was a cornerstone of the Manhattan Project, and it played a major role in the risks and consequences faced by those involved in the development of the atomic bomb. While secrecy was deemed necessary to protect the project from espionage, it also created an environment in which workers and scientists were not informed about the potential dangers they faced. The lack of transparency meant that individuals working on the project were not fully aware of the risks they were taking.

The secrecy surrounding the project also had ethical implications. Workers were not given adequate information about the dangers of radiation exposure, nor were they told of the potential long-term health effects. The project's leaders, including General Groves and Oppenheimer, made decisions about the safety of workers without fully understanding the long-term consequences of radiation exposure. This lack of transparency and accountability meant that many workers were exposed to serious health risks without their consent.

The issue of secrecy and its consequences became even more pronounced in the years following the war. As the health effects of radiation exposure became more apparent, there was little acknowledgment of the role the Manhattan Project had played in causing these illnesses. The workers who had contributed so much to the development of nuclear weapons were left to deal with the aftermath on their own, with little support or recognition from the government or the scientific community.

5. The Legacy of the Manhattan Project's Human Cost-

The Manhattan Project may have been an incredible scientific achievement, but it came at a tremendous human cost. The health risks, secrecy, and personal sacrifices faced by those involved in the project are an integral part of the story of nuclear weapons development. The long-term effects of radiation exposure, the emotional and psychological toll of working on such a destructive project, and the lack of accountability and transparency all contribute to the human cost of the atomic bomb.

The legacy of the Manhattan Project is not just about the creation of nuclear weapons—it is also about the people who worked on the project, the risks they faced, and the moral and ethical dilemmas they had to confront. The human cost of the Manhattan Project is a sobering reminder of the consequences of technological advancements and the toll they can take on those involved. As we reflect on the legacy of the atomic bomb, we must also remember the individuals whose lives were forever changed by their involvement in one of the most significant and controversial projects in history.

Acknowledgment and recognition in later years-

The acknowledgment and recognition of individuals involved in the Manhattan Project and the subsequent development of nuclear weapons is a complex and multi-faceted story. While the contributions of many scientists, engineers, and workers were celebrated at the time, the long-term recognition of their efforts has been marked by a mix of neglect, partial acknowledgment, and, in some cases, delayed or contested recognition. This narrative extends far beyond the successful development of the atomic bomb—it touches on the moral, ethical, and psychological aftermath that haunted those who played a pivotal role in the creation of one of the most powerful and destructive weapons in human history.

The story of recognition begins with the Manhattan Project's immediate aftermath, when the public was largely unaware of the scope of the project and its personnel. Following the bombings of Hiroshima and Nagasaki, the U.S. government quickly moved to classify the details of the atomic bomb's creation, keeping much of the work and its participants shrouded in secrecy. This period of post-war secrecy left many workers and scientists without recognition, despite their central roles in achieving the project's success.

However, over time, the increasing public knowledge of the Manhattan Project and the development of nuclear weapons prompted a reckoning of sorts. The moral and ethical questions surrounding the bomb's use, along with the evolving discourse on nuclear weapons and disarmament, led to a reevaluation of the contributions of the scientists and workers involved. This complex process of acknowledgment and recognition unfolded over decades, as individuals and organizations grappled with the legacy of the atomic bomb, the long-term health effects on workers, and the ethical consequences of unleashing nuclear weapons.

This exploration of acknowledgment and recognition in later years touches on several key themes, including the immediate post-war period, the delayed recognition of scientists and workers, the impact of the Cold War and arms race on public perception, the moral reckoning with the bomb's use, the acknowledgment of contributions by women and minorities, the legal and political struggles for compensation and recognition of the workers' sacrifices, and the broader reflection on the role of science in warfare. It also considers the evolving public discourse about the Manhattan Project's moral implications, the contested nature of scientific recognition, and the role of institutions in shaping the historical narrative.

1. The Immediate Post-War Period: Secrecy and the Forgotten Heroes-

Following the successful detonation of the first atomic bomb at the Trinity test site in New Mexico on July 16, 1945, and the subsequent bombings of Hiroshima and Nagasaki in August 1945, the United States government immediately classified the details of the Manhattan Project. This secrecy led to a lack of recognition for the tens of thousands of people who contributed to the project. While the U.S. military and political leaders, including President Harry Truman, received public acknowledgment, the scientists, engineers, and workers who made the project possible were largely left out of the narrative.

At the time, the development of the atomic bomb was considered a national security issue, and there was little public acknowledgment of the individuals who had worked on the project. Many of the key scientists, including J. Robert Oppenheimer, Enrico Fermi, and Niels Bohr, were renowned in their respective fields, but their work on the Manhattan Project was kept secret until the government declassified the details decades later. As a result, the general public had little understanding of the scale and scope of the effort behind the bomb's creation.

Moreover, the workers who labored at sites like Los Alamos, Oak Ridge, and Hanford, often without full understanding of the significance of their work, were not given any public acknowledgment for their contributions. Many of these workers, who performed menial or technical tasks, did not receive recognition or fame. The secrecy surrounding the Manhattan Project meant that they could not discuss their work with their families, communities, or even colleagues in the scientific community. This created a sense of isolation and, in many cases, a lack of acknowledgment for their vital contributions to one of the most important scientific endeavors in history.

For decades, the workers who contributed to the Manhattan Project remained largely anonymous. Their work was overshadowed by the secrecy of the project, and they were unable to fully grasp the monumental impact their contributions had on the world. The bombings of Hiroshima and Nagasaki, while marking the end of World War II, also ushered in a new era of geopolitical tension, which further marginalized the individuals involved in the bomb's creation.

2. Cold War Politics: The Arms Race and Its Impact on Recognition-

The Cold War that followed World War II had a significant impact on how the Manhattan Project and its contributors were viewed in the public eye. As the United States and the Soviet Union engaged in an arms race, the development and deployment of nuclear weapons became central to the ideological and military standoff between the two superpowers. The atomic bomb, which had been developed in secrecy and with moral ambiguity, was now the cornerstone of global power dynamics.

As the Cold War intensified, recognition for those involved in the Manhattan Project remained a contentious issue. On the one hand, some scientists, including Oppenheimer, were lauded for their contributions to the war effort. On the other hand, the moral and political implications of the bomb's use began to take center stage. The legacy of the bomb was increasingly viewed through the lens of its role in shaping global politics, with the bomb becoming a symbol of nuclear deterrence, arms proliferation, and the looming threat of nuclear war.

While some individuals were recognized for their role in the project, others, particularly those who had expressed reservations about the bomb's use or who had advocated for international control of nuclear weapons, faced scrutiny. Oppenheimer, for example, was called before the U.S. Atomic Energy Commission in 1954 for a security hearing, during which he was questioned about his past associations with left-wing groups and his opposition to the development of the hydrogen bomb. Despite his central role in the development of the atomic bomb, Oppenheimer's political views made him a target of the U.S. government's anti-communist hysteria, and he was stripped of his security clearance. This marked a dark chapter in the history of scientific recognition, as Oppenheimer was punished for his views on nuclear weapons, despite his pivotal role in their creation.

In contrast, the scientists who continued to support the development of more powerful nuclear weapons during the Cold War were often celebrated and given prominent positions in the scientific and political community. The recognition of these individuals was shaped by the geopolitical needs of the United

States during the Cold War, as nuclear weapons were seen as central to maintaining military superiority over the Soviet Union.

3. The Ethical Reckoning: Delayed Recognition and Moral Reflection-

As time passed, the ethical and moral questions surrounding the use of nuclear weapons became more pronounced. The devastation caused by the bombings of Hiroshima and Nagasaki, coupled with the long-term effects of radiation exposure, led many to question whether the use of the atomic bomb had been justified. In the years following the bombings, some of the scientists who had worked on the Manhattan Project expressed regret over their involvement, and many advocated for nuclear disarmament. This growing sense of moral responsibility would eventually lead to a delayed recognition of the contributions of those involved in the project, but this acknowledgment would be framed by a complex and painful ethical reckoning.

Oppenheimer, in particular, became a central figure in this moral reckoning. In the years after the war, he expressed regret over the use of the atomic bomb, famously remarking, "Now I am become Death, the destroyer of worlds." His statement, drawn from the Hindu scripture the Bhagavad Gita, encapsulated the inner conflict he felt about the bomb's destructive power and the role he had played in its creation. Oppenheimer's ethical reflection was shared by many of his colleagues, including Leo Szilard, who had advocated for a peaceful resolution to the war with Japan and had tried to prevent the use of the bomb on civilian targets. Over time, the moral ambiguity surrounding the use of the atomic bomb became an integral part of the story of the Manhattan Project, and those who had contributed to the project were forced to reconcile their scientific achievements with the devastating consequences of their work.

As the ethical implications of nuclear weapons became more apparent, the recognition of the scientists and workers involved in the Manhattan Project began to shift. The narrative surrounding their contributions evolved, with greater emphasis placed on the human costs of the atomic bomb and the need for responsible scientific research. Recognition of their work was no longer solely framed in terms of military success, but also in terms of the responsibility that comes with creating a weapon of mass destruction.

4. The Role of Women and Minorities in the Manhattan Project-

One of the most significant aspects of later recognition involved the acknowledgment of the contributions of women and minorities to the Manhattan Project. During World War II, the war effort created new opportunities for women and people of color in science and industry. Many women played key roles in the success of the Manhattan Project, working as technicians, mathematicians, and physicists. These women, however, were often relegated to the background in the historical narrative, with their contributions overshadowed by their male counterparts.

Some of the most notable women involved in the project included Katharine Way, who was a chemist at the Oak Ridge National Laboratory, and Leona Woods, who worked on the Chicago Pile-1, the first nuclear reactor. Women like Way and Woods made vital contributions to the scientific and technical aspects of the project, but their achievements were often overlooked in the post-war narrative. It was only much later that the full extent of their contributions came to light, as historians began to recognize the roles that women had played in the success of the Manhattan Project.

Similarly, the contributions of African American workers, including those who worked at Oak Ridge, were often ignored or underappreciated. Despite facing racial segregation and discrimination, African American men and women played critical roles in the success of the Manhattan Project, working in fields ranging from technical labor to administrative positions. The stories of these workers, like those of the women, were largely absent from the public discourse about the atomic bomb's creation.

In recent years, efforts have been made to recognize the contributions of women and minorities to the Manhattan Project. Museums, books, and documentaries have sought to uncover the hidden histories of these individuals and give them the recognition they deserve. This process of rediscovery and acknowledgment is part of a broader trend of reassessing the roles of women and minorities in the history of science and technology.

5. The Complex Legacy of Acknowledgment and Recognition-
The recognition of the individuals who contributed to the Manhattan Project is a story of delayed acknowledgment, moral reflection, and, in some cases, the eventual recognition of overlooked contributions. The atomic bomb, while viewed as a scientific triumph during and immediately after World War II, has become a symbol of the complex relationship between science and warfare, and the ethical responsibility of scientists who develop technologies with the potential for mass destruction.

Over time, many of the scientists, engineers, and workers involved in the Manhattan Project have been recognized for their contributions, but this recognition has often been accompanied by moral and ethical reflection. The legacy of the atomic bomb is a double-edged sword, and the recognition of those involved in its creation is inevitably tied to questions of responsibility, justice, and the human cost of technological progress.

In the end, the story of acknowledgment and recognition in the context of the Manhattan Project is not simply about celebrating scientific achievements. It is about reckoning with the profound implications of those achievements, understanding the sacrifices made by those who worked on the project, and grappling with the moral and ethical questions that continue to shape the legacy of nuclear weapons. The recognition of these individuals—both the well-known figures and those whose names have been forgotten—is part of a larger conversation about the role of science in shaping the future of humanity and the responsibility that comes with the power to create technologies of mass destruction.

CHAPTER ELEVEN

REFLECTIONS ON POWER – LESSONS FOR THE FUTURE

The Manhattan Project, despite its immense achievements, offers critical lessons that remain relevant for future generations in various domains, from scientific research to international policy, ethics, and global security. The project's legacy provides insights into the balance between scientific progress, moral responsibility, and the potential consequences of technological innovation. As we continue to advance in areas such as artificial intelligence, genetic engineering, and nanotechnology, the lessons from the Manhattan Project are more important than ever. Below are some key lessons that can guide future endeavors:

1. The Responsibility of Scientific Innovation-

One of the most significant lessons from the Manhattan Project is the immense responsibility that comes with scientific and technological advancement. While the project was intended to bring an end to World War II, the development of nuclear weapons led to unintended, catastrophic consequences. The moral and ethical questions surrounding the use of the atomic bomb remain contentious to this day, serving as a stark reminder of the importance of considering the potential impacts of new technologies.

Future researchers and engineers must recognize that their work does not exist in a vacuum. Scientific progress can bring great benefits, but it also has the potential to cause harm. Whether working on cutting-edge technologies or developing new industrial methods, scientists must consider the broader implications of their work, including environmental, societal, and ethical consequences.

Lesson: As scientific knowledge advances, there must be a parallel emphasis on understanding the moral and ethical consequences of technological innovations, ensuring that progress benefits humanity without causing harm.

2. The Importance of Transparency and Accountability-

The secrecy that surrounded the Manhattan Project, while necessary during wartime, led to a lack of accountability and transparency. The workers involved in the project, as well as the general public, were largely kept in the dark about the potential consequences of their work. The long-term health risks faced by workers at the Los Alamos, Oak Ridge, and Hanford sites, many of whom were unaware of the dangers of radiation exposure, highlight the importance of transparency in scientific endeavors.

In future scientific and technological projects, especially those with significant potential impacts on human health, the environment, or global security, transparency is essential. Researchers, governments, and corporations should be required to disclose information regarding risks, safety measures, and potential consequences. Additionally, there should be mechanisms in place to hold individuals and organizations accountable for any harmful consequences of their actions.

Lesson: Future projects must balance the need for confidentiality with the necessity of transparency to ensure informed public discussion, accountability, and ethical oversight.

3. The Need for Ethical Oversight in Military and Scientific Collaboration-

The Manhattan Project also highlights the potential dangers when scientific research is aligned too closely with military or political objectives. The close relationship between the U.S. military and the scientific community during the project allowed for rapid progress but also led to the development of weapons that have been widely criticized for their devastating effects. The ethical dilemma faced by many of the scientists involved in the project—particularly those who later expressed regret about the bomb's use—underscores the need for ethical oversight in any scientific endeavor with potential military applications.

As military and scientific research continue to intersect, it is crucial to establish clear ethical guidelines and independent oversight bodies to ensure that the development of new technologies is done in a responsible manner. Scientists must be able to challenge and question the ethical implications of their work, particularly when it has the potential to be used for violence or oppression.

Lesson: Strong ethical oversight must be integrated into military and scientific collaborations to ensure that technologies developed for national security do not harm innocent populations or violate human rights.

4. The Need for Multilateral Diplomacy and International Cooperation-

The development of the atomic bomb and the subsequent arms race between the United States and the Soviet Union during the Cold War highlighted the potential dangers of nuclear proliferation. The rush to develop more advanced and powerful nuclear weapons fueled tensions between nations and created an atmosphere of mistrust and fear. This underscores the importance of international cooperation in regulating and controlling the spread of dangerous technologies.

In the future, global challenges such as climate change, pandemics, and emerging technologies will require unprecedented levels of international collaboration. The Manhattan Project's legacy serves as a warning of the dangers of an arms race and emphasizes the importance of multilateral diplomacy in addressing global threats. Through treaties like the Non-Proliferation Treaty (NPT) and the International Atomic Energy Agency (IAEA), the international community has made significant progress in controlling the spread of nuclear weapons. However, as new technologies emerge, similar frameworks for international cooperation will be necessary to ensure that global challenges are addressed collectively.

Lesson: Multilateral diplomacy, international cooperation, and the creation of effective global frameworks are essential to address shared global risks, from nuclear weapons to emerging technologies.

5. Balancing National Security and Global Security-

The Manhattan Project was driven by the urgency of winning World War II and securing national security for the United States. The threat of Nazi Germany developing atomic weapons created a race to develop the bomb first, a race that was largely dictated by national interests. However, the aftermath of World War II demonstrated that the creation of nuclear weapons not only impacted national security but also global security, as the entire world was now under the shadow of nuclear warfare.

In future conflicts, nations must balance their own security concerns with the broader need for global security. Technologies that can enhance national security, such as advanced cyber capabilities, biotechnology, and artificial intelligence, must be developed with an understanding of their global implications. Nations must work together to ensure that the benefits of technological advancements are shared equitably and that risks are mitigated through cooperative efforts.

Lesson: Future global security strategies must balance national interests with the long-term stability and security of the entire planet, ensuring that technological advancements are used for the common good.

6. The Ethical Duty to Consider Long-Term Effects-

The Manhattan Project's legacy is not just about the immediate impacts of nuclear weapons on warfare—it is also about the long-term consequences. The environmental damage caused by radiation from nuclear testing and the health issues faced by workers who were exposed to radiation are long-term consequences that were not fully understood at the time of the project's development.

Future technological innovations must be developed with a long-term perspective. Researchers and policymakers need to consider not only the immediate benefits of a new technology but also its potential impact on future generations. This is particularly relevant in fields such as genetic engineering, artificial intelligence, and climate change, where the effects of current decisions may be felt for centuries. Decision-makers must adopt a precautionary approach and carefully weigh the long-term consequences of their actions.

Lesson: Future technological development must take into account the long-term consequences, both for people and the environment, and incorporate sustainability and foresight into the decision-making process.

7. Recognizing the Human Cost of Technological Progress-

One of the most sobering lessons of the Manhattan Project is the human cost of technological progress. Thousands of workers, including those at Hanford and Oak Ridge, were exposed to harmful radiation, leading to long-term health issues, and many individuals unknowingly paid the price for the success of the project. The lives of survivors in Hiroshima and Nagasaki also serve as a tragic reminder of the human toll of nuclear weapons.

In future projects, it is essential to prioritize the well-being of workers and communities, particularly those who may be exposed to dangerous or harmful substances. The stories of those affected by the Manhattan Project highlight the importance of worker protections, informed consent, and safety measures in any large-scale scientific endeavor. Additionally, it is essential to provide support and compensation for those who suffer the consequences of new technologies.

Lesson: The human cost of technological progress must never be overlooked. Ethical responsibility should include care for the well-being of workers and communities, as well as efforts to mitigate harm.

8. The Necessity of Public Engagement and Education-

The Manhattan Project unfolded largely behind closed doors, with little public knowledge of its development or consequences. In later years, as the true nature of the bomb's impact became clearer, public sentiment shifted dramatically. If the public had been more informed about the potential consequences of nuclear weapons, there may have been more vocal opposition or demand for different courses of action.

For future technologies, it is crucial to involve the public in discussions about their development, ethical implications, and potential risks. Transparency and education are key to ensuring that society as a whole can engage in informed debate and make decisions about how technologies are used. This is particularly important in areas like artificial intelligence, biotechnology, and nanotechnology, where the implications are vast and often not fully understood.

Lesson: Public engagement, transparency, and education are essential for ensuring that new technologies are developed in a socially responsible way, with input from a broad range of stakeholders.

9. Learning from the Past to Shape the Future-

Finally, the Manhattan Project teaches us the importance of learning from history to avoid repeating past mistakes. The development and use of nuclear weapons during World War II and the subsequent Cold War arms race are stark reminders of the potential dangers of unchecked technological progress. The atomic bomb is not just a scientific achievement but a cautionary tale about the destructive power of human innovation.

By studying the past, including the successes and failures of the Manhattan Project, future generations can better navigate the ethical, political, and technological challenges they face. History offers valuable lessons in how to balance scientific progress with ethical responsibility, how to mitigate the risks of new technologies, and how to approach global cooperation in an increasingly interconnected world.

Lesson: By learning from the past, especially from moments of technological innovation with global consequences, future generations can make informed decisions that prioritize humanity's long-term well-being and security.

,The lessons from the Manhattan Project are invaluable for shaping the future of scientific research, technological development, and global governance. As we move forward in the 21st century, we must recognize the profound responsibility that comes with the power to shape the world through innovation. The Manhattan Project reminds us that scientific progress is not just about discovery and achievement but also about ensuring that progress serves humanity as a whole, without causing harm or exacerbating global risks. Through careful consideration of ethics, transparency, international cooperation, and a long-term vision, we can navigate the complex challenges posed by new technologies while avoiding the pitfalls of the past.

Biography Collection

J. Robert Oppenheimer (1904–1967)

Early Life and Education: J. Robert Oppenheimer was born on April 22, 1904, in New York City to a wealthy Jewish family. His father, Julius Oppenheimer, was a successful textile importer, and his mother, Ella Friedman, was an artist. Oppenheimer's early education was marked by academic excellence, showing a particular affinity for literature and science. He attended the Ethical Culture Fieldston School, a progressive institution that fostered intellectual curiosity and social consciousness.

Oppenheimer's intellectual brilliance was evident from a young age. He entered Harvard University at the age of 18, where he initially studied chemistry before shifting his focus to physics. His time at Harvard was marked by deep philosophical reflections on the nature of science and a growing interest in theoretical physics. He graduated in 1925 with a degree in chemistry, having also dabbled in literature, and he went on to pursue graduate studies in physics at the University of Cambridge and later at the University of Göttingen in Germany. It was at Göttingen that Oppenheimer worked under the guidance of renowned physicist Max Born, where he became deeply immersed in quantum mechanics.

Scientific Career: Oppenheimer's return to the United States in the late 1920s saw him establish a distinguished career in academia. He became a professor of physics at the University of California, Berkeley, where he developed a reputation as a brilliant and unorthodox thinker. His research spanned various fields of theoretical physics, including quantum mechanics, nuclear physics, and astrophysics. Oppenheimer made key contributions to understanding the behavior of subatomic particles and the nature of the atomic nucleus, including the Oppenheimer-Phillips process in nuclear reactions and his work on the theory of black holes.

Despite his rising prominence as a theoretical physicist, Oppenheimer's political and personal views were more complicated. He developed a strong interest in leftist politics during the 1930s, particularly in response to the economic hardships caused by the Great Depression. Though he was never a member of the Communist Party, his associations with left-leaning intellectuals, including his relationship with members of the Communist Party, would later lead to intense scrutiny during the Cold War.

Role in the Manhattan Project: In 1942, as the United States entered World War II, the U.S. government launched the Manhattan Project, a secret initiative to develop an atomic bomb before Nazi Germany. Oppenheimer was appointed as the scientific director of the project and played a crucial role in bringing together the best minds in physics, engineering, and other disciplines at the Los Alamos Laboratory in New Mexico.

Under Oppenheimer's leadership, the project achieved remarkable scientific and engineering breakthroughs, including the creation of the first controlled nuclear chain reaction. Despite his relative inexperience in nuclear weapons technology, Oppenheimer's intellectual brilliance, ability to manage complex projects, and skill at coordinating diverse scientific teams made him the ideal leader. The success of the Manhattan Project culminated in the Trinity Test on July 16, 1945, where the world witnessed the first detonation of an atomic bomb in the New Mexico desert.

Although Oppenheimer was deeply proud of the scientific achievement, he was also aware of the immense moral implications of creating a weapon of mass destruction. The atomic bomb's destructive power was demonstrated shortly thereafter with the bombings of Hiroshima and Nagasaki in August 1945, leading to Japan's surrender and the end of World War II.

Post-War Advocacy and Political Controversy: Following the war, Oppenheimer became a prominent voice in discussions surrounding nuclear policy. He advocated for international control of nuclear weapons and was a member of the General Advisory Committee to the Atomic Energy Commission (AEC). His stance was that nuclear weapons should be subject to strict international oversight to prevent their proliferation and the potential for future warfare. He pushed for the peaceful use of nuclear energy and played a pivotal role in the creation of the U.S. Atomic Energy Commission's post-war policies.

However, Oppenheimer's political associations from the pre-war era, particularly his ties to individuals with Communist affiliations, came back to haunt him during the early stages of the Cold War. In 1954, amidst growing fears of communism and Soviet espionage, Oppenheimer's past was scrutinized during a highly publicized security hearing. The U.S. government questioned his loyalty, and his earlier political affiliations were used against him. Despite his significant contributions to the nation's wartime efforts, the Atomic Energy Commission stripped Oppenheimer of his security clearance, effectively ending his influence in U.S. government policy.

The hearings were highly controversial, and many felt that the charges against Oppenheimer were politically motivated, driven by the climate of fear and suspicion surrounding the Red Scare. In the years following the hearing, Oppenheimer's reputation was tarnished, though he continued to contribute to the academic community and maintain his intellectual standing.

Later Years and Legacy: After the security hearings, Oppenheimer withdrew from public life, and he returned to academia. He served as a professor at Princeton University's Institute for Advanced Study and continued to write and lecture on a wide range of scientific and philosophical topics. Despite the personal and professional setbacks, he maintained his interest in the ethical and political implications of nuclear technology, offering reflections on the responsibility of scientists in the modern world.

Oppenheimer's legacy is multifaceted. He is remembered as one of the leading scientists of the 20th century, whose leadership in the Manhattan Project helped shape the outcome of World War II and the nature of global politics in the nuclear age. His contributions to physics were substantial, and his intellectual curiosity and leadership qualities set him apart as one of the great scientific minds of his time.

However, Oppenheimer's story is also one of tragedy, torn between scientific achievement and the moral cost of his work. The development of nuclear weapons—and the subsequent arms race during the Cold War—led to a new era of global instability, one in which the very existence of humanity was threatened by the destructive power that Oppenheimer and his colleagues had helped unleash. The guilt and moral doubts that Oppenheimer expressed in the years following the bombings of Hiroshima and Nagasaki reflect the deep inner conflict faced by many scientists involved in the project.

In his later years, Oppenheimer remarked, famously quoting from the Bhagavad Gita, "Now I am become Death, the destroyer of worlds." This statement encapsulated his complex feelings of responsibility and regret over the bomb's use.

Oppenheimer died on February 18, 1967, of throat cancer at the age of 62. Despite the controversies that clouded his later life, his work and legacy as the "father" of the atomic bomb have been indelibly marked in history. His contributions to the development of nuclear weapons fundamentally changed the course of human history, making him a figure both of admiration and of deep moral reflection.

Legacy and Reflection:

Oppenheimer's legacy has evolved over time, from being seen as a hero who ended World War II to a more complex figure whose work raised profound ethical questions. He is now regarded as a cautionary figure in the history of science and technology. The scientific community continues to study his work and ponder the broader implications of scientific progress, particularly in the development of weapons of mass destruction.

In the decades following his death, Oppenheimer's views on the dangers of nuclear weapons have gained even more relevance. As the global community continues to grapple with the challenges posed by nuclear proliferation and the ongoing development of more advanced technologies, Oppenheimer's life and legacy serve as a stark reminder of the profound ethical responsibilities that come with scientific discovery. His cautionary tale urges scientists, policymakers, and the general public to approach technological advancements with careful consideration of their potential consequences for humanity and the world.

General Leslie R. Groves (1896–1970)

Early Life and Military Career: Leslie Richard Groves was born on August 17, 1896, in Albany, New York, to a middle-class family. His father, a U.S. Army officer, provided him with a strong military background, and Groves showed an early interest in engineering. He attended the U.S. Military Academy at West Point, graduating in 1918 with a degree in engineering. His military career began shortly after graduation during the closing years of World War I, but his contributions to military engineering would become most significant during World War II.

After the war, Groves continued to serve in various engineering capacities within the Army, including assignments with the Army Corps of Engineers, which would prepare him for his most critical role during World War II. He gained experience working on large infrastructure projects, including the construction of military installations and the development of dams, which would later serve him well in the management of the Manhattan Project's massive scale.

By the late 1930s and early 1940s, Groves had risen to the rank of brigadier general, and his reputation as a competent and highly organized officer was well-established. His leadership capabilities and track record in overseeing large-scale engineering projects made him an ideal candidate to oversee the Manhattan Project.

Role in the Manhattan Project: In September 1942, General Leslie Groves was appointed as the military director of the Manhattan Project, the U.S. government's top-secret initiative to develop atomic weapons during World War II. Groves was tasked with overseeing all aspects of the project, from securing the necessary resources and facilities to managing its personnel and ensuring the project's success under extreme secrecy. His leadership would prove critical to the completion of the project in a remarkably short time frame.

Groves took a hands-on, no-nonsense approach to the project. His primary responsibility was to ensure that the Manhattan Project remained efficient, secure, and focused on its objective: the creation of nuclear weapons. He had little tolerance for inefficiency or delays, and he famously drove the project forward with an iron fist, balancing the technical challenges of the project with the need to maintain secrecy and prevent leaks of sensitive information.

One of Groves's first major decisions was to select Los Alamos, New Mexico, as the site for the central laboratory where the atomic bomb would be designed and tested. Groves worked with scientists, including J. Robert Oppenheimer, to establish the laboratory at a remote location, far from public attention. His decision to select the site was based on the region's isolation, its potential for secrecy, and its ability to accommodate the project's large-scale operations. Los Alamos became the heart of the Manhattan Project, where the theoretical and practical challenges of atomic bomb design were tackled.

In addition to Los Alamos, Groves was responsible for the construction and management of two other key facilities: Oak Ridge, Tennessee, and Hanford, Washington. Oak Ridge was crucial for the production of enriched uranium, while Hanford was responsible for producing plutonium. Groves oversaw the construction of vast industrial complexes at both sites, ensuring that they were equipped with the necessary resources to carry out the chemical and physical processes that would lead to the creation of atomic bombs.

Groves's military background allowed him to manage the logistical and operational aspects of the project with remarkable efficiency. Under his leadership, the Manhattan Project grew into one of the largest and most secretive scientific endeavors in history, *employing over 130,000 people and costing approximately $2 billion (equivalent to about $30 billion today). Groves coordinated the efforts of scientists, engineers, and laborers, ensuring that each phase of the project was completed on time and within budget.*

Leadership Style: Groves was known for his pragmatic, authoritarian leadership style. He was a demanding and at times abrasive leader, pushing his subordinates to work quickly and efficiently. However, despite his tough approach, Groves had a deep respect for the scientific talent that was driving the Manhattan Project. He worked closely with scientists like Oppenheimer, ensuring that they had the resources and support they needed to make progress.

Groves's leadership was also marked by his ability to make tough decisions under pressure. For example, when it became clear that the U.S. needed to produce enough enriched uranium and plutonium for atomic weapons, Groves made the critical decision to expand Oak Ridge and Hanford, creating entirely new facilities that could scale up production. He also negotiated with local governments and private companies to secure the necessary resources, despite the enormous logistical challenges involved.

Groves's ability to manage people was equally critical. The Manhattan Project was a highly diverse and interdisciplinary project, requiring collaboration between military personnel, civilian scientists, and industrial engineers. Groves had to bridge the gap between the military and scientific communities, ensuring that both sides understood the importance of the mission and worked together to achieve its goals. Although he was not a scientist himself, Groves demonstrated a keen understanding of the technical challenges of the project and worked to create an environment where scientists could focus on their work without being bogged down by administrative obstacles.

Groves's leadership style was not without controversy. His authoritarian methods sometimes led to tensions with scientific staff, particularly when he overruled their decisions or placed the project's needs ahead of personal preferences. For instance, when a group of scientists questioned the ethics of using nuclear weapons, Groves remained focused on the military necessity of completing the project. His single-minded focus on the bomb's development sometimes led to criticism from those who felt that the human cost of the project was being overlooked.

The Trinity Test and the Bombings of Hiroshima and Nagasaki: Groves's leadership reached its zenith on July 16, 1945, when the first successful test of an atomic bomb was conducted at the Trinity test site in New Mexico. Groves played a central role in organizing the test, ensuring that the site was secure and that all necessary preparations were made. The test was a success, confirming the scientific theories that had been developed at Los Alamos, and paving the way for the use of atomic bombs on Japan.

In the weeks following the Trinity test, Groves was involved in the decision to drop atomic bombs on the Japanese cities of Hiroshima and Nagasaki. Despite the devastating consequences of these bombings, Groves believed that the use of atomic bombs was necessary to bring about Japan's surrender and end the war quickly. He argued that the bombings would save countless American and Japanese lives by avoiding a prolonged invasion of Japan.

Groves was intimately involved in the logistics of the bombings, overseeing the preparations for the aircraft that would carry the bombs and ensuring that the necessary personnel were in place. His unwavering commitment to the mission, even in the face of ethical questions raised by the bombings, helped seal his place in history as a key figure in the creation of nuclear weapons.

Post-War and Later Years: After the war, Groves continued to serve in the U.S. Army, retiring as a lieutenant general in 1948. He was briefly involved in the development of the U.S. nuclear program, overseeing efforts to protect nuclear secrets and prevent the spread of atomic technology to the Soviet Union. He also played a role in the early stages of the Cold War, helping to shape the U.S. military's nuclear strategy.

Following his retirement from the Army, Groves worked in the private sector, advising on large-scale construction and infrastructure projects. He also wrote a memoir, "Now It Can Be Told," published in 1962, in which he detailed his role in the Manhattan Project and offered his perspective on the ethical and political implications of nuclear weapons.

Groves died on July 13, 1970, at the age of 73. His legacy, like that of many figures involved in the Manhattan Project, is complex. While he played a critical role in ensuring the success of the project and the development of nuclear weapons, his actions have been the subject of much debate, particularly in the context of the bombings of Hiroshima and Nagasaki. His commitment to military objectives and the efficiency of the Manhattan Project came at a significant human cost, and his leadership was marked by both admiration and criticism.

Legacy and Reflection: General Leslie Groves is remembered as one of the most important military figures in the history of the Manhattan Project, a man whose pragmatic leadership and unwavering dedication to the mission helped bring about the creation of atomic weapons. His contributions to the development of nuclear technology played a decisive role in ending World War

II, but his legacy is also marked by the ethical and moral questions that the use of nuclear weapons has raised in the years since.

Groves's leadership was instrumental in the success of the Manhattan Project, but it is also a reminder of the complexities and moral dilemmas that accompany technological advancements. His story is one of scientific triumph mixed with deep ethical concerns, a tension that continues to define the role of nuclear weapons in global politics.

Enrico Fermi (1901–1954)

Early Life and Education: Enrico Fermi was born on September 29, 1901, in Rome, Italy, into a middle-class family. His father, Alberto Fermi, was a government official, and his mother, Ida de Gattis, was a schoolteacher. From a young age, Fermi displayed a remarkable aptitude for mathematics and physics, excelling in his studies. He attended the prestigious Scuola Normale Superiore in Pisa, where he completed his degree in physics in 1922, graduating with high honors. His talent for theoretical and experimental physics soon became apparent, and he began working under the guidance of some of the leading scientists of the time.

Fermi's early work focused on the behavior of atoms and atomic nuclei. In the mid-1920s, he made significant contributions to the development of quantum mechanics, and by 1926, he had formulated what would later become known as the "Fermi-Dirac statistics," a mathematical framework that helped explain the behavior of particles in quantum mechanics. This work earned him widespread recognition in the scientific community and established him as one of the leading physicists of his generation.

Move to the United States and Early Nuclear Work: Fermi's career took a pivotal turn in the early 1930s when he became involved in experiments related to radioactivity and nuclear reactions. His work in these areas laid the foundation for his later contributions to nuclear physics. In 1938, Fermi was awarded the Nobel Prize in Physics for his work on induced radioactivity in elements. That same year, he and his team discovered that the bombarding of uranium with neutrons could produce a new element, an important finding that would later play a crucial role in the development of nuclear energy.

The rise of fascism in Italy and the increasing anti-Semitic policies of Benito Mussolini's regime eventually forced Fermi and his wife, Laura, to leave Italy. In 1939, Fermi moved to the United States, where he was appointed to a professorship at the University of Chicago. His decision to leave Italy was heavily influenced by the fascist regime's growing hostility toward Jews, as Fermi's wife was of Jewish descent. After relocating to the U.S., Fermi became a naturalized American citizen and embarked on a path that would lead to his pivotal role in the Manhattan Project.

Role in the Manhattan Project: Fermi's contributions to the development of nuclear physics and his expertise in experimental physics made him a crucial figure in the success of the Manhattan Project. In the early 1940s, as the United States became embroiled in World War II, the U.S. government initiated the Manhattan Project, a top-secret research effort to build an atomic bomb. Fermi, with his wealth of knowledge in nuclear physics, was quickly brought on board, and he was assigned to the University of Chicago, where a central laboratory was established to conduct research on nuclear reactions.

Fermi's primary contribution to the Manhattan Project was his leadership in the creation of the first controlled nuclear chain reaction. This achievement, which took place on December 2, 1942, at the University of Chicago, was one of the most important milestones in the development of nuclear energy and the atomic bomb. Known as Chicago Pile-1 (CP-1), the reactor was the world's first nuclear reactor to achieve a self-sustaining chain reaction. This momentous event marked the beginning of a new era in science and technology, opening the door to the harnessing of nuclear energy for military and civilian purposes.

Fermi's understanding of nuclear reactions and his innovative approach to experimental physics were key to the success of CP-1. He was instrumental in designing the reactor, which consisted of uranium fuel and graphite moderators arranged in a spherical shape. The reactor was placed under a stadium at the University of Chicago, and its first successful operation proved that a controlled nuclear chain reaction was not only theoretically possible but could be sustained. This breakthrough laid the foundation for the later development of reactors capable of producing the materials necessary for the atomic bomb.

Fermi's work at Chicago was crucial to the overall success of the Manhattan Project. The ability to achieve a controlled chain reaction enabled the production of plutonium, a critical element for the development of the bomb. At the time, the theoretical basis for nuclear fission and chain reactions was still in its infancy, and Fermi's experiments provided the necessary experimental validation to confirm that nuclear reactions could be harnessed to release vast amounts of energy.

In addition to his work on the chain reaction, Fermi played a pivotal role in many of the theoretical aspects of the Manhattan Project. He contributed to the development of the theoretical models that explained how uranium and plutonium could be used to create a nuclear explosion. His expertise in experimental design and theoretical analysis allowed him to advise other physicists and engineers working on the project, helping them to navigate the complexities of nuclear physics and reactor design.

Fermi's role in the Manhattan Project also extended beyond the laboratory. He served as a mentor to many of the younger scientists working on the project, imparting his knowledge and experience to the next generation of nuclear physicists. His calm demeanor and ability to simplify complex problems earned him the respect and admiration of his colleagues, and he became one of the most respected figures in the scientific community.

Theoretical and Experimental Contributions: Fermi's theoretical and experimental contributions to nuclear physics were groundbreaking. He is perhaps best known for his work on neutron-induced fission, a process in which a neutron collides with an atomic nucleus, causing the nucleus to split and release energy. This process would later form the basis for nuclear reactors and atomic bombs. Fermi's research demonstrated that uranium atoms could undergo fission when bombarded by neutrons, a finding that had profound implications for the development of nuclear energy.

Fermi's work on fission also led to the discovery of the concept of the nuclear chain reaction. A nuclear chain reaction occurs when the fission of one atom releases additional neutrons that go on to induce the fission of other atoms, creating a self-sustaining reaction. This discovery was crucial to the development of the atomic bomb, as it allowed scientists to design a weapon that would release an enormous amount of energy in a very short time.

In addition to his work on fission, Fermi made significant contributions to the understanding of nuclear decay and the behavior of subatomic particles. His work on beta decay, in which a neutron in an unstable atomic nucleus transforms into a proton, was instrumental in developing the theory of weak interactions in particle physics. This work would later be recognized as a key contribution to the development of the Standard Model of particle physics.

Fermi's contributions to nuclear physics were not limited to theoretical work. He was also a brilliant experimentalist, and his ability to design and conduct groundbreaking experiments set him apart from many of his contemporaries. Fermi's experiments with neutrons and atomic nuclei led to a deeper understanding of the forces that govern the behavior of matter at the atomic level. His experimental work provided the empirical evidence necessary to confirm many of the theoretical concepts that were being developed in the field of nuclear physics.

Legacy and Later Life: Following the success of the Manhattan Project and the development of the atomic bomb, Fermi continued to contribute to the field of physics. In the postwar years, Fermi's work on nuclear reactors and particle physics continued to influence the scientific community. He became a professor at the University of Chicago, where he continued his research and mentored young physicists. Fermi also played a key role in the establishment of the Argonne National Laboratory, one of the first national laboratories in the United States dedicated to nuclear research.

Despite his achievements, Fermi was deeply conflicted about the use of atomic bombs. Like many of his colleagues in the Manhattan Project, Fermi was initially motivated by a desire to end the war and prevent Nazi Germany from developing nuclear weapons. However, after witnessing the devastation caused by the bombings of Hiroshima and Nagasaki, Fermi, like many of the *scientists involved in the project, expressed regret and concern over the use of atomic weapons.*

Fermi continued to work in physics until his death on November 28, 1954, from stomach cancer, which some believe was linked to his work with radioactive materials. He was survived by his wife, Laura, and their children. Fermi's legacy in the field of nuclear physics is enduring, and his contributions to both theoretical and experimental physics have had a lasting impact on science, technology, and global politics.

Enrico Fermi was one of the most important and influential physicists of the 20th century, whose work in nuclear physics was foundational to the development of atomic energy and weapons. His leadership in the development of the first controlled nuclear chain reaction and his contributions to the theoretical understanding of nuclear fission were key to the success of the Manhattan Project. Fermi's legacy continues to shape the field of nuclear physics, and his achievements are a testament to his brilliance as both a theoretical and experimental physicist.

Niels Bohr (1885–1962)

Early Life and Education: Niels Bohr was born on October 7, 1885, in Copenhagen, Denmark, into a distinguished family. His father, Christian Bohr, was a professor of physiology, and his mother, Ellen, was a talented woman with a strong interest in science. From a young age, Bohr showed a keen interest in the natural world, which was fostered by his family's academic background. He attended the University of Copenhagen, where he initially studied philosophy but later shifted his focus to physics. In 1911, he earned his doctorate in physics, after which he moved to England to work with renowned physicist J.J. Thomson at the University of Cambridge.

Bohr's early career was marked by a deep engagement with the emerging field of atomic theory. In 1913, he developed the Bohr model of the atom, which was groundbreaking in its attempt to explain the structure of the atom and the behavior of electrons. This model, which introduced the idea of quantized energy levels, was pivotal in the development of quantum mechanics and earned Bohr a reputation as one of the foremost physicists of his time. His work on atomic structure and quantum mechanics was integral to the early understanding of the nature of matter and energy.

The Copenhagen Interpretation of Quantum Mechanics: Bohr's most significant contribution to theoretical physics was his development of the Copenhagen interpretation of quantum mechanics, which became the standard framework for understanding the behavior of subatomic particles. Bohr, along with Werner Heisenberg, was a key figure in the formulation of this interpretation, which posited that particles such as electrons do not have definite properties like position and momentum until they are measured. Instead, the act of observation collapses the wavefunction, giving rise to specific outcomes. This theory was revolutionary and laid the foundation for much of modern quantum mechanics.

The Copenhagen interpretation also introduced the concept of complementarity, which held that different experimental setups could reveal different aspects of the same quantum phenomenon. Bohr's ideas on quantum mechanics sparked a philosophical debate about the nature of reality and the limits of human knowledge. He was known for his discussions with Albert Einstein on the interpretation of quantum mechanics, where Bohr famously argued that quantum mechanics did not require a complete and deterministic description of reality, while Einstein contended that there must be underlying physical laws that could explain quantum phenomena in more detail.

Bohr's work not only advanced the understanding of atomic structure but also set the stage for the development of the quantum theory of matter. His ideas were influential in shaping the direction of physics in the 20th century, and they earned him the Nobel Prize in Physics in 1922 for his investigation of the structure of atoms and the radiation emanating from them.

Niels Bohr and the Rise of Nuclear Fission: In the 1930s, the focus of Bohr's work shifted toward nuclear physics. In 1938, physicists Otto Hahn and Fritz Strassmann discovered nuclear fission, the process by which the nucleus of an atom splits into two smaller nuclei, releasing a vast amount of energy. This discovery quickly became a focal point for scientific research, particularly after it became clear that nuclear fission could be harnessed for both energy production and, potentially, the development of powerful new weapons.

Bohr recognized the significance of the discovery of fission, both for its scientific potential and its political implications. He began collaborating with other physicists to better understand nuclear fission and how it could be applied practically. Bohr's insights into nuclear reactions were critical in explaining the underlying principles of fission and its ability to release tremendous amounts of energy. He worked on theoretical models that demonstrated how uranium could be used as a fuel for chain reactions, which would be essential for both nuclear reactors and bombs.

In 1939, Bohr fled Denmark to escape the threat of Nazi occupation and moved to the United States, where he would become a crucial figure in the Manhattan Project. Before his departure, Bohr had been involved in important discussions with physicists such as Hahn and Strassmann, as well as scientists in the U.S. and Britain, about the possibility of building an atomic bomb. His expertise in nuclear fission made him an invaluable asset to the Allied scientific community.

Role in the Manhattan Project: Although Bohr was not directly involved in the day-to-day operations of the Manhattan Project, his contributions to the project were profound. He served as a consultant and advisor to the project, providing crucial insights into nuclear fission and its weaponization potential. Bohr's knowledge of nuclear reactions and his theoretical work on chain reactions were vital in helping the project's leaders understand how to harness fission to create an atomic bomb.

Bohr also played a key role in advising on the selection of materials for the bomb, including the use of uranium-235 and plutonium-239, which were the isotopes needed for nuclear weapons. His work on the development of nuclear reactors, particularly in understanding how to control chain reactions, was instrumental in shaping the design of the reactors at Oak Ridge and Hanford, which produced the fissile materials necessary for the bomb.

Perhaps Bohr's most important contribution to the Manhattan Project was his advocacy for international cooperation and his warnings about the dangers of a global arms race. Bohr believed that the development of nuclear weapons must be accompanied by a moral and political framework for their control and regulation. He was deeply concerned about the potential for nuclear weapons to lead to a catastrophic arms race and an escalation of global tensions. In 1944, Bohr proposed a plan for international cooperation on atomic energy, which he presented to the U.S. government. His proposal called for the establishment of an *international body to oversee the peaceful use of nuclear energy and to prevent the proliferation of nuclear weapons.*

Bohr's calls for international cooperation were largely ignored by U.S. officials, who were more focused on the immediate military objectives of the Manhattan Project and the use of nuclear weapons against Japan. Despite this, Bohr's ideas continued to influence discussions about the control of nuclear technology in the years following World War II.

Post-War Activities and Advocacy for Peace: After the end of World War II, Bohr remained a strong advocate for the peaceful use of nuclear technology and international collaboration. He continued to emphasize the need for an international framework for nuclear control, arguing that the development of atomic energy should be used to benefit humanity rather than to fuel further conflict. In 1945, shortly after the bombing of Hiroshima and Nagasaki, Bohr met with President Franklin D. Roosevelt and other U.S. officials to discuss the implications of nuclear weapons. He continued to promote his vision of a global approach to nuclear control, but his proposals were met with resistance from many of the leaders of the time.

Bohr's advocacy for nuclear disarmament and his warnings about the dangers of the atomic arms race made him a target of suspicion during the Cold War. His association with the Manhattan Project, along with his vocal support for international cooperation, led to tensions with the U.S. government, particularly during the early years of the Cold War when fears of Soviet espionage and the spread of communism were at their height. Bohr's concerns about the increasing militarization of nuclear technology and his calls for peaceful coexistence were at odds with the increasingly polarized political climate.

In 1949, Bohr was invited to visit the Soviet Union, where he met with Soviet physicists and discussed the possibility of nuclear cooperation between the U.S. and the Soviet Union. His visit was controversial and sparked fears of espionage, as some in the U.S. government believed that Bohr's interactions with Soviet officials could compromise national security. Despite these concerns, Bohr continued to advocate for scientific collaboration and dialogue between nations, believing that open communication was essential to preventing nuclear war.

Philosophical Views and Legacy: Bohr was not only a brilliant physicist but also a deep thinker who reflected on the broader implications of science and technology. He believed that science should be used for the betterment of humanity, and he was profoundly concerned about the potential for scientific discoveries to be misused for destructive purposes. His philosophical views were shaped by his experiences during the development and use of atomic weapons, and he became a vocal proponent of international cooperation and peaceful applications of science.

Bohr's legacy extends far beyond his work on the Manhattan Project. He is widely regarded as one of the founding fathers of quantum mechanics, and his contributions to atomic theory and nuclear physics remain foundational to modern physics. His work on the Bohr model of the atom, his contributions to the development of quantum mechanics, and his leadership in the field of nuclear physics helped shape the course of scientific discovery in the 20th century.

Bohr's advocacy for nuclear disarmament, his calls for international cooperation, and his commitment to the peaceful use of atomic energy have made him a symbol of the moral responsibility of scientists. His legacy continues to inspire those who work in science and technology to consider the broader ethical implications of their work, particularly in the context of nuclear energy and weapons.

Niels Bohr was a towering figure in the development of modern physics and played a crucial role in the advancement of nuclear science. His contributions to quantum mechanics, atomic theory, and nuclear fission were instrumental in the success of the Manhattan Project and in shaping the future of nuclear technology. Bohr's moral and philosophical approach to science, his advocacy for international cooperation, and his warnings about the dangers of nuclear weapons have left a lasting legacy that continues to influence discussions about nuclear policy, disarmament, and the ethical responsibilities of scientists.

Edward Teller (1908–2003)

Early Life and Education: Edward Teller was born on January 15, 1908, in Budapest, Hungary, to a Jewish family. Teller's early academic pursuits reflected his natural aptitude for science and mathematics. In 1926, he moved to Germany to study chemical engineering at the University of Karlsruhe. However, his interests soon shifted toward theoretical physics, and he transitioned to studying under the renowned physicist Werner Heisenberg in Leipzig, Germany. Teller received his Ph.D. in physics from the University of Leipzig in 1933. During his studies, he was particularly influenced by the growing body of work in quantum mechanics and the emerging field of nuclear physics.

In 1933, with the rise of the Nazi regime, Teller moved to the United States, where he would become a key figure in the development of nuclear science and weapons. He began working at the University of Michigan and then at George Washington

University, where he continued his research in physics. Teller's expertise in quantum mechanics and his ability to think through complex scientific problems quickly earned him a reputation as one of the leading minds in the emerging field of nuclear physics.

The Manhattan Project and Nuclear Fission: While Teller's involvement in the Manhattan Project was not as direct or central as other scientists such as J. Robert Oppenheimer or Enrico Fermi, his contributions to the project were nonetheless significant. Teller, who had been working in nuclear physics in Europe before his immigration to the United States, was recruited to the project in the early 1940s. His work primarily revolved around theoretical aspects of nuclear reactions, particularly in the development of nuclear chain reactions that would become the basis for both the atomic bomb and later thermonuclear weapons.

Teller initially worked on the theoretical modeling of the atomic bomb, particularly in understanding how uranium-235 and plutonium-239 could undergo fission in a chain reaction. He helped refine the bomb's design, contributing ideas that led to better understanding of the critical mass necessary for a successful explosion. However, Teller was not at the center of the atomic bomb's development; his role was more secondary compared to the leadership of physicists like Oppenheimer and the engineering and experimental work done by Fermi, Leo Szilard, and others at the Manhattan Project's laboratories.

Teller's real legacy within the Manhattan Project comes from his consistent focus on advancing nuclear weapons technology beyond the atomic bomb, specifically his advocacy for the development of the hydrogen bomb, or thermonuclear bomb. His work on the atomic bomb provided him with the background and tools necessary for thinking about the next step in nuclear weaponry.

The Hydrogen Bomb and Thermonuclear Weapons: Following the success of the atomic bomb and the end of World War II, Teller became increasingly focused on the next frontier of nuclear weapons development: the hydrogen bomb. In the early years of the Cold War, tensions between the United States and the Soviet Union escalated, and the question of how to maintain military superiority over the Soviet Union became central to American defense policy. Teller, along with other physicists, began to seriously consider the possibility of a more powerful nuclear weapon—one that harnessed not just nuclear fission but also nuclear fusion.

Teller became one of the leading proponents of the hydrogen bomb, a weapon that relied on the fusion of hydrogen isotopes (deuterium and tritium) rather than the fission of uranium or plutonium. The theoretical basis for the hydrogen bomb was rooted in the idea that if an atomic bomb could provide the necessary temperature and pressure to trigger a fusion reaction, a much more powerful explosion could result. This idea was formulated by physicists such as Teller, Hans Bethe, and Stanislaw Ulam.

Teller's push for the development of the hydrogen bomb was met with skepticism and opposition from some of his peers, including J. Robert Oppenheimer. Oppenheimer and many others on the Manhattan Project were wary of developing a weapon of such immense destructive power, fearing it would lead to further escalation in the arms race and potentially set the stage for catastrophic global warfare. Some physicists even questioned the necessity of the weapon, given the devastating effects of the atomic bomb already demonstrated in Hiroshima and Nagasaki.

Despite the opposition, Teller remained a staunch advocate for the hydrogen bomb, arguing that the Soviet Union's potential development of similar weapons posed a grave threat to U.S. national security. He believed that the United States needed to maintain its technological edge in nuclear weapons, and that the hydrogen bomb was an essential part of this strategy. Teller's insistence on moving forward with the hydrogen bomb led to the development of the first thermonuclear weapon, the "Ivy Mike" test, conducted by the U.S. in 1952. The success of the test proved the viability of the hydrogen bomb, marking a pivotal moment in the Cold War arms race.

Debate Over the Ethics of Nuclear Weapons: Teller's advocacy for advanced nuclear weapons, particularly the hydrogen bomb, placed him at the center of intense ethical debates. While the atomic bomb was already an immensely destructive weapon, the hydrogen bomb represented a leap in destructive power that many physicists, politicians, and ethicists viewed as irresponsible. The implications of hydrogen bombs, which could devastate entire cities with a single detonation, raised serious concerns about the future of warfare, the survival of humanity, and the ethics of developing such powerful weapons.

Teller was a polarizing figure in these debates. His unwavering commitment to the development of the hydrogen bomb earned him admiration from some military and political leaders, who saw his work as crucial for ensuring U.S. dominance in the arms race. However, his position also attracted significant criticism. Many scientists, including Oppenheimer and other Manhattan Project veterans, were horrified by the idea of pursuing such a dangerous weapon, arguing that the human cost would be too great and that the pursuit of even greater nuclear weapons would inevitably lead to an escalation of global tensions.

Teller's focus on the hydrogen bomb was especially contentious after the destruction caused by the atomic bombs dropped on

Hiroshima and Nagasaki in 1945. The effects of these bombings left deep scars on the global conscience, leading to growing calls for arms control and disarmament. Some believed that the development of the hydrogen bomb would only fuel the arms race and make nuclear war even more likely.

In 1954, Teller's controversial role in the hydrogen bomb's development came into sharp focus during the hearings of the U.S. Atomic Energy Commission (AEC). Teller's vigorous push for thermonuclear weapons, combined with his accusations of Soviet espionage, led to a bitter fallout with his colleagues, particularly Oppenheimer. Oppenheimer had advocated for caution in the development of nuclear weapons and had expressed concerns about the potential dangers of pursuing further nuclear escalation. This disagreement between Teller and Oppenheimer became a defining moment in Teller's career, as it led to a public and professional rift that affected his reputation.

The Cold War Arms Race and Nuclear Proliferation: The successful development of the hydrogen bomb by the United States was followed by the Soviet Union's successful test of its own thermonuclear weapon in 1953. The ensuing arms race between the U.S. and the Soviet Union led to the rapid development of increasingly powerful nuclear weapons, including multi-stage thermonuclear bombs and intercontinental ballistic missiles (ICBMs). Teller's work on the hydrogen bomb provided the foundation for this escalation in weapons development.

Teller's support for the continuous development of nuclear weapons was framed by his belief that nuclear deterrence was the key to preventing global conflict. He advocated for a policy of "peace through strength," arguing that the possession of an overwhelming nuclear arsenal would deter any potential adversary from launching an attack. However, this philosophy of nuclear deterrence also contributed to the ever-increasing stockpiles of nuclear weapons held by both the U.S. and the Soviet Union, leading to the looming threat of mutually assured destruction (MAD).

Despite Teller's advocacy for further nuclear development, his position on nuclear weapons was not entirely static. In later years, he acknowledged the dangers of nuclear proliferation and became an advocate for some forms of arms control, including the Partial Test Ban Treaty of 1963. However, his support for nuclear weapons and his push for new technologies like missile defense systems remained a significant part of his political and scientific identity.

Teller's Later Years and Legacy: In the years following his work on the hydrogen bomb, Edward Teller became a prominent figure in the broader scientific and political landscape, frequently testifying before government committees and advocating for nuclear policy. He was an outspoken supporter of President Ronald Reagan's Strategic Defense Initiative (SDI), a controversial missile defense program. Teller continued to be an advocate for the development of new military technologies, including advanced missile defense systems and space-based defense systems, throughout his career.

Teller's legacy is complex. He is seen by some as a visionary who helped ensure the United States' dominance in the Cold War by developing the hydrogen bomb, a weapon that fundamentally changed the nature of international relations. To others, Teller is a symbol of the ethical dilemmas faced by scientists who are involved in the development of potentially catastrophic technologies. His unyielding push for advanced nuclear weapons, particularly the hydrogen bomb, continues to spark debate about the moral responsibilities of scientists and the potential consequences of their work.

Conclusion: Edward Teller's contributions to nuclear science, particularly his work on the hydrogen bomb, made him one of the most important figures in the history of nuclear weapons development. While his work in the Manhattan Project and subsequent advocacy for thermonuclear weapons helped shape the course of the Cold War, it also placed him at the center of intense ethical debates about the role of science in warfare and the potential consequences of creating ever more powerful weapons. Teller's legacy remains controversial, but his influence on nuclear policy, arms control, and the development of advanced weapons technologies is undeniable. His career offers a poignant reminder of the profound ethical challenges that scientists face when their discoveries have the potential to reshape the world in both destructive and transformative ways.

Author Biography

I am Adeeb Jamal, an author and researcher with a focused interest in the realms of technology, innovation, and their far-reaching implications. Currently an 11th-grade student, in Allen House Public School in Khalasi Line with a deep passion for understanding scientific and technological phenomena.

My journey into the world of research and professional development began with a strong curiosity about the fields of robotics, cybersecurity, and quantum computing. These areas have shaped my academic trajectory, and over the years, I have dedicated considerable time to exploring the broader impact of emerging technologies on society, security, and global dynamics.

Professionally, I have earned multiple certificates from prestigious institutions like John Hopkins, Standford University , University of London, In Subjects like cybersecurity, quantum computing, and project management From Multiple Platforms. These certifications have not only enriched my technical knowledge but also helped me develop a holistic understanding of how emerging technologies intersect with business, ethics, and global security.

In addition to my academic interests, I am deeply invested in research. I have had the opportunity to publish several research papers, including papers like- Exploring quantum computational synergies in business operations, Cyber Physical System security in hyperconnected global supply chains, Neural symbiolic integration for autonomus social media marketing platfors,In well-regarded Journals like IRJET, IRJMETS and IJPREMS which has further fueled my interest in exploring how cutting-edge technologies can shape the future. This work has allowed me to contribute to the ongoing discourse on the potential of technology to drive innovation while also considering its ethical and societal implications.Also I am the author of another book Titans of Trade and Power.

This book is a product of my passion for speculative theories on nuclear weapons and their future potential. Through this exploration, I hope to challenge conventional thinking and encourage readers to think critically about the technological advancements that may shape the future of global security. My aim is to continue contributing to meaningful discussions on the responsible development and application of advanced technologies, ensuring that innovation is guided by both scientific curiosity and ethical responsibility.